SAFETY IN MUSEUMS AND GALLERIES

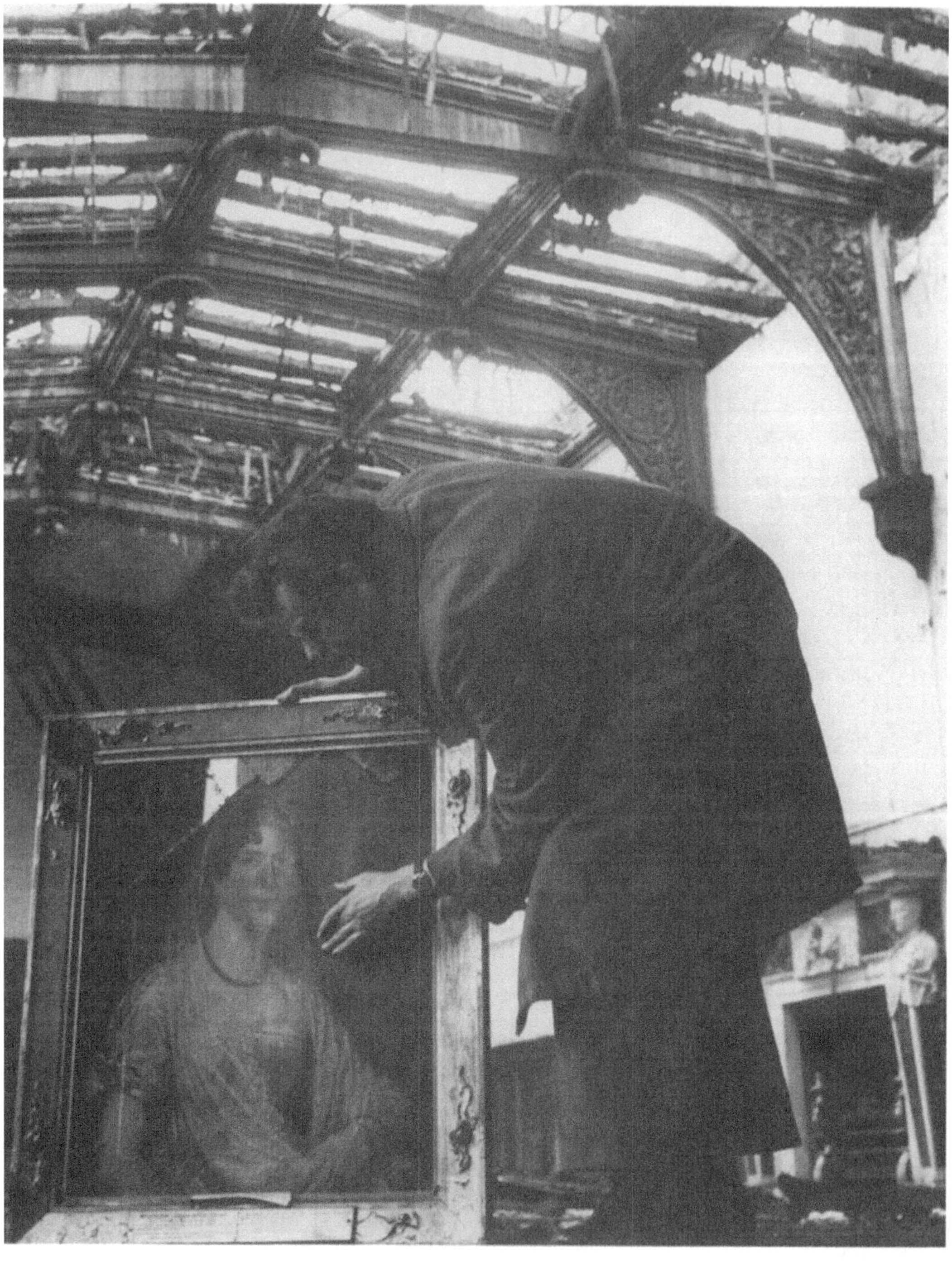

Aftermath of the Newstead Abbey Fire in 1965, in which the picture salon was badly damaged and the Italian Renaissance ceiling destroyed. Here the curator is examining a damaged oil-painting of Byron's mother. (Photo: Raymonds of Derby)

SAFETY IN MUSEUMS AND GALLERIES

Editor

F. Howie

Museum Safety Officer,
British Museum (Natural History), London

Published in association with

The International Journal of

MUSEUM MANAGEMENT AND CURATORSHIP

Edited by

Peter and Caroline Cannon-Brookes

Butterworths

London Boston Durban Singapore Sydney Toronto Wellington

First published 1987

British Library Cataloguing in Publication Data

Safety in museums and galleries: special
supplement to The International journal
of museum management and curatorship.
1. Museums – Safety measures 2. Museums
– Hygiene aspects
I. Howie, F. II. The International journal
of museum management and curatorship;
ISSN 0260-4779
363.1'19069 AM7

ISBN 0-408-02362-7

Library of Congress Cataloguing-in-Publication Data

Safety in museums and galleries.

Special supplement to The International journal of
museum management and curatorship.
Bibliography: p.
Includes index.
1. Museums – Security measures. 2. Museums –
Safety measures. 3. Museum conservation methods.
I. Howie, F. (Frank) II. International journal of museum
management and curatorship. Supplement.
AM148.S34 1987 069.5'028'9 87-23896
ISBN 0-408-02362-7

Photoset by Butterworths Litho Preparation Department

Printed in Great Britain by
Henry Ling Ltd., at the Dorset Press, Dorchester, Dorset

Foreword

The Health and Safety at Work Etc. Act 1974 has proved to be a far-reaching legislative instrument that now regulates working practices in every place of employment. Museums and galleries are not, I imagine, commonly regarded as high-risk places of employment, but nevertheless there have been many changes as they have responded in getting to grips with the requirements of the Act.

It is appropriate, therefore, that the Museums' Association, the United Kingdom Institute for Conservation and the British Museum (Natural History) should jointly have taken the initiative in organizing the 1985 Conference on Safety in Museums and Galleries, whose proceedings substantially form the contents of this volume, for there has been a marked change in attitude towards safety practices over the past decade. From an initial tendency to regard health and safety at work as requiring simply the continuation of the common-sense attitude that had long prevailed there has been a shift to the present situation of a shared responsibility between management, staff and their unions in providing a safe and conducive working environment.

The chapters in this volume authoritatively review the past ten years and examine the present status of health and safety legislation, policy, and practice in our museums and galleries, and I commend the volume to all who work in them. Clearly much has been achieved, but equally there can be no place for complacency. A healthy and safe working environment is not the product of chance but derives from a responsible attitude by all towards the securing and maintenance of optimum conditions in which to work. It is to this end that this volume is devoted.

A. C. Bishop
Deputy Director
British Museum (Natural History)
London

January 1987

Preface

Originally conceived as the 'Proceedings of the Safety in Museums Meeting' held in the autumn of 1985 in London, this Special Supplement to *The International Journal of Museum Management and Curatorship* has developed from that meeting, which was jointly organized by the Museums Association (United Kingdom), the International Institute for Conservation (IIC), and the British Museum (Natural History) to review the state of play regarding both approaches to occupational safety in museums and the extent to which they had been successful, or not, in handling problems, chiefly as they affected staff but also, to some extent, the visiting public. Hence, this volume follows closely the original organization of the meeting and is divided into four sections, each covering a major topic of fundamental importance to institutions large and small.

The original meeting, held over two days, was too short to enable every aspect of occupational and visitor safety in museums and galleries to be considered, and it was agreed that the 'Proceedings' should be expanded to cover at least some of the important topics which had to be omitted in 1985. Consequently, this Special Supplement has been designed primarily to illustrate the 'state of the art' regarding knowledge, awareness and approaches to safety in museums and galleries, and to highlight some of the problem areas, general and specific, which are met by curators, conservators and administrators. It was neither the intention of the 1985 meeting nor that of the Editors to produce a text detailing every specific hazard and its control. Such data are readily available in an increasing number of current textbooks and journals and are, of course, constantly changing with improving knowledge.

Section One, 'Legal and Administrative Framework', is designed to give an overview of the legal and administrative background, commencing with a résumé of developments during the past decade within the framework of United Kingdom safety legislation. Other chapters here cover the need for, and structure of, safety policies and their use in managing health and safety in museums; risk management in museums and the penalties, legal and financial, for failing to comply with simple precautions; the legal liabilities of museum employers and employees, and the special situation of visitors and contractors; and finally the role that the governmental regulatory agencies play in museum activities.

Section Two, 'Aspects of Museum Safety', commences with an examination, in some detail, of the particular problems met by conservators, drawing on experience gained in museums in both the United States of America and the United Kingdom. These include pest control and related fumigation hazards, the control of a wide range of hazards stemming from toxic chemicals to the handling of fragile art objects, and the activities of the Centre for Occupational Hazards in New York in respect of the safety of museum personnel and visitors. The following chapters cover the importance of collecting and assessing accident statistics in museums as the basis for safety training priority and the design of safe systems of operation, and, finally, the importance of considering a multidisciplinary approach to solving specific museum safety problems.

The third section, 'Hazards and Their Control', which has been considerably expanded from the topics covered at the 1985 meeting, contains seven chapters discussing basic elements of hazard recognition and control. Toxicology and its importance in the practice of conservation is outlined; the use of local exhaust ventilation with 'dos' and 'don'ts' for the control of hazardous volatile materials at source is described; the fundamental importance of careful planning for safe practice, whether in the laboratory, workshop or studio, is outlined; and a chapter devoted to fire safety details the obligations of all those who work in museums. There then follow three chapters which cover the basic approaches to maintaining individual safety, through the use of protective equipment such as guards and eye protection in workshops, and by the avoidance of biological hazards such as sensitizing materials.

The fourth and final section, 'Information Sources and Training in Safety', covers access to health and safety information through the use of both conventional and computer-based data retrieval systems and approaches to safety training by professional organizations.

The Special Supplement concludes with a bibliography and appendices which cover useful standards, books and journals on occupational health and safety and fire safety, safety organizations in the UK and USA, and a model safety inspection checklist. However, lists of manufacturers, suppliers and distributors are not included for the reason that addresses, and even the names of companies, have the habit of changing so rapidly as to render their inclusion unhelpful.

F. Howie
Museum Safety Officer
British Museum (Natural History)
London

January 1987

Contents

Contributors

Michael R. Bailey is Safety Officer and Occupational Safety Adviser at the London School of Hygiene and Tropical Medicine. He holds an MSc in radiation biology, and spent several years in University College Hospital and The National Institute for Medical Research with particular responsibilities for radiation protection and safety organization. In his present post, as well as School Safety Officer, he teaches safety management and radiation safety and is involved in research and consultancy work, particularly on Legionnaires' disease and AIDS-related problems.

Ian Bartlett is occupational hygienist at the London School of Hygiene and Tropical Medicine. He obtained an MSc in hygiene at the school and helped to co-ordinate the school's occupational medicine hygiene service. He is currently involved in research into safety problems in the textile industry, in particular with the development of dust sampling methods and the development of field techniques for protective clothing.

Jake Bharier started work as a paint technologist in the laboratories of a large paint company. He became the company's group health and safety officer in 1976, and moved to the Courtalds Group Safety Department in 1980. He has a particular interest in chemical hazards and their control, and in the quality of information available in this area.

Gordon Chapman is Director of Occupational Safety at The Royal Society for the Prevention of Accidents (ROSPA). After many years' experience in industry, firstly as plant and production engineer and later as safety engineer, he joined ROSPA in 1973 as Training Manager for the industrial safety training centre in Birmingham. Here he developed 'in company' safety training courses tailored to the needs of individual companies. He is now responsible for all occupational safety matters in ROSPA, including training, journals, booklets, posters, conferences and exhibitions.

Peter Constable is the Deputy Medical Adviser with the Civil Service Occupational Health Service, which provides a comprehensive occupational health service to the National Museums. Apart from a keen interest in museum hazards the author's other interests include agricultural medicine and a wide range of malted barley products.

Paul Double is a barrister who specializes in parliamentary work. Previously he was in chambers dealing mainly with personal injury and professional negligence claims. He was a member of a government legislation review unit which monitored the development of many of the new health and safety laws brought in under the Health and Safety at Work Act 1974. He has also been Secretary of the Health and Safety Commission Printing Industry Committee's Working Part on isocyanates and Subcommittee on chemicals, producing publications on safety in the use of inks, varnishes and lacquers cured by ultraviolet light (HMSO, 1986), and the provision of health and safety information by importers and suppliers (HMSO, 1986). Apart from lecturing to government personnel on health and safety law, Mr Double is a lecturer for London University's external Bachelor of Laws degree, and is editor of a casebook on the Law of Evidence.

Elizabeth A. Griffiths is the Administrator of The Phillips Collection in Washington, DC. She was formerly the Business Manager at Monticello, the home of Thomas Jefferson, in Charlottesville, Virginia. She received her undergraduate degree in English from Trinity College in Washington, DC, and a masters degree in business administration from the Colgate Darden Graduate School of Business Administration at the University of Virginia, where until recently she taught a course in business communications.

Frank Howie was appointed the first full-time Safety Officer at the British Museum (Natural History) in 1984 after several years working as Conservator in the Museum's Paleontology Department. He is author of a number of papers and has lectured widely in Europe and North America on both conservation and safety topics. He has chaired a number of safety committees including the London (Southern) Occupational Health and Safety Group, and has acted as a consultant on various aspects of museum technology.

Donald Hughes graduated in physics in 1951 and was later awarded a PhD for research into the magnetic properties of uranium. He has worked in industry, at the Royal Marsden Hospital Institute of Cancer Research, London, and was a Medical Research Council Follow at the University of Leeds. He then served as the university's Radiation Protection Officer, apart from periods as a Visiting Lecturer at the University of Minnesota and as the World Health Organization Consultant in Radiological Health in Iran. He is now the University of Leeds' Radiation Protection Adviser and Head of the Radiation Protection Service. Donald Hughes is the author or editor of over 80 scientific publications, including the Science Reviews Series of Monographs on Occupational Hygiene, the British Occupational Hygiene Society's Technical Guide Series, and the HHSC Handbook Series. He has been involved in the design of fumecupboards and ventilation systems since the 1960s, and has often acted as a consultant in this field.

Sheila Pantry BA, ALA, is a qualified librarian with many years' experience in library and information work. A varied career in iron and steel, engineering, research and the coal industry culminated in 1977 at the Health and Safety Executive, where she is Head of Library and Information Services. Author of many papers and a well-known speaker, Sheila Pantry has become a leading authority in the UK on the wide-ranging information associated with health and safety at work. She has also carried out consultancy work for Occupational Safety and Health organizations in Canada, Australia (Canberra), Jordan and Dublin, and is a computer addict.

Hani Raafat is a lecturer in Health and Safety at the Department of Chemical Engineering, Aston University. Dr Raafat has produced over 20 publications, and 3 books on reliability, risk assessment and machinery safety. He is a member of the British and European Standards Committees on Fluid Power Machinery Safety, and his main research interests are machinery risk assessment and human reliability analysis.

Monona Rossol is a potter, chemist and art teacher, with a special interest in the hazards of the materials used in art and art conservation. She holds a BS in chemistry, an MS in ceramics and sculpture, and an MFA from the University of Wisconsin-Madison. In 1977 Monona Rossol helped to found the Centre for Occupational Hazards, and is currently its President and the Director of its Art Hazards Information Center. She lectures and consults nationally about hazards in the arts, conservation and theatre. She has written over 20 data sheets for the COH and regularly contributes to the *Art Hazard News*. She has also written a book on theatre hazards and is working currently on a book about ceramics hazards.

Shane Rowles is an occupational hygienist who qualified and worked at the London School of Hygiene and Tropical Medicine. She now works as Lead Occupational Hygiene Consultant for Casella Environmental Services.

Elisabeth Sherman is Principal Inspector of Factories with many years' involvement with several London Museums. From a background in food microbiology and water chemistry she has worked in the Health and Safety Executive, on the production of the Lead Regulation and on negotiations on the EC Lead Directive, as well as inspecting all types of establishments in the London area.

Roger Slade graduated in chemistry from Hull University. In 1969 he was appointed lecturer at Queen Elizabeth College London. He became safety officer for the Chemistry Department in 1972 and for the next six years chaired the college's safety committee. In 1978 he was appointed College Safety Officer on a part-time basis. Following the merger of King's, Queen Elizabeth and Chelsea Colleges in August 1985 he became Kensington Campus Safety Officer and then, in October 1986, he was appointed the first full-time Safety Officer for King's College London (KQC). His particular interests are in fire and electrical safety, and workplace environmental monitoring. Dr Slade has lectured and written widely on these and other topics, and is a member of the Institute of University Safety Officers and the Association of University Radiation Protection Officers.

Allan St John Holt is managing director of E. St John Holt and Associates Limited, an occupational health and safety consultancy based in Southampton, England. A fellow and past president of the Institution of Occupational Safety and Health, he spends much of his time travelling, lecturing and writing on behavioural aspects of health and safety at work. Allan St John Holt represents IOSH on the Board of the Federation of Associations of Specialists in Occupational Safety and Health (FAS), of which he is Vice-President. He is a member of the American Society of Safety Engineers and Vererans of Safety, and is the only European elected to the Construction Section Executive of the American National Safety Council. He is co-author of the recent SCAUM Manual, *Health and Safety in Archaeology.*

Frank Swaine is a Senior Area Director for the Health and Safety Executive. Trained as a physicist, he spent several years working on legislation for the control and use of flammable liquids and on the EC directive on packaging and labelling regulations. He is actively involved with problems in the construction industry.

Anthony Waldron is consultant physician in occupational medicine to University College Hospital, London, consultant to the Occupational Health Department of the Hospital for Sick Children, London, and senior lecturer in occupational medicine at the London School of Hygiene & Tropical Medicine. He is Editor of the *British Journal of Industrial Medicine*, and is the author of a number of books on occupational medicine.

Section 1. Legal and Administrative Framework

Every museum and gallery has a two-fold responsibility, to protect both its employees (and those who use the collections) and the public who visit the premises to view the exhibits. Museum management is thus charged with important duties of care for all who enter their premises, including their grounds, buildings and, where applicable, the exhibits themselves. Failure to carry out these duties in a reasonable manner could result, if a member of staff or the public is injured, in a civil claim for damages or, where a breach of statutory obligation has been committed, a criminal action being brought against the museum.

Safety and health statutory legislation in both the United Kingdom and the United States of America is composed of enabling Acts. The major pieces of this legislation are The Health and Safety at Work Etc. Act 1974 in the United Kingdom, and the Occupational Safety and Health Act 1970 in the United States of America. Both are comparatively recent and are continuously being reinforced by statutory regulations and non-statutory guidance. Under these Acts and regulations employers and employees have specific duties, both absolute and conditional, to ensure that the place of work is kept free from hazards.

However, perhaps the most important legal redress available to an individual working in the United Kingdom who wishes to seek compensation from his or her employer for a work-related illness or injury is through the civil court, where claims under common law are heard. Possibly contrary to popular belief, the phrase 'safe system of work' was not defined by any action brought under a safety law, but under common law.

This section encompasses a wide range of views on the application of both common law and safety law to situations encountered in museums, and commences with an overview of developments in United Kingdom safety legislation during the past decade. The rest of the section covers the following topics:

- Reasonable practicability in safety legislation
- Museums and liability
- The individual and liability
- Contractors and liability
- The Occupiers' Liability Act
- Why have a safety policy at all?
- Constructing a safety policy
- Safety policy objectives
- Policy organization and arrangements
- Publicizing the policy
- Responsibility for policy
- The role of the inspector
- How inspections are carried out in museums
- Some museum problems
- Enforcement
- Improvement and prohibition notices
- Museums and insurance
- Risk management in museums
- Implementation of a museum risk programme

1.1 HASAWA—the Health and Safety at Work Act

The First Ten Years

F. J. Swaine

To a readership which is generally concerned with conserving historic artifacts, the last 10 years seems a very short time indeed. However, it is useful to go back to examine what happened at the beginning of those 10years. The Robens Commission was set up in 1972 to carry out a study into health and safety at work in the United Kingdom, and into the basic legal requirements which were then extant. These were essentially, the Factory Acts and the health and safety Act relating to Offices, Shops and Railway Premises. There was a considerable body of regulations relating to these Acts and much of it was very outdated. This legislation was difficult to interpret and was fragmentary in the sense that, for example, certain risks from lead were covered by regulations while other risks from lead were not, although there were the same risks to health in both cases.

The Robens Committee formed the view that the existing legislation should be simplified, and that it should be all-embracing, dealing not only with the risk to the worker, as did previous legislation, but with risks to the general public or anybody else who might be affected by work activities. To a large extent the wishes of Robens have been carried through. There is, however, one important observation to be made here—that whilst there is still a vast amount of legislation, much of it yet to be simplified, it deals with people at large and with risks to everybody. The Act itself has embodied as a criminal requirement, in accordance with Robens's suggestion, the sorts of risk that were hitherto considered solely the province of civil law, the law of tort (i.e. civil wrongs). These formerly gave cause for civil action but not to criminal action. This requirement is tailored by the words 'reasonably practicable', a concept which had received considerable attention in the courts, much of it long before the Health and Safety at Work Etc. Act was enacted in 1974.

'Reasonably practicable' means, in relation to health and safety legislation, that the risk of an activity is placed on one side of the scale and on the other you place the cost of removing that risk, whether in terms of money, expertise, manpower, and so on. It is, however, all very well in a legal judgement to make that sort of balance, but it is often in different terms. The cost of providing a protective guard or an operating improvement may be so much, but the cost of the mischief may be difficult to determine and express in monetary terms. Nevertheless it can be done, and during these 10 years a philosophical approach to 'reasonably practicable' has developed, perhaps to the extent that it is now central to the very being of the Health and Safety Commission (HSC). This is effectively a quango and quite distinct from the Health and Safety Executive (HSE), which employs the inspectors and policy workers who develop health and safety techniques. The inspectorate is described in more detail by Sherman later in this section in Chapter 1.4.

The Commission examines what the Health and Safety Executive is doing and often asks for things to be done, but it does not intervene in individual cases, and it does not say that you must prosecute this place of work or you must not prosecute that one. The Health and Safety Commission is composed of three representatives proposed by the Trades Union Congress, three by the Confederation of British Industry (the employers' side of industry), and two local authority representatives. Ever since its inception these two local authority representatives have been politically split—one Tory and one Labour. There is therefore a political complexion to the Commission and there is a balance to be struck. The Chairman is there but hardly ever gives a deciding vote. His job is to obtain a consensus, and basically this is what is sought throughout. The balance is present when preparing 'Regulations', 'Codes of Practice', 'Guidance Notes', and so on. A great deal of time is spent reaching a consensus, and this is achieved by speaking to technical and professional associations and bodies that may have a particular interest in the issue at hand.

The Health and Safety Executive publishes consultative documents on the gist of proposed new legislation, and anybody in the United Kingdom is encouraged to comment on the proposals. A great many comments are received from a large number of associations and from industry, and a fair number from individuals who are of the opinion that something ought to be put right. Sometimes a letter from a member of the public suggests that something is wrong and that another provision is needed.

Consultation works reasonably well, but the simplification of legal requirements is extremely difficult to effect. For instance, some time ago the present author, faced by an audience of Chief Fire Officers, was asked how on earth the Health and Safety at Work Etc. Act 1974 could apply to what they did since they provided in-depth training to deal with very dangerous situations. To answer their queries they had to be made aware that the Health and Safety at Work Act applies to everybody at work, to acrobats, to high-wire walkers, and even to people who put their heads in lions' mouths. There are obviously circumstances in the dangerous professions where extra caution needs to be taken: high-wire walkers must be very sure that wire will not break under them and that the supports for it are satisfactory to keep them from the utmost peril. There is no easy answer to this question, and it is no answer at all to suggest that somebody should be exempt just because they are involved in a dangerous activity. In those heady days of 10 years ago, it had only to be suggested that more expertise or more inspectors were needed and within a short time they materialized. For the past 5 years, however, the Factory Inspectorate, the largest part of the Executive and that which enforces the legislation, has had a policy of no recruitment. This has produced strains already, and will bring further strains in the future. As good Civil Servants, of course, what the Health and Safety Executive has to do is to make the best use of the resources available, e.g. by using computers for their work programmes to identify premises for priority attention.

From an inspector's point of view, what is the main thrust of the Health and Safety at Work Act? There are two ways in which inspectors can operate. They can find a poor factory or an unsafe museum that is badly managed and then work away to improve the premises using all the powers at their disposal: advice, prohibition notices and prosecution to improve that unsafe workplace. There are, however, some much more fundamental things that they should seek to do—they must try to change attitudes. In 1833, when the first inspectors were appointed, attitudes towards children in work were appalling. Few would now accept such work conditions and today, in a radically different world from that of the 1830s, most people would say 'What dreadful people they must have been!' We are, however, all creatures of our time, and in another 100 years or so our descendants will perhaps also be saying 'What dreadful people they must have been! Look at all that asbestos they sprayed around the country, acres of it, thousands of square miles!' A major change of attitude in recent times has been displayed by many members of senior management. When the present author joined the Factory Inspectorate in 1957, it was sometimes possible to discuss problems with senior management, but frequently it was an approach that had little lasting effect. However, senior management of large companies have significantly changed their attitude to safety matters within the last 10 years. Every safety policy now requires a named person at high level to be personally responsible for carrying out the provisions of the policy. Indeed a Director of Roads in a local authority, and a Managing Director of a large engineering company have been prosecuted as individuals under the Health and Safety at Work Act.

There is another significant change, for which the Health and Safety Executive and the Atomic Energy Authority can jointly claim credit, and that is the approach to high-risk areas, such as the Canvey Island problem. Sir Bernard Braine, a hard-hitting Member of Parliament, pursued the question of the safety of his constituents on Canvey Island who lived amidst some five oil refineries and similar high-risk premises. The Health and Safety Executive spent a large sum on an assessment of the risks, including societal risks and the risks specific to those living on Canvey Island. This approach set the scene for the rest of the world regarding the societal study of high-risk areas. In a similar way the laboratories of the Health and Safety Executive have taken on board the question of gas cloud dispersion, in an attempt to predict levels of risk on an international scale. The population at large is now far more wary of large stocks maintained at chemical works, and these fears were tragically realized at Flixborough with the total devastation of that chemical works and considerable loss of life. It had been forecast that the really large man-made disasters would be due to release of toxic substances rather than fire and explosion, and this has now, of course, occurred at Bhopal with colossal loss of life. Not long before, there was a very serious fire and explosion at Mexico City. Television makes disasters impinge on each of us, and almost every day a plane crash or a major fire is brought within minutes into our living rooms. This has led to a frightening change in perception of risk amongst the general public. Sometimes this may be an appropriate reaction, and sometimes it may be misplaced, but in each case assurance is required.

The Health and Safety practitioner of today is dealing with very difficult concepts. When members of the public are involved and worried, responses often develop political dimensions, and of course Members of Parliament need to consider their constituents' requirements for preserving the health and safety of the community at large. An example of this perception was the impact of the San Carlos Camp-site disaster almost 10 years ago, when a tanker carrying liquid gas broke down outside the camp-site and subsequently exploded, killing more than 200 people. This immediately led to a demand for regulations to be introduced, to control the transport by road of dangerous substances. The European Economic Community (EEC), a few months later, obliged and we now, quite rightly, enjoy the benefits of extensive legislation on the transport of dangerous goods. From the conveyance of dangerous substances in the United Kingdom there has been only one death recorded in recent years—that of a lady who abandoned her car when there was a spillage of a corrosive material, and was virtually dissolved in that spillage.

Most practitioners would like regulations to be both comprehensive and sufficiently flexible to allow for a number of variations on a particular theme of safety to encourage innovations. To a certain extent this is inherent in the flexibility of much safety legislation. Approved Codes of Practice can be produced by the Health and Safety

Executive or, for example, by the British Standards Institution. What this means is that in relation to that particular risk, or array of risks, the Commission has approved, with the agreement of the Secretary of State, a way of dealing with the particular problems. Failure to comply with a Code of Practice could be used as evidence that all that was 'reasonably practicable' had not been carried out, and in that case the onus would fall on the accused to show that their measures were either as good as the Code of Practice or better. This is, of course, quite convenient and useful for large companies who are in the forefront of developments in health and safety. They can develop a system that at least does what is immediately required by the law and develop from there. But, nevertheless, there are many smaller industrial concerns which find it difficult to decide exactly what they should do, and the concept of what is reasonably practicable is not much help to them. The Health and Safety Executive produce a fair body of detailed requirements which, given some guidance, the smaller firms and less professional or less expert people will be able to follow and should keep them free from health and safety problems.

During its heyday, the asbestos industry spread some 300 000 tons of crocidolite, or blue asbestos, around the country. As it was frequently mixed with varying amounts of other types of asbestos, the acreage of the most dangerous type is enormous. There is a very substantial risk to the men who work with it, but there is also, for the general public, a very slight risk involved.

Entry into Europe has brought to the United Kingdom a number of changes in legislation, and the present author's chief responsibility has been with regard to the Classification, Packaging and Labelling (CPL) Regulations. (It has been estimated that there is enough work in Brussels for at least 10 000 years in relation to Classification, Packaging and Labelling!) The regulations initially incorporated the Brussels requirements. These, however, change at least once a year, not in general terms, but in the lists of the substances covered. Further complications arise because the regulations incorporate the United Nations requirements for conveyance of substances by road. There are differences between the two sets of requirements and if, for instance, a carcinogenic material is on board a lorry, unless the carrier/driver actually spends the whole of his life loading the lorry with this carcinogen, the risk from it is very slight indeed. This situation would require somewhat different labelling from the supply of the same substance to a household or to a chemical works, and so on, but the Conveyancing, Packaging and Labelling (CPL) Regulations came into effect on 1 January 1986. There are considerable difficulties, some brought about by the administrative system under which the Directives are written in Brussels, and of course a number of deals have been struck, some in the open and some more covert, amongst the European nations who are part of the Community. However, labelling will be standardized and will also bear risk and safety phrases. Though these are not always sufficiently detailed to protect all people in all uses of the material, the labels do at least give a warning to whoever should pick up a bottle or a box that it contains something that needs further inquiry. These regulations are likely to be directly relevant to museums.

In the construction industry, there are at least 150 fatalities a year. Included amongst those fatalities are members of the general public, and it is a factor, particularly on the maintenance side, that affects us all. It certainly affects museums not only in respect of building maintenance but also the more simple maintenance tasks. All expose people to a certain degree of risk, and the unfortunate part is, of course, that the law of gravity continues to operate throughout, and that gives rise to a substantial number of serious and maiming accidents. Other problems in the construction industry are old ones. Asbestos is all-pervading, whilst involved in almost anything related to demolition is lead. Probably one of our oldest poisons, it is still a risk, and should you burn debris that is lead-painted, the fumes poison whoever is in charge of the operation. We have made only a start on the way towards our Citizen of 100 years hence, who will look back and condemn us, but it can be said honestly that we have at least made that start.

1.2 Safety Legislation for Museums, and Their Directors and Conservators

Paul Double

Since the Health and Safety at Work Etc. Act 1974, and other safety legislation, is adequately covered in other chapters, the purpose of this contribution is not to discuss in detail its provisions. Rather it is to introduce some of the general principles of liability which arise in relation to safety, and to illustrate the sort of thinking that goes into a finding of liability in circumstances which may be encountered in the museum world.

Museums and Liability

Those who work in museums, as well as those who are responsible for operating them, are likely to find themselves at some time or another involved with the law of safety. Generally this will stem from an accident after which, in the normal run of affairs, people will tend to point an accusing finger and you are one of the selection of people at whom the finger can most appropriately be pointed. If you are the operator of a museum, or a member of the workforce in the museum's laboratories or workshops, you may find yourself responsible for not only the actions of museum staff and the activities of contractors, but also for those of outside visitors who have come along to view the museum, or indeed people such as salesmen who are unconnected with your primary activities in the museum. Generally speaking, whether or not you are going to be found liable in any given case will depend on whether or not you have been careful, and in the law, both under the Health and Safety at Work Etc. Act 1974[1] and at common law, what a court assesses is whether or not the person who is alleged to be at fault exercised 'reasonable care'. Now that is rather like saying 'how long is a piece of string?', because it depends on the circumstances, and if you ask a lawyer 'what do you mean by reasonable care?' his answer will be just that. There are, however, some guidelines.

The first is the *degree of risk*. The degree of care which the law requires people to take depends on the degree of risk, so the greater the risk, the more care needs to be taken. For example, no one would usually criticize a museum operator for not arranging that someone check every three months to make sure that the roof of the exhibition hall was not going to fall down on the people below. However, if the museum had reason to know that the roof was full of dry rot, that might be a perfectly reasonable thing to expect, and if it were not done the museum might be liable in the event of an accident.

A second consideration is the *likelihood of injury*. The likelihood of injury or damage being caused is a matter which a court will take into account in deciding how much care should have been taken in particular circumstances and, to use the words of one judge, 'People must guard against reasonable probabilities but not fantastic possibilities'. Every situation depends on its own facts. If a blind person visits a museum it is clearly not going to be terribly useful to illustrate a hazard, such as a hole in the floor, by putting up a notice. Of course, if there were no expectation that blind persons would visit the premises, the situation might well be different.

A third consideration is the *nature of the consequences* which flow from the event concerned. The degree of care required of a person or organization is proportional to the gravity of the consequences if the degree of care is not met. Clearly it is incumbent upon someone in a museum laboratory to exercise more care in using cyanide than in using domestic bleach, because the likely result of exposure to those two chemicals is, of course, widely different in seriousness.

Fourth, there is a *consideration of cost*. The cost of adopting precautionary measures is relevant, but its relevance declines as the magnitude of the risk and the seriousness of the result increases. Thus, whilst it would be appropriate in assessing liability to consider the cost of a precaution for guarding a machine where a failure to guard it could result in a broken finger nail, if the machine were a power press which could cause very serious injury, the cost factor would be very much less influential.

Liability and the Individual

The four considerations above are perhaps those which are most frequently used by the courts in assessing liability. Most of the examples cited have assumed that we are talking about the liability of a museum operator, but of course the individuals who work in musems may also themselves be liable, either at common law or under the Health and Safety at Work Act 1974. If individual employees fail to exercise reasonable care in relation to their own actions (the cyanide example above is one), then they may be liable in criminal proceedings under Section 7 of the Health and Safety at Work Act 1974. It is more normal, however, for the employer—the operator of the museum—to be the party against whom proceedings are taken, whether at common law or under the 1974 Act. The law makes an employer liable for the acts of employees, so if an employee does not take reasonable care, and damage or injury is caused, the museum operator will be liable as well as the employee. The employer is not, however, liable for all acts of employees, but only those done in the course of employment, that is, related to the employees' work. So if one employee decides to put a pin on a colleague's chair and, as a result,that colleague contracts blood poisoning and dies, the employer is very unlikely to be found liable. However, the current trend is to make the employer liable for more rather than fewer acts of employees, and some recent cases have shown a tendency to regard what might have been previously dismissed as pranks to be within the course of the employees' work, thus making the employer liable.[2] The employer may be required to provide people who are not his employees with information that is necessary to ensure that his own employees are safe. Thus, if a museum operator brings in a contractor to perform some specialist restoration work and the contractor's employees wrongly use chemicals which asphyxiate members of museum staff, then it is possible that the museum operator may be found liable on the basis that he failed to give information to the contrator's employees to ensure that his own employees were safe.[3] The activities of contractors are covered in more detail below because they raise special problems.

Liability and Contractors

Liability for safety matters, as for most other things, can arise in a number of different ways, and with contractors it is necessary to consider the situation first under the general common law and then under the Occupier's Liability Act 1957. People in museums may wish to hire contractors for a number of different purposes. Normally, however, they are hired to undertake particular tasks, often in an 'expert' capacity. Generally, an employer is not liable for the failure of a contractor, or the contractor's employees, to exercise reasonable care in the execution of work which the contractor has been engaged to carry out. This general rule is, however, subject to important exceptions. If you, as a museum operator, engage an independent contractor to do something which is unlawful, such as trespass for example, then you will certainly not avoid liability by saying that the contractor was the person who trespassed. More importantly, from the museum's point of view, where a contractor's work involves the creation of a dangerous thing, such as fire, caustic or explosive vapours, and things of that sort, then the person who engages the contractor will be liable if, through the fault of the contractor, some catastrophe ensues because the contractor or his employees have failed to take reasonable care. So, for example, if you as a museum operator engage a firm to remove a large central-heating tank, and the contractor's chemist samples the atmosphere and says it is safe to cut the tank, and if, through the chemist's fault, the atmosphere is in fact flammable so that the tank explodes when oxyacetylene cutting equipment is used, then the museum operator will be liable for the damage caused by the explosion.[4]

A similar rule applies to work undertaken on or near highways. For example, a museum operator wishes to remove, or receive, a large exhibit at its premises, and a specialist contractor is engaged to perform the task of removing or placing the exhibit in the building, employing a lorry-mounted crane parked on the adjacent roadway for the purpose. Then, through lack of care, an accident occurs when the load becomes unstable. In those circumstances the museum operator, as occupier of the premises, is liable to the highway users injured as a result of the occurrence. This principle is not strictly limited to dangers created on the highway, but extends to dangers created anywhere where other persons are lawfully passing.[5] Finally, it should be mentioned that, at common law, if a person engages an independent contractor to discharge a statutory duty put on that person, which the contractor then fails to perform, the person who engaged the contractor will still be liable. So, for example, under the Factories Act, a person who engages a contractor to guard machinery in a workshop cannot raise a defence on a suggestion that it is not his failure but that of the independent contractor which has given rise to any contravention, if that person is subsequently alleged to have contravened the Act by not guarding the machinery properly.[6]

Museums and the Occupiers' Liability Act

The above is the general common law position, but mention should also be made of the Occupiers Liability Act, 1957.[7] This Act lays down a general code of liability for occupiers of premises that invite visitors—a broad term meaning more or less everyone except trespassers—and that category does of course include museums. The same standard of care—reasonable care—is required under the Act, but there are some provisions which are of particular relevance in relation to contractors. Section 2(3)(b) of the Act says that an occupier may expect that a person in the exercise of his calling will appreciate and guard against any special risks which are part and parcel of that person's business. Section 2(4)(b) states that where damage is caused by a danger due to faulty execution of any work of construction, maintenance or repair, by an independent contractor employed by the occupier, the occupier is not liable if he had acted reasonably in entrusting the work to an independent contractor and had taken reasonable steps to satisfy himself that the contractor was competent and that the work had been properly done.

The practical result of these two provisions is that when, for example, a contract electrician visits a museum to perform some work, there is no requirement for the museum operator to tell him about the dangers arising from electricity. He is expected to know them. If the electrician does the work badly and someone working at or visiting the museum is injured, then the museum will not be liable if it can be shown that it was reasonable to engage a specialist for the sort of work undertaken, and that there was no reason to suppose anything was wrong with the work which had been done. It is, of course, perfectly reasonable to engage an electrician to do electrical work because that is not within the sphere of competence of ordinary people without specialist training. So, too, if that electrician has held himself out as competent through, say, an advertisement and there is nothing to indicate that the work has been poorly performed—no bare wires emerging from walls and so on—then the museum will have an effective defence under the Act.

The Occupiers' Liability Act is not a criminal statute, but the Health and Safety at Work Act embodies many of the principles which are to be found in this earlier Act. They are not explicitly stated, and as is well known, the Act is content to describe duties in the broadest terms, but liability under the 'general duties' sections of the Act will doubtless oblige any court to consider matters relevant at common law in assessing reasonableness under the 1974 Act. There is as yet little legal authority to illustrate this, although at least one case (involving asbestos) has arisen in which the court adopted a similar line in assessing the liability of the employer for the acts of an asbestos-removal contractor to those already mentioned under the common law.[8]

Conclusion

This is necessarily a brief look at a very wide subject area. In assessing the risks occasioned by activities within a museum, the guidelines referred to should, however, provide an indication of the sort of situations in which liability may arise.

Notes

1. 1974: Chapter 37. A detailed discussion of the legal principles underlying the 'new style' legislation is given in Drake and Wright's *Law of Health and Safety at Work—The New Approach* (Sweet and Maxwell, 1983). The Health and Safety Executive publishes a number of free general guidance documents on the application of the 1974 Act.
2. For a recent example see *Harrison* v. *Michelin Tyre Co.* (1985) 1 All England Law Reports 918.
3. As an example see *R* v. *Swan Hunter Shipbuilders* (1981) Industrial Case Reports 831.
4. Applying *Rylands* v. *Fletcher* (1868) Law Reports, 3 House of Lords Series 330.
5. *Packard* v. *Smith* (1861) 10 Common Bench Reports (New Series) 470.
6. The Pass of Ballater (1942) 2 All England Law Reports 79.
7. 1957: Chapter 31. This Act did not cover trespassers, now dealt with under the Occupiers' Liability Act 1984 (1984: Chapter 3).
8. *T. Kilroe & Sons* v. *Gower;* Liverpool Crown Court (not reproduced in the Law Reports).

1.3 Safety Policies in Museums: Why and How

Allan St John Holt

Accidents at work are easy to dismiss as due merely to a lack of care and attention on the part of employees. They are thought to be difficult to predict, expensive if not actually impossible to control, and anyway infrequent on the premises of museums and conservation activities. Accidents are indeed relatively infrequent, but their consequences can be devastating to individuals and to an organization. The only alternative to trusting to luck is to plan—for health as well as safety—since exposure to some of the sophisticated and toxic chemicals currently in use for conservation work can be responsible for slow, long-term damage to the body. Serious accidents are mercifully rare events, but an awareness of this fact can encourage the complacency so often cited at the top of the list of reasons why safety is given a low priority.

There is relatively little precise information available concerning accidents in United Kingdom museums. Accidents in industry have been widely studied, though, and some of the information obtained is of value to non-industrial organizations. The Health and Safety Executive recently studied fatal accidents due to transport, occurring in industry between 1978 and 1980. During that period, an astonishing 362 people died. More than a quarter of all work fatalities involve transport, and there are many more accidents which result in serious injuries or costly damage to plant. Their study, *Transport Kills*, makes interesting and sobering reading, especially the section which comes to the conclusion that 86 per cent of those deaths could have been prevented by reasonably practicable precautions, and that this percentage is common to other studies undertaken in different industries, not just in the field of transport.

The Health and Safety Executive concluded that the most common causes were poor management organization, failure to establish and follow a safe system of work, and inadequate training, information and instruction. Nobody goes to work consciously prepared to suffer serious injury or to die, and no one will admit to lacking that magic ingredient, common sense. Common sense is, of course, a necessary ingredient, but it is not in itself sufficient to prevent accidents. Everyone has perfect vision in hindsight; the difficult part is to put the hindsight where the foresight should be!

Why Have a Safety Policy?

Every activity has associated risks. The basic job of managing safety consists of identifying the potential for harm, evaluating the likelihood of harm, and controlling those circumstances where the risk is unacceptable by reason of the potential severity or frequency (or both) of harm. This is what is required by society, by the law and also by good business sense, because accidents and their consequences are expensive. More than 10 years after the introduction of the Health and Safety at Work Etc. Act 1974 it is still not uncommon to find senior officers in the public services saying 'I didn't know those

Regulations applied to me'. Managers seem especially surprised to learn that the Act applies to them, and that they are usually subject to the requirement to produce a written policy statement on health and safety which includes details of their specific organization and the arrangements made for the health and safety of their employees.

Guidance on these matters need not be expensive or hard to find and, contrary to popular belief, the control measures which are effective are usually those which cost little money. However, they do require commitment from management. The plain fact is that the comments in *Transport Kills* are not unique to transport safety. They apply to all industries, and only the remedying of them will provide a guarantee that health and safety at work is being efficiently managed. Luck is not a feature of a planned safety programme, nor is the blind following of rules and regulations all that is needed. Modern regulations are designed to avoid giving a list of 'dos and don'ts', but rather set a standard to be achieved by the employer without specifying how to do it.

Constructing a Safety Policy

The last sixty years have taught us much about the many ways in which accidents happen and the good sense of doing something about prevention in even the smallest organization. So where is one to start in managing safety? The simplest place to begin is with the safety policy statement. Constructing or revising this document is a useful exercise in its own right, as it concentrates the attention of senior managers on health and safety matters and satisfies a legal requirement on nearly all employers. Section 2(3) of the Health and Safety at Work Act (which applies to every employing organization, however large or small) requires every employer to:

> . . . prepare and revise when necessary a written statement of its general policy with respect to the health and safety at work of its employees and the organisation and arrangements for the time being in force for carrying out that policy, and to bring the statement and any revision of it to the notice of all its employees.

At present, the only exception is for an employer who employs fewer than five employees. Government discussions in 1986–1987 indicate that some relaxation of this rule may be forthcoming, with a view to raising the limit from five to a suggested twenty employees. Today, though, the present requirement affects the majority of employers, even though it is believed that as many as a third have not yet complied. Fines of £500 have been imposed on employers prosecuted for not having a safety policy. If the job of writing it has been delegated to you, the reader, the case of *Herron* v. *Armour* should be read, since the Director of Roads of Strathclyde Regional Council was prosecuted personally for neglect after failing to draw up a Departmental Policy as instructed by the Council. He lost the subsequent appeal.

There is no standard or model policy, and each employing organization must devise its own to cater for its own needs. However, nearly all policies will have common elements, such as are discussed below. It is most unlikely that a one-page policy statement with no cross-references to other documents will satisfy the requirements.

Safety policy statements are quasi-legal documents: that is to say they are not only required to be produced by law but they can also be used by the law-enforcement process against their compilers. In claims, they can be used by the plaintiff to illustrate that the employer has not carried out his own undertaking as alleged. In prosecution under the criminal law of the Act, managers may be charged with 'neglect', a term that requires some reference point or yardstick to measure what was done or omitted against what should have been done. That standard is what the employer said should be done, and is written down in the policy, which contains, as it must, details of responsibilities and duties. There is every reason not to entrust the writing of such a document to those with little knowledge of the organization's needs, or what may be reasonably achievable. One can quote the plight of the managing director of a national company who was in danger of personal prosecution. An accident to an employee in a distant part of the country was determined to be partially due to lack of training. On examination, the safety policy was found by an Inspector to delegate the responsibility for safety training to the managing director, who felt that this was clearly not achievable for him under the circumstances. 'Well,' said the Inspector, 'this may be so, but in that case your safety policy should not have made you responsible for it. Since it does, you are clearly negligent!' In the event, prosecution did not follow, but there was a rapid revision of the safety policy.

Policy Objectives

The first element of the safety policy will be a simple statement of objectives which can be met. It would be pious and unwise to claim that 'the employer will do everything possible to prevent accidents'. This is more than the law itself requires, and is most unlikely to represent the employer's real intentions, or even capabilities. A statement which is both readable and reasonable might begin: 'The organization will carry out work in the safest practicable manner, consistent with good practice'. Other components of this general statement should be: (a) a commitment to health and safety as a management responsibility, ranking as high in importance as anything else the organization does; (b) mention of the need for workforce cooperation; (c) a commitment to support employees in the event of conflict between the demands of safety and the work in hand if they reasonably choose the safety of employees or third parties as the priority; (d) the signature of the most senior member of the management team; and (e) the date of issue or revision.

Policy Organization and Arrangements

'Organization and arrangements' are harder to define. 'Organization' means the systematic delegation of responsibility, to the appropriate degree, to all levels in the organization. This is more complex in a large organization, but can be explained using a 'family tree' and listing the responsibilities for safety at each level of the structure. What is needed is an easy indication to employees of who is responsible for what, what are their own duties, and who is to be asked for advice.

'Arrangements' covers systems and procedures for safe working. What do employees need to know? Simple arrangements on how to report accidents, fire drill and escape instructions, and first-aid facilities, are easy to write down. More complex topics—such as training (assessment and provision), documentation, local safety rules, composition, terms of reference and function of the safety committee (if you have one), arrangements negotiated with trade union-appointed safety representatives, involvement of employees in health and safety matters, and the means of reviewing the safety policy itself—must all be considered and expressed in simple and yet precise terms. Special procedures to cover specific hazards may also form part of the arrangements to be included, or they can be cross-referenced if they already form part of another set of documents. Examples of this are special-access problems, safe storage of finds, unusual fire protection systems, chemical storage and handling in laboratories, and entry into work areas by the general public. If there is a known special-risk activity, it should be covered, or at least referred to, by way of cross-references to other documentation.

It is also recommended that third-party risks should be examined, and arrangements set out in writing inside the policy, although this is not a legal requirement. Relationships with contractors, such as cleaners, and with visitors should be considered: some may require special mention. At all points in the policy, references should be to named individuals where possible, rather than to job titles.

Publicizing the Policy

The written document has to be 'brought to the notice of' all employees, though there is no specified way of doing this. If it is short enough, everyone can have their own copy, but it is sufficient to make people aware of the policy, by means of a note in the pay packet or elsewhere, such as a noticeboard, and then displaying the policy at places where it can be easily read, such as a folder in each department. Obviously, a short, well-written policy will be more likely to be absorbed than one which is too long, legalistic and places excessive emphasis on employee duties. Any policy longer than about 10 A4 pages is probably in this category, and would constitute a manual rather than a practical policy.

The end-product should be readable, practical, and describe what actually happens for safety rather than a collection of pious hopes. Informed and aware managers are in a better position to do the actual writing or revision than a solicitor or even a safety consultant. The latter can and often does prepare draft versions for consideration, but the final say should rest with those who have to operate it. Consultation with employees during drafting is vital to success.

Responsibility for the Policy

At first, the writing or revising of a safety policy statement should be a responsibility given to one senior person, who will then become knowledgeable about the health and safety problems within the organization. Many employers have little idea about these or the rules which aim to control them, so appointing a task force is useful. The exercise will probably uncover potential sources of liability to the public, or activities which are already subject to specific legislation requiring minimum standards to be observed. For example, it may be found that the Factories Act can apply to workshops, the Offices, Shops and Railway Premises Act applies to offices(!) and that the Construction Regulations may apply to certain field operations. Failure to warn of hazards can be grounds for a successful claim for damages after injury, despite the conditions of entry to premises. Since 1977 the Unfair Contract Terms Act has rendered invalid exclusion clauses attempting to limit or exclude liability for death or personal injury.

Once management has put effort into the control of health and safety matters, attention can be turned to the employees. Training in responsibilities, the law, hazard detection and prevention, as well as in day-to-day safe working is essential for managers, supervisory staff and employees. The safety policy will contain brief details on how this will be done. Information should be available on special training requirements which may be required by law. For example, there are still those who are unaware that it is illegal for employees on premises within the scope of the Factories Act to change an abrasive wheel or cutting disc unless specifically trained and appointed in writing to do so by the employer. (In all other premises and work, such a provision would be 'reasonably practicable' under the terms of the main Act.) There will also be knowledge of previous accidents, within the organization and nationally, which will give pointers for the direction training should take.

Conclusions

Health and safety at work is one of the most-documented subjects of modern times, but that documentation is not all in one place and easy to find. In itself, that is a plus for the safety policy statement, because this practical document is where you should expect to find condensed practical advice on not having an accident. A bonus for the United Kingdom is that, although other countries now recognize the value of formal safety programmes and policies, it was and still is the only country where such a document is a legal requirement for all employing organizations except the very small. It is the core of safety in the organization, and the barometer, for if there is no adequate policy there is no adequate organization, and without that we play the kind of Russian roulette which brings death for several hundred ordinary people each year, and crippling injury for thousands of others.

Bibliography

Some useful publications issued by the Health and Safety Executive and available from Her Majesty's Stationery Office (HMSO):

Writing Your Health and Safety Policy Statement, (1986)
Writing a Safety Policy Statement—Advice to Employers (HSC 6)
Guidance on the Implementation of Safety Policies (IAC/L1)
Written Safety Policy Statements: Guidance for Local Authorities (LAA1/A/3/3)
Effective Policies for Health and Safety (Accident Prevention Advisory Unit, 1980)
Transport Kills: A Study of Fatal Accidents in Industry, 1978–1980 (1982)

Appendix: Health and Safety Policy Statement Assessment*

General statement:
- Clear declaration of intent
- Protection of employees and others
- Signed and dated
- Enlists employee support and cooperation

Organization:
- Traceable management structure
- Duties clearly defined
- Arrangements for joint consultation
- Constitution of safety committees
- Commitment of resources to health and safety

Arrangements:
- Common hazards (housekeeping, fire, ladders, abrasive wheels)
- Special hazards of the trade or business
- Inspection and maintenance of plant and equipment
- Processes for new plant, substances, processes
- Provision and use of protective clothing
- Accident reporting, investigation procedures
- Welfare facilities
- Emergency procedures
- Monitoring policy and rectifying shortcomings
- Reference to other documentation
- Training

* As adopted by the Greater London Council Compliance Unit.

1.4 Museums and the Health and Safety Inspectorate

ELISABETH SHERMAN

The Health and Safety Executive (HSE) is responsible for enforcement policy, development of new legislation, provision of information, setting standards and international liaison. Within the framework of the legislation the HSE's inspectors are responsible for putting the enforcement policy into practice, and Figure 1 shows how the operational inspector fits into the overall structure. The main Act is the Health and

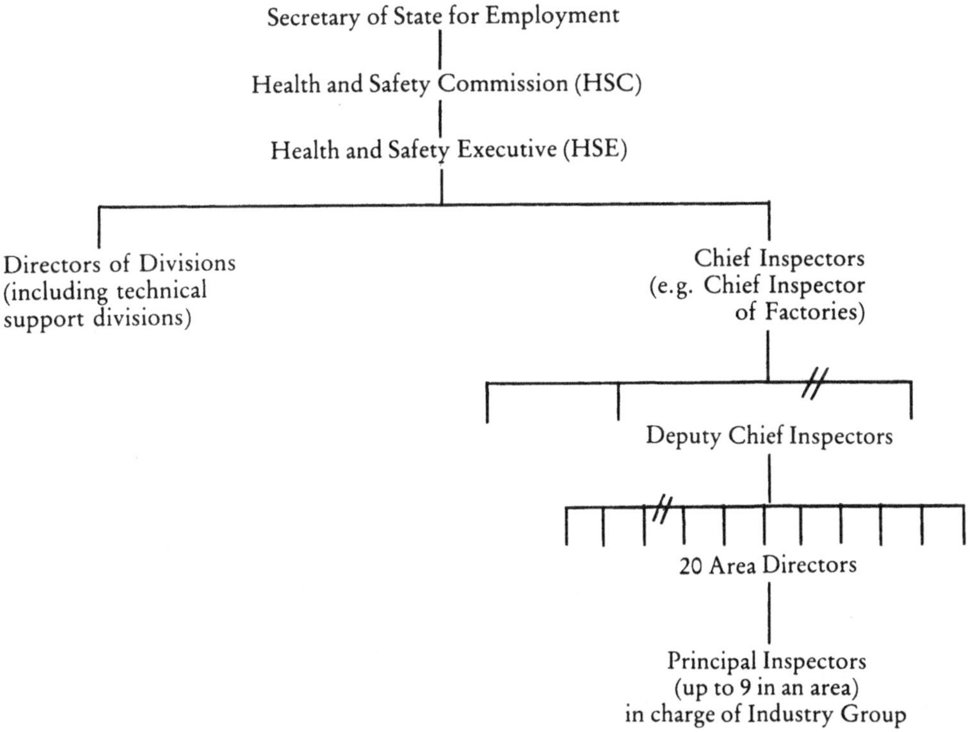

1. How the operational inspector fits into the overall structure of the United Kingdom health and safety system

Safety at Work Etc. Act 1974, whilst the subordinate legislation includes a number of Acts, e.g. the Factories Act, and the Offices Shops and Railway Premises Act, which apply to specific types of workplace.

There is also a large number of sets of regulations which usually apply to specific processes, e.g. Control of Lead at Work Regulations 1980 which apply to work with lead and lead compounds and derivatives. The Acts and Regulations are passed by Parliament and have to be complied with in toto, but there are also Approved Codes of Practice (ACOP), e.g. Approved Code of Practice for the Control of Lead at Work, which are drawn up by the Health and Safety Commission after consultation with unions, management and other interested bodies. ACOPs are enforceable at law but there is a fundamental difference between these and the Parliamentary legislation in that it is acceptable to achieve an equivalent standard by a system different from that set out in the ACOP.

The Inspector's Role

The role of the inspector is the enforcement of the legislation, and this is achieved by inspection, education and advice. If these softer approaches do not prove to be successful then consideration would be given to enforcement by Improvement Notices, Prohibition Notices and, ultimately, by prosecution. With those functions go quite wide powers which are laid down in the Health and Safety at Work Etc. Act. Inspectors have right of entry into premises at all reasonable times, which is interpreted basically as the times when the premises are occupied. There are certain circumstances, however, under which entry might be essential outside normal working hours, e.g. if there are major risks. Inspectors have powers of examination and investigation, can take samples and possession of articles and substances. They can require production of relevant documents, and take copies of these, an important provision in such cases as checking air monitoring results to assess levels of exposure to hazardous substances. Finally, they have any other power necessary to enforce legislation.

Inspectors' visits follow varied patterns. There are routine inspections carried out at broadly fixed intervals, visits to investigate accidents, incidents and complaints, special surveys, and visits at the request of management or the unions. Routine inspections could be by arrangement or by surprise visit. In the past, when they were basically Factory Inspectors, they on principle always made surprise visits, but nowadays the much larger field of work covered means that they carry out more arranged visits, though they nevertheless retain the authority to make unannounced visits.

In organizations like museums, however, the only way to see specific people is to make an appointment and arrange the visit. Before such routine inspections both the management and the safety representatives are informed so that a properly organized visit can take place. (Those who have been inspected already know the system.) During the visit the inspector will try to make contact with both management and workforce: management because they have the power to change what is going on and have the duty to comply with the Regulations and Acts. In actual fact, management is almost invariably held to be responsible for whatever is going wrong. Safety representatives have a vested interest in what the inspectors do, because they are representing the workforce who are those most likely to be adversely affected by non-compliance with the legislation. An important part of the inspector's role is to try to put health and safety matters into perspective.

Inspections

During an inspection the inspectors try to identify hazards, check if there is any organization or system there to deal with them, and ensure that the appropriate action is taken. They ask to see the Safety Policy, because this should indicate which member of senior management is responsible for health and safety, and also the organization and arrangements for putting the policy into practice. Where serious risks are identified, follow-up visits are arranged to ensure that appropriate action has been taken.

Some Problems in Museums

Manual Handling of Objects and Loads

A wide range of hazards is to be found in museums, and one probably common to all is the manual handling of awkwardly shaped objects. A wide range of shapes, sizes and weights of objects has to be handled, and to compound the problem, there is often a considerable shortage of space, so that storage space tends to be at a premium. Some objects are stored in odd corners, on high shelves and in cramped conditions, all of which makes handling difficult.

In 1982 some 90 000 accidents in the United Kingdom resulted from manual handling activities, and 1.6 million working days were lost due to back injuries. When the cost of the lost time (probably about £60 million), apart from all the pain and suffering, is considered, it is obviously worth trying to improve manual handling techniques in any field. It is estimated that 90 per cent of the British working adult population can safely lift up to about 16 kilograms, whilst with special training a further 10 per cent can lift up to 55 kilograms. New regulations are in the pipeline to counter this hazard. The current draft regulation says that a person shall not be employed to handle manually any load likely to injure him or her. It goes on to say that due account should be taken of the weight, shape, size or lack of rigidity of the load (a big floppy load is much more difficult to lift than a small compact load) and the frequency with which that load is handled. Back injuries tend to develop over a period of time and those who are constantly lifting loads are likely to sustain an injury sooner rather than later. The other matter to take into account is the conditions under which the load is handled. The present author recalls observing, in a museum, what looked like a fairly lightweight load being handled. This consisted of some very large prints stacked in an awkward corner. The woman moving the prints had to stand to one side of shelf and push down or lift up at a very awkward angle. The overall weight was low, but the amount of twisting and moving around to lift out the prints was such that she was heading straight for a back injury. The Regulations do not specify an upper weight limit for lifting, but they do specify the conditions under which the load is to be handled. When looking at manual handling the risks can be minimized by better design of the storage system to reduce the need for manual handling. In the aforementioned museum, consideration was being given to handling the prints mechanically by means of a forklift truck or a hand-truck designed for the job. Another proposal was to move the stacks to a more easily accessible position, something which is easier said than done in most museums because of lack of storage space.

Consideration should also be given to effective matching of the manual handling task with the strength and capacities of the individual. There are some jobs where a larger, stronger person is needed to lift loads that would cause problems for a youngster or a physically handicapped person. Planned action is required to ensure the introduction and continuing observance of good, safe, manual handling practice. In relation to all safety matters, good management is needed to design a system and ensure that it is used. You need to take note of the techniques employed for handling an object of that size and weight, including the height to or from which it is to be moved, and the position (e.g. is a twisting movement needed?). How repetitive is the job? Do you need personal protection (e.g. is there also a risk from broken glass or corrosive chemicals if the load were to be dropped?). Visibility (can the operator see what he is doing or where he is going?)—obviously if you can see what you are doing you are less likely to be injured, and working in dark corners increases the accident risk. Another point to consider is the labelling of loads; some of them have been in the average museum store for a very long time and the weight may not be known. Before moving any large object you need to assess whether a team of people or mechanical handling gear is needed to move it.

To sum up, heavy objects should be labelled with their weight and perhaps even the technique for moving them. Finally, and perhaps most important, training is often needed. Training is important in all areas of work, not just for lifting. People need training so that a concern for safety becomes ingrained, and this means not only initial training but also refresher training. Training should not just say 'do this', it should also explain what the hazard is and the reasons for the precautions laid down. Practical as well as theoretical training is essential, because it should be work-related, not just discussed in the rarefied atmosphere of a training room.

Hazards Inspections

As stated earlier, inspections include the identification of hazards and checking whether there is a safety policy and an organization to deal with the hazards. This is something which should be drawn up by top management. Normally there should be three parts to a safety policy:

1. The general policy which states that the management policy is in compliance with the Health and Safety at Work Act, and that all possible steps will be taken to maintain a healthy and safe place of work.
2. The part that contains the organization and arrangements for carrying out that policy—this should state the senior person on the board of management responsible for the organization's safety effort, followed by a description of the management system down to first line supervision, and the responsibility for putting the policy into practice.
3. Finally, the practical system for telling everybody about the policy and monitoring its performance and effect.

One obvious method of monitoring a policy is to check accident rates either within the museum during specified periods (e.g. annually) or by comparing the museum's accident rates with local or national figures (e.g. the national figures for back injuries could be compared with the back-injury rate in museums). Another form of monitoring is talking about the job with the workpeople concerned, and this can reveal practical problems which are not very obvious to the outsider (see St John Holt's chapter for a detailed discussion on the subject of safety policy preparation and monitoring). Furthermore, there is the need to follow the job through. In the asbestos example given and during the discussions with management about moving the awkwardly stored prints, it became obvious that they had not talked to the women who were actually doing the job, and consequently did not appreciate the awkwardness of the storage position and the risks involved for the women in carrying out this part of their job.

As well as physical hazards, there can be health hazards attending some work in museums. A brief explanation of the Control of Lead at Work Regulations will serve as an example of the modern approach to health hazards. These Regulations, which came into force in 1980, are relatively modern. They follow a logical sequence, and the first thing they require is assessment of the problem. Examination of the use of lead at work—for example, in lead-based paints or working with stained glass—is the basis for an assessment of the risk to personnel, and then training and information should be given to those people handling the lead. Appropriate controls should be provided and these should be monitored to ensure that they are working effectively. If necessary the people working with the substance should be monitored for lead absorption and for its effects. Things should not reach this stage, but should a person be found to have absorbed an excessive amount of lead, he or she should be suspended from working with the substance.

The assessment procedure is vital, and it is something new to be brought into the sphere of Regulations. Assessment will be incorporated into the Control of Substances Hazardous to Health Regulations, which are proposed (from 1987/88) to cover all work-related aspects of the use of hazardous substances, and they will follow a very similar pattern to the Lead Regulations. The purpose of assessment in the Lead Regulations is to determine: (a) compliance with the Lead in Air Standard; (b) whether exposure to lead is significant; (c) what action is required; and (d) any risk to other people. Obviously, the more lead there is in the workplace, and the more complex the process, the more detailed the assessment will need to be.

First of all, you should look at the type of work: Where is it done? Who does it? Who else may be affected? When, for example, in a large multi-user area (such as a conservation studio) lead paint is being stripped off a wooden structure by a group of people at one end of the room while a different activity is going on at the other, with informal eating facilities in the middle, there may well be several problems. Such an area is not entirely suitable for working with lead, since other people may be at risk and the food may be contaminated. All these factors should be taken into account in the assessment.

Secondly, you should consider (a) the nature of the lead: Is it dust, fume or vapour? Is there any risk from ingestion or inhalation? In the chosen example, the main problem was dust. The people doing the job were wearing their respirators, but there was still a considerable risk of their hands being contaminated. Meanwhile, the people at the other end of the room were not protected. (b) You should look at the amount of lead involved (or, in this case, likely to be released): How long is it used for? Is the process continuous or intermittent? Lead is one of these substances which has a half-life in the body; but it can be excreted, and providing it is not taken in faster than it is excreted, there should not be a major problem.

Next, the level of exposure should be assessed, and this may include consideration of the 'lead in air' levels, the blood-lead results and the degree of contamination of the hands and face. The assessment should include information about the control measures, including any dust extraction system used, its maintenance schedule and efficiency. Finally, a check should be made of any past records.

The Regulations apply anywhere lead is used at work; but some of the Regulations apply only if there is *significant* exposure to lead, otherwise the cost of the precautions would be completely out of proportion to the risk. Significant exposure means exposure to above half the Lead in Air Standard or to work where there is a substantial risk of ingesting lead. The risk of skin absorption from lead alkyls is probably not relevant to museum work. Unless there is gross contamination the only way of proving an ingestion risk is by biological tests such as blood-lead determination.

The Lead in Air Standard relates to personal exposure, and so it means wearing a personal sampler for the Lead in Air measurements (personal sampling equipment is specified in HSE Guidance Note EH28). The Lead in Air Standard is an 8-hour time-weighted average; it relates to the amount of lead to which you are exposed over 8 hours, and is a flexible figure which allows up to three times the Standard (to take into account the varying nature of lead compounds) provided that the blood-lead levels are acceptable. Where there is lead exposure, even below the Lead in Air Standard, the employer has to reduce such exposure as much as is reasonably practicable. The most recent version of the proposed Control of Substances Hazardous to Health requirements is almost identical to the Control of Lead at Work Regulations. The Lead in Air Standard was one of the early controlled limits, produced before 'Control Limits' of exposure were published by HSE (1984). These are agreed, after consultation with both sides of industry, by the Health and Safety Commission. Control Limits are judged to be reasonably practicable by most of industry, and they should not normally be exceeded. However, they are not the *safe* level; therefore, wherever and whenever possible, exposure should be to a much lower level.

Enforcement

Inspectors have quite strong powers of enforcement, as illustrated by the following incident. In a building infested with cockroaches, a tradesman and his mate were instructed to drill holes in the walls to allow the introduction of a pesticide fatal to cockroaches. The rooms continued in occupation while the men were drilling the holes. When all the holes had been drilled, someone said 'this looks like asbestos'—an observation that came rather too late because by then the workmen had drilled one-inch holes all over the place. A panic ensued, the two men stopped work and everybody who had remained in the room during the drilling moved out. The men had been exposed to quite high levels of asbestos: this could be ascertained from knowledge of the type of work they had been doing and the type of drill used. Also, there was considerable asbestos contamination of the floor and other surfaces. Not only had the two men been exposed to asbestos but so had all the other people in the room, however at a relatively smaller risk compared with the risk to the workmen.

On investigation, it was found that the tradesman and his mate had received virtually no training in the use of, nor the dangers from, asbestos. In addition, their supervisor was ignorant of the hazards. It was also found that in the past a systematic programme had been set up to try and identify asbestos in this complex of buildings. This particular building had not been surveyed but nobody had thought to tell the people doing the job how far the survey programme had progressed. Buried in the records was evidence of asbestos in this building, and if somebody had taken the trouble to consult the records they would have been aware of the presence of asbestos. The Inspectorate decided to prosecute the tradesmen's employer, who also owned the building, under Sections 2 and 3 of the Health and Safety at Work Act. The tradesmen's employer was prosecuted for exposing both them and the occupants of the room to asbestos. The people occupying the building were not prosecuted because they had no control over it and were not in a position to know about the presence of asbestos.

In certain circumstances it may be necessary to invoke enforcement action by serving a notice on the employer or occupier. There are two types of notice—Improvement Notices and Prohibition Notices. An Improvement Notice can be used only where there has been a breach of the Health and Safety at Work Act. The breach has to be remedied within a set period, and at least 3 weeks has to be allowed in order to give time for an appeal, which has to be lodged within that period. There is automatic prosecution at the end of the specified time if the work has not been done. A Crown Improvement Notice follows a similar pattern but the Inspectorate cannot prosecute at the end of it. Most of the national museums have been maintained by the Property Services Agency (PSA), who are Crown Agents. There are many improvements which the museum authorities cannot undertake themselves because only the PSA has the authority. If there is a breach of the Act's provisions, therefore, it is not the museum but the PSA that receives a Crown Notice. Other museums, administered by local authorities and universities, will be served ordinary Improvement Notices as they cannot claim Crown Immunity. Usually attached to a Notice is a schedule which lists the action to be taken. The work does not necessarily have to be carried out exactly as the inspector specifies, but an equivalent or higher standard should be achieved.

The other type of notice is a Prohibition Notice, and to illustrate the difference between the two types an actual example may be quoted. An Improvement Notice was served on a museum where the security staff needed to cross the roof. In wet weather they were skidding about on wet broken planks with no handrails, and in places they faced a 50-foot drop. Where the staff risked falling off the edge of the walkway or falling through glass, a Prohibition Notice was placed, stating that there should be *no access* until the walkways were repaired and handrails fitted. This Notice took effect immediately. However, on the less hazardous section, where the security staff risked slipping, but not falling over the edge, an Improvement Notice was posted, saying that it should be repaired within three months. A Prohibition Notice is used where there is risk of *serious* personal injury. If there is an imminent risk, the job is stopped immediately; otherwise a time delay is usually allowed before the Notice comes into effect.

1.5 Liability Risk Management for Museums

ELIZABETH A. GRIFFITH

In a violent windstorm, visitors to the historic house take cover. A woman ventures into the open and is struck by the branch of a tree, sustaining minor but permanent brain damage. She sues the museum and six of its employees for negligence, asking $5 million in damages. The woman's lawyers uncover no sign of negligence. However, in order to avoid a jury trial (and the possibility of a large 'sympathy settlement'), the museum's insurers settle out of court for $500 000, and give notice that they will not renew insurance coverage at any price.

This story is true. It happened at Monticello, the home of Thomas Jefferson in Virginia, and a similar accident could happen at any museum with high visitation, jeopardizing its ability to obtain insurance and stay open.

The Insurance Crisis and Museums

The insurance crisis is here, and it is striking hardest at service industries and organizations which have contact with large numbers of people. Hotels, restaurants, hospitals, transit systems, retailers, city governments—these are some of the businesses that are seeing premiums increase four and five times for coverage decreases of up to 90 percent. Museums, despite their lack of clear hazards, are thrown into the same category by underwriters who see only large numbers of people and their propensity to slip and fall. In the present era of conservative underwriting, even museums with good safety records are subject to large premium increases, penalized by an environment in which the public is increasingly likely to sue the owners of the property on which they sustain life's inevitable minor accidents.

Most museum administrators, when they think of insurance at all, think in terms of coverage for their collections and loan items. Fine arts insurance, however, is just one part of the total insurance coverage a museum should carry. Coverage should include:

1. a *package* policy, which insures the buildings and contents (exclusive of the collection) against loss or damage;
2. a *fine arts* policy, which insures the collection and loan items, both at home and in transit;
3. a *liability* policy, which protects the museum's assets and staff against suits arising from personal injury or property damage sustained by visitors to the museum;
4. an *umbrella* policy, which extends the liability coverage to higher limits in the event of extremely large claims;
5. *workers' compensation* coverage, for claims by employees for injuries sustained on the job;
6. *automobile* coverage, for any museum-owned vehicles; and

7. *directors' and officers'* coverage, which protects the directors and officers against suits arising from personal injury or property damage sustained by visitors to the museum.

The components of this package most adversely affected by the insurance crisis are the *liability, umbrella* and *directors' and officers'* coverage.

Museums unable to obtain such coverage face an unpleasant choice: closing their doors to visitors, or remaining open without coverage—'going bare' as it is known in the business. Museums without coverage leave their assets open to claims by accident sufferers; one large claim could, in the worst case, force liquidation of the collection and endowment for payment. An alternative to closing, often considered by museums and other businesses unable to obtain liability coverage, is that of requiring visitors to sign claims waiver forms. Experience has shown, however, that these forms often fail to hold up in court. Once a museum has sustained a large claim, it has a serious insurance problem; the best it can hope for is a large premium increase. More likely, as in the case of Monticello, it will face discontinuation of coverage by its current carrier, and a lack of interest from other carriers. In the absence of convincing evidence to the contrary, other carriers will assume that the circumstances leading up to the first claim still exist, leaving them open to similar losses.

A Primer on Insurance

The insurance business began in earnest in Venice, during the Renaissance, to protect the fortunes of the great merchant shippers. The practice of insuring gradually spread to cover land-bound activities. From this came the term, still used, *inland–marine* insurance, used to signify the insurance of goods against loss or damage, and often applied to fine arts policies. Businesses today purchase insurance from an underwriter or carrier, which insures many types of businesses. Coverage is rarely purchased directly, however; most often a business goes through an agency, or broker, whose business it is to know the insured's business and assist with loss control and the filing of claims. Agents can range from an individual licensed to do business with one or two carriers to an international firm able to tap many *markets,* the term often used by agents to refer to carriers. Carriers evaluate the desirability of a given account by evaluating its *risk experience* and *loss history.* The risk experience of a business is a summary of any claims filed against it, usually for the past 5 years. The risk experience summary will include claims for which no payments were made, as well as claims which resulted in payments. A firm's loss history consists of just those claims which resulted in payments by the carrier.

From the loss history and the policy premiums the *loss ratio* is derived. The loss ratio is the most important single factor in determining a firm's desirability to an insurer. It equals the premium paid for a given year, divided by the claims paid during that year. Loss ratios of less than one represent a net loss to the carrier and render coverage extremely difficult to obtain. Ideally, a museum will bid out its business once every three years, to assure a competitive price. To do this, it submits a summary of the coverage it wishes to obtain to one or more agents for circulation to interested underwriters. This list should include:

1. an appraisal of its collection;
2. valuations of its buildings at current replacement costs;
3. a list of all its non-collection property at current replacement costs;
4. a list of vehicles and drivers;

5. the names of all directors and officers;
6. information on visitation, sales and other activities;
7. premiums paid for the past five years; and
8. its risk experience and loss history for the past five years.

The Insurance Market and Museums

Museums with excellent loss histories, low loss ratios and little claims potential should be able to use the bidding system to their advantage, with a number of carriers competing for their business on the basis of price. Other museums—those with unattractive loss histories, high loss ratios or simply the potential for large claims by virtue of high visitation and a large physical plant—may find themselves in the position of trying to interest just one or two carriers in their business. Their managers must present their operations in the most favorable light just to obtain a quote. Waiting until an accident occurs to begin an accident prevention and response program is a serious mistake. Such programs established after an accident occurs are far less convincing to the carrier, and can sometimes increase the likelihood of an unfavorable settlement by implying negligence on the part of the management. Instead, preventing and responding to accidents should be an ongoing part of your museum's operations. To begin, ask yourself two questions about your museum's operations:

- How would your museum look to an insurer who is thinking about assuming your risk?
- How would your museum look to a court deciding a personal injury case in which you are the defendent?

Risk Management

What can a museum do to avoid a liability disaster? It can, and should, manage its risk. An understanding of the concept of risk management by the director and staff is necessary for any museum which seeks to reduce its liability exposure. Many organizations regard accidents, such as the one described above, as uncontrollable events. 'That's why we have insurance,' they say. Insurers, however, do not see it quite that way, and have begun to avoid writing policies for organizations guided by this belief. Insurers today insist on seeing an attitude of risk management among their insured clients. They rightly see themselves in business to insure pure risk—not the risk occasioned by sloppy maintenance of a heavily visited site or the indifferent attitude of management.

Insurers do not demand risk-free environments. They simply want to know that a museum is doing its best to reduce its manageable risk—they will insure the rest. Likewise, courts do not decide cases from a zero-risk standpoint. While a few cases involving high settlements on spurious grounds have been widely publicized, most cases are decided using the 'reasonable man' principle; organizations which take steps a reasonable man would be expected to take to reduce its guests' risk are usually found not liable for negligence. How can museum managers apply the 'reasonable man' rule to their museum's operations? A good first step is to survey other, similar museums and see what they do to minimize *their* risk. If you can demonstrate that you are doing as much or more than other museums, chances are courts will find that you are acting as a 'reasonable man' would.

Thomas Jefferson Memorial Foundation, Inc.

Accident Report

Name of injured____________________ Age (estimate if necessary)________

Address____________________

____________________ Phone #__________

Location of accident____________________

Day: S M T W Th F S Date____________ Time________

Eyewitnesses:

name	address	phone # (include area code)
1.		
2.		
3.		

Monticello staff response:

First aid at scene of accident? yes no From whom?____________

Nature and extent of injuries and first aid given:

Rescue unit response:

Was rescue unit called? yes no Which unit responded?____________

Treatment administered by rescue unit:

Hospital information:

Was injured taken to hospital? yes no Which one? ____________

By whom? ____________

Status report(s):

date and time **report**

General information:

Injured's version of how accident occured:

Comments at scene of accident:

speaker	comment	phone # (include area code)

ART comments and recommendations:

By:____________

Date:____________

1. The Monticello accident report.

Two Kinds of Risk

Risk experts understand that there are essentially two kinds of risk, which I call *manageable risk* and *pure risk*. By *pure risk* I mean the risk which cannot be reasonably avoided or diminished. *Manageable risk*, on the other hand, can and should be diminished as far as it is possible to do so. The incident of the tree branch offers a good example. 'Pure risk!' many would say. But is it? Clearly the windstorm is a pure risk, but other aspects of this incident are arguably manageable, such as the maintenance of trees and the training of employees to deal with extreme weather conditions, crowd control and first aid. This experience caused the staff at Monticello to think long and hard about visitor safety and to implement a number of changes, many of them surprisingly inexpensive, to achieve a higher level of safety. Other sites can learn from this experience, so do not wait for disaster to strike before taking preventive measures!

Three Steps to Greater Protection

To carry out an accident prevention and response program, museums must:

1. *identify* their areas of greatest liability;
2. *prioritize* their needs; and
3. *implement* the program.

Identifying Risk Areas

Identifying areas of greatest liability can begin with the Director of Security, Grounds or Maintenance, clipboard in hand, taking a walk around the property. Where could visitors slip and fall? Hit their heads? Stumble in the dark or in inclement weather? Taking a look at the premises through a loss control expert's glasses is a simple but effective way to identify areas of risk. Once a liability risk management program is in effect, the best method of identifying high-risk areas is through accidents reports. The Monticello accident report is included as an example (Figure 1). These reports should include space for:

1. the name, address, phone number and age of the injured person;
2. a specific description of the area in which the accident took place;
3. the weather conditions at the time of the accident (particularly if it took place outside the building);
4. names, addresses and phone numbers of eyewitnesses;
5. staff response;
6. rescue unit and hospital response;
7. comments at the scene from the accident sufferer and eyewitnesses; and
8. comments from the staff.

Clear patterns will often emerge, leading to clear solutions. For example,reports at Monticello during the first year of its program showed that the majority of accidents were taking place on a certain walking trail during rain. Closing the trail on wet days has effectively reduced these slip-and-fall incidents.

Prioritizing Risk Projects

A museum assessing its liability risk for the first time will be faced with a daunting list of

Thomas Jefferson Memorial Foundation, Inc.

Accident Prevention and Response at Monticello

The policy of the Foundation is that every employee should be aware of potential accident hazards, and that senior management should respond immediately to hazardous situations. To this end one member of the senior staff has been designated Director of Security and given broad authority to respond to security and safety considerations.

The Accident Response Team, formed and headed by the Director of Security, serves Monticello by offering prompt, consistent treatment to all visitors suffering accidents or medical problems at Monticello. The Team consists of six members on a seven-day rotation. At least two members of the team are available during all public hours.

Most members of the Accident Response Team have had some prior experience in accident response by working with a rescue squad, volunteer fire department or hospital emergency room. In addition, each member receives training in First Aid, CPR, visitor communications and accident reporting, as well as a briefing on the Foundaiton's liability insurance coverage.

Monticello employees are instructed to summon a member of the Accident Response Team when a visitor has an accident or a medical problem in their area. The Team Member offers comfort and First Aid (from one of Monticello's three First Aid stations) where appropriate; decides whether to summon the Rescue Squad; and obtains information about the circumstances of the mishap, including eyewitness accounts and names, addresses and telephone numbers of the eyewitnesses.

The Team files an Accident Report (form attached) within 12 hours of the accident with the Director, the Director of Security and the Controller. The Director of Security is responsible for determinig if a hazardous situation exists and, if so, for referring it to the proper staff member for prompt preventative response. A copy of each form is sent to the insurance agent as well. Accident patterns are analyzed on a seasonal basis for further preventative measures.

The Director of Security maintains a network of outside professionals and has regular contact with local police and fire officials, fire and building code administrators and the local Rescue Squad.

6/11/86

2. The Monticello policy on accident prevention and response.

things to do. To keep the list from overwhelming the staff, realistic priorities need to be set. By the time it reaches the prioritization stage, a museum's administration is usually ready to articulate an accident prevention and response policy. This is an important step to securing the support of the staff and board. The Monticello policy is included as an example (Figure 2).

Implementing a Risk Program

Implementing a risk reduction plan is, in the long run, often less costly than a manager might expect. Expenditures fall into one of these categories:

1. major, one-time capital expenditures;
2. minor training costs incurred at regular intervals; or
3. minor, ongoing costs of stepped-up maintenance.

A frequent pattern is for the initial liability survey to turn up one or two major items requiring capital expenditures. Once these expenditures have been made, however, future surveys are likely to reveal procedural matters which cost little or nothing to implement. It is easy to be overwhelmed by an initial survey which indicates the need, for example, to spend $25 000 on fire detection/suppression hardware. Museum managers, however, must guard against this tendency. While insurers would ideally like to see well-protected properties, they are most interested in seeing a commitment to safety, and recognize, especially in the case of not-for-profit organizations, the need to phase in large capital items.

It is important for managers to take a long-term look at their risk management program. One-time purchases of necessary equipment, regular training and ongoing stepped-up maintenance are all part of a good prevention program. Each of these activities should be monitored regularly by a committee composed of the Director, the Directors of Grounds, Security and Maintenance and the person responsible for administering the insurance program.

Accident Response at Monticello

While accident prevention at Monticello is the responsibility of all the staff, accident response centers around a few, select individuals who comprise the Accident Response Team (ART). The ART was formed by the Director of Security to assure prompt, professional treatment to all visitors suffering accidents or medical problems while visiting Monticello. Most members of the ART had some prior experience in accident response through working with a rescue squad, volunteer fire department or hospital emergency room. After being selected for the ART, each member received further instruction in First Aid, CPR, visitor communications, accident reporting and Monticello's insurance package. Detection of an incident likely to give rise to a liability claim is an important step in accident response. Monticello employees have been taught to recognize such a situation, and to call the ART in the event of one. The ART is taught the importance of responding appropriately and consistently, always mindful of the public relations impact of their actions. Each of these elements is detailed below.

Appropriateness of Response

The appropriateness of the response depends to a great extent on the laws of the jurisdiction in which the museum lies. For most American museums, first aid and CPR by trained personnel are protected by 'Good Samaritan' laws; that is, staff cannot be sued for injuries sustained during a good-faith effort to be of assistance. Further help, however, including moving the accident sufferer, is not. The Director of Security should investigate the location and response time of the nearest hospital and rescue squad, and should undertake to acquaint the staff of these organizations with the museum and its needs. Notices with these telephone numbers should be available to museum staff for use in time of need.

Consistency of Response

Consistency of response is the best way to ensure that staff members do not lose their heads in an emergency, doing or saying something detrimental to the museum's well-being. Trained staff do not panic or make statements implying museum negligence. As in warfare, the team that is trained the best beforehand performs best in action, and the more disastrous the potential incident the more important the training. The Monticello Accident Response Team is grilled regularly on the 'worst-case' scenarios. What would you do in the case of a severe seizure? A bus accident? A sudden death? ART members must learn to respond unhesitatingly with a legitimate plan of action—one that holds up under the 'reasonable man' rule. The catch is that what seems 'reasonable' to a court of law in the calm of the chambers would not necessarily occur to a young museum employee faced with disaster. Regular training and evaluation help to bridge this gap. A crucially important aspect of this training should be the recording of remarks at the site of an accident. Verbatim quotations of the accident sufferer's remarks of those around him not only help to capture the nature of the incident to those reading the report afterwards, they often provide a solid defense in the event of future suit (and indeed forestall suits by those who remember that their candid comments were recorded).

The Public Relations Aspect of Good Response

The public relations content of a museum's response to an accident is crucial. It is important that the response should represent the museum well, because it will be heard by the accident sufferer's family, friends and traveling companions as well as other visitors in the location. Watching your employees in action will shape their impression of your museum at least as much as the exhibit they visited. Some museums go to great lengths to leave a favorable impression on visitors in distress. One large American historical museum actually provides any visitor needing medical attention, regardless of the circumstances, with a pass to the local emergency room to be treated at the museum's expense. Managers at this museum consider that this investment has paid off handsomely for them in goodwill and reduced lawsuits.

Commitment of Top Management

Like any program that requires money and staff time, an accident response program will not function without commitment from top management and an ongoing, closely monitored program. Ideally, the director should circulate a memorandum to all staff on risk-reduction and -response measures as they are developed. The Monticello director's memorandum to the staff on the Accident Response Team is included as an example (Figure 3).

May 20, 1986

TO: All Monticello Employees
FROM: Dan Jordan

RE: Accident Response Team

The Monticello Accident Response Team, formed by Glen Slosson in March, serves the Foundation by offering prompt, professional treatment to all visitors suffering accidents or medical problems at Monticello. The Team consists of Glen, Al Goodwin, David Robinson, Warren Wood and Davy Layne, all members of the Transportation staff, and Rob Maddex, the Visitors Center Superintendent. The Team is important for reducing our liability risks as well as for enhancing visitor and public relations.

Most members of the Accident Response Team have had some prior experience in accident response by working with a rescue squad, volunteer fire department or hospital emergency room. In addition, each member receives training in First Aid, CPR, visitor communications, and accident reporting, as well as a briefing on the Foundation's liability insurance coverage.

In its relatively short existence the Team has already contributed significantly to the Foundation's well-being. But, to do its work most effectively, the Team must have the cooperation of all Monticello employees. When a visitor has an accident or a medical problem in your area, please:

1. Call the Ticket Office at extension 322 (or, after closing, the shuttle station pay phone at 972-9577) and give your location and the nature of the accident. The Ticket Office will dispatch a member of the Team to your location.

2. Make the visitor as comfortable as possible while waiting for the Team member to arrive.

3. When the Team member arrives, offer help. If none is needed, please resume your normal duties.

4. Once a Team member is on the scene, no other employee should offer advice or assistance to the injured visitor, or discuss the accident or the circumstances surrounding it with any visitor.

3. Memo on Accident Response Team at Monticello.

Conclusion

Risk management, as an intrinsic part of managing a museum, is here to stay. Clearly, the costs associated with operating a public facility are increasing, and insurance premiums are just one part of the picture. The expense of making a facility safe and secure for visitors, as well as for the collection, is rising as well. Museums must remember, however, that the costs of increased premiums, maintenance, personnel and training are insignificant when compared with the worst-case alternative—closing their doors to the public.

Section 2. Aspects of Museum Safety

Embodied in Section 2 of Part 1 of the Health and Safety at Work Etc. Act 1974 is the duty of *every* employer to ensure the health and safety of the workforce. In particular, this duty covers the provision of equipment and systems for the safe storage and use of substances and articles, and the provision and maintenance of a working environment free from risks to health.

This particular aspect of the Act is to be strengthened by the introduction of the Control of Substances Hazardous to Health Regulations. These far-reaching regulations will affect museums primarily in their laboratories and workshops, and their main thrust will be to introduce the concept of occupational hygiene and health principles into every workplace.

In the past, the risk assessment of using a particular process or substance has been left very much to the individual worker, often without much in the way of guidance from supervisors. All too often this has led, in the museum context, to extreme risk-taking with dangerous substances, for example, exposure to benzene and methylene chloride. Assessments have often been carried out on an uninformed basis, sometimes by guesswork and usually by laypersons with little or no knowledge either of monitoring exposure to hazardous agents or of health surveillance in the workplace.

The following three chapters set out some of the ground-rules for appraising the risks, both potential and actual, associated with museum work, and approaches to mediating such risks through contol systems. The following aspects are covered:

- Steps in controlling health hazards
- Health and safety programmes for museums
- Emergency evacuation plans
- Hazards in maintaining and renovating museum buildings
- Medical surveillance
- Accident recording and prevention
- Monitoring and controlling exposure to hazardous agents
- Health problems in restoration and conservation work
- Fumigation processes

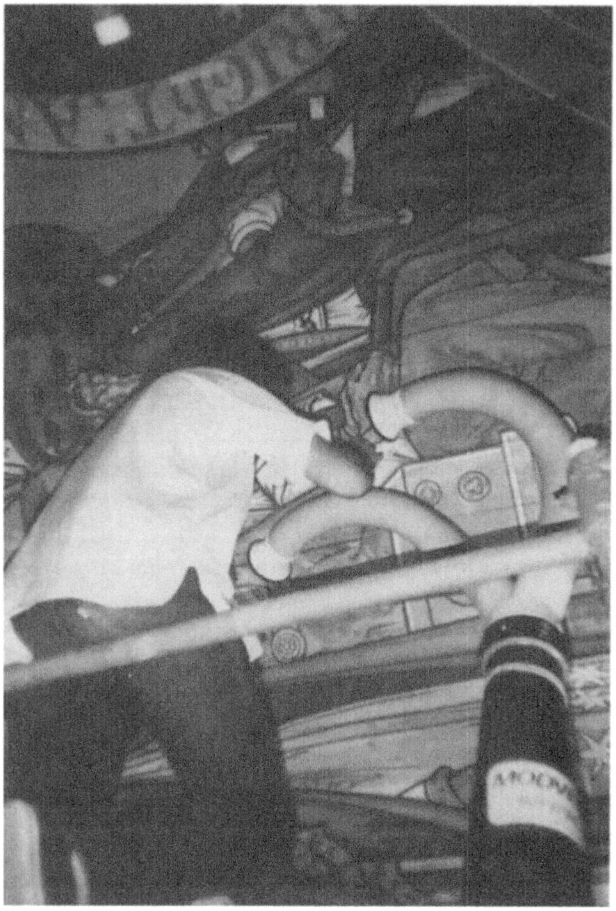

Mobile local exhaust system in use for the removal of fumes during ceiling painting restoration at Ely Cathedral. (Photo: Buyvital Limited)

2.1 Care and Preservation of Museum Personnel

Monona Rossol

As an industrial hygienist who specializes in art and theater occupational hazards, the present author finds the hazards involved with museum work particularly challenging. Museum conservators, for example, may employ especially toxic solvents, pesticides, fumigants, preservatives, polymeric treatment chemicals (epoxy resins, urethane resins, and the like), and many more such substances. These toxic materials are applied to objects of every age, size, and condition—objects which may then become hazardous to handle, not just for conservators, but for anyone who works in a museum. Artifacts and works of art may be contaminated with arsenic, DDT, or mercury compounds from previous pesticide treatments; or they may release ethylene oxide or other toxic gases and vapors from recent fumigation. Artifacts containing animal products may be contaminated with anthrax and other biological hazards, whilst old or flaking pigments may contain lead, cadmium, mercury, arsenic, uranium, and many other toxic metals.

In addition to hazards posed by the artifacts themselves and the materials used to conserve them, more are to be found in museum departments outside the galleries, storage areas, and conservation laboratories. Places where material is packed for shipping, where displays and exhibitions are designed and fabricated, or where maintenance chemicals and materials are stored or used can be also sites where museum workers undertake hazardous industrial processes. These processes include woodworking, tooling, polymerization and foaming of plastics, painting, and the dyeing and fireproofing of textiles, as well as cleaning and treating surfaces using a variety of substances. The vast array of substances, methods, and materials used in museums has the potential to adversely affect not only museum employees, but visitors as well. Ethylene oxide fumigation, for example, presents some severe health risks for those who undertake the actual fumigation, but, should some of the fumigating gas escape accidentally, it could harm unprotected co-workers and the visiting public.

In the United States of America, occupational and environmental hazards are monitored and regulated by federal agencies such as the Occupational Safety and Health Administration (OSHA), the National Institute for Occupational Safety and Health (NIOSH), and the Environmental Protection Agency (EPA). In addition, a variety of state and local government agencies also have jurisdiction over many aspects of museum work. These agencies, for example, grant building permits, inspect premises for violations of fire, electrical, and health codes, and exercise many other responsibilities. Besides federal, state, and local governments which set such controls in America, private non-governmental groups, like trade unions, trade associations, and standard-setting professional associations, also promulgate health and safety guidelines. The standards they encourage are usually the most stringent of all, but most experts now agree that it is wiser to follow them in preference to the various government standards and regulations, which provide for only the minimum standard of protection.

Despite these controls and recommendations, many American museum administrators and employees at all levels know alarmingly little about the health and safety regulations which apply to their work. For instance, in 1982 the Center for Occupational Hazards (COH) and the New York City Department of Health cooperated on a survey of New York City museums. Twenty-seven museums returned questionnaires, telling how they used pesticides and fumigants. Of the twenty-seven, only thirteen used any sort of protective equipment, and whilst seven said they used respiratory protection, only one used the proper type. Nine museums used ethylene oxide fumigation, but none monitored these operations for leaks or residual outgassing of ethylene oxide, despite the fact that federal regulations demand such monitoring. Dangerous practices like these persist in part because museums often escape the notice of inspectors and authorities. Unfortunately it sometimes takes an accident or a lawsuit to alert museum personnel to their responsibilities for health and safety precautions, or to prompt initiation of inspections and enforcement of legal requirements. To avoid such consequences, prudent museum staff should establish a health and safety program which functions to oversee health and safety problems, to study the relevant regulations and laws, and to act as a liaison with other workers, visiting inspectors, industrial hygienists, and other experts when necessary.

Steps in Controlling Health Hazards

An essential first step in establishing a health and safety program is to identify potential dangers such as toxic materials, hazardous working conditions, dangerous restoration or conservation materials, equipment and procedures, and the potential sources of fires and accidents throughout the museum. For instance, a health and safety committee, or officer, might undertake or arrange preliminary analyses of objects selected for preservation in order to detect any toxic substances with which museum personnel will have to cope. In specimens prepared by taxidermists, for instance, that analysis should include the examination of both the specimens and their records for evidence of use of arsenic, DDT, or other pesticides in earlier stages of preparation. In decaying paints or gesso, one must look for lead and other toxic metals. It is crucial to identify any such toxic materials during the earliest planning stages of a health and safety program, because short-range project budgets and long-range program budgets (which will include various project budgets) must provide for any costly precautions needed to work safely with these materials.

After identifying toxic materials, the next step in a health and safety program is to develop precautionary procedures. The program should provide for training the supervisor, foreman or another responsible individual, as well as a number of workers, about chemical hazards, emergency procedures, the use of personal protective equipment, etc. In the United States of America, federal or state laws often require such training. Once those responsible for the program have selected appropriate procedures and materials for the various jobs, they should then gather information about the products, methods, and equipment which will be used. These museum staff members will have to study the relevant government and industry regulations and guidelines. Sources for such information can include product information, labels, material safety data sheets, and government regulations—each of which is discussed below.

1. Product information. Several suppliers and manufacturers of chemicals and equipment used in museum work and conservation have prepared safety manuals or information booklets which provide essential safety information about their products, and major manufacturers and suppliers sometimes have experts on their staffs who are willing to advise interested persons on safe use of their products. However, safety information may have to be requested specifically, because manufacturers and suppliers sometimes will not provide it spontaneously or gratuitously—this is particularly true in the case of raw materials and common consumer products. One must be very careful, however, when deciphering or interpreting the literature which accompanies products or has been requested. Facts relevant to health and safety are all too often hidden or buried in the prose and illustrations of such material. Rarely, for example, do the specially posed photographs reproduced in promotional leaflets show a worker wearing protective equipment other than gloves or a hard hat, even when the models in these pictures are demonstrating a process such as chemical spraying, for which the real-life user must wear an appropriate respiratory protective device.

2. Labels. Product labels can often be useful sources of information. Labels on laboratory chemicals usually provide detailed technical information, even listing trace impurities. This kind of detailed information is needed in conservation and other museum work, not only to protect your health, but also to protect the integrity of the art object, artifact, or historical relic being treated. Industrial and consumer product labels are far less informative than labels on laboratory chemicals. Some do not list the ingredients and provide only a trade name for the product. Health warnings on labels are usually limited to *acute* exposure warnings only. *Chronic* hazards—such as cancer, birth defects, and the effects of repeated low-dose exposure—are not usually mentioned. Under the current United States laws (labelling provisions of the Federal Hazardous Substances Act), products with chronic hazards may even be labelled 'non-toxic'. However informative a label may seem, it is essential to obtain formal information in the form of a Material Safety Data Sheet.

3. Material Safety Data Sheet (MSDS). A Material Safety Data Sheet should be acquired for every product used in the museum. These may be obtained from responsible manufacturers, distributors, or importers of the products (laws in some states of the United States require making MSDSs available to employees). Occasionally an MSDS will state that a product's composition is 'proprietary', meaning that its actual ingredients are a trade secret. Avoid these products, if possible, and if not, check on them with museums and universities that conduct research in conservation and preservation. They may know already what the product contains; if not, they may be able to analyze it. In addition to lists of ingredients, MSDSs should provide other valuable information like physical data (boiling-point, vapor pressure, etc.), fire hazards, protective equipment and ventilation requirements, and methods to be employed for cleaning up spills and disposing of wastes. Once you have MSDSs in hand, the health and safety officer or committee (or group of persons designated in the health and safety program) should review them, rejecting or replacing products for which the information is incomplete or inadequate, particularly when the MSDS indicates that the product is too dangerous or otherwise unsuitable for the proposed job. The health and safety program should maintain a central file of MSDSs and make copies available to employees. The program should arrange also to teach all workers how to understand and use an MSDS, and indeed in the United States some states mandate such training.

4. Government Regulations. Once the inherent hazards of both the site and the products in use have been assessed, the relevant governmental regulations should be investigated. For example, in the United States of America the government has set standards for exposure to many of the chemicals museums use, and these government standards should be known and complied with. Several COH data sheets and handbooks (see the chapter bibliography) are particularly helpful in familiarizing museum personnel with safety standards and United States regulations.

Special Aspects of Museum Health and Safety Programs

All institutions need health and safety programs in order to evaluate and control hazards, plan for emergencies, and educate and train employees and administrators alike. However, museums have some particular needs due to the special nature of their work and their environments. Some of these are related to the need to control pests, handle various toxic chemicals, and vacate the premises in an emergency, together with ongoing maintenance and the occasional renovation and remodelling, and ongoing medical surveillance. Each topic is discussed separately in the following sections.

Museum Pest Control

All institutions need to control pests as part of both their health and safety and conservation programs, but museums need specially efficient methods because the objects for which they have assumed responsibility can be, and in some cases have been, devastated by insects or other kinds of pest damage. Indeed, entire collections can be ruined by pests. Pest control is made even more difficult in museums because collections can be contaminated by outside influences, and not just by in-house activity. Members of the visiting public can unwittingly contaminate objects if they have close access to exhibits and collection materials, or to areas housing them, whilst traveling exhibitions and new acquisitions can also bring pests into a museum. Pest control requires constant vigilance as well. If curators or other staff members do not inspect stored objects frequently, pest damage may not become apparent until it is too late. Fear of such infestation often leads museums to undertake wholesale fumigation on both emergency and maintenance bases, but unfortunately such fumigation is extremely hazardous and may harm the staff, or even the visiting public. Pesticides, however, bring their own particular problems with them and they too are potential sources of harm to people. Less obviously, some pesticides react with, alter, or otherwise damage collections. What is worse, the effects of pesticides on many materials are not known, and the little which is known consists primarily of data accumulated by trial and error, and not through traditional scientific research. Information about the reactivity and health effects of some of the most commonly used museum fumigants is summarized in Table 1. More recently, conservators and others in library and museum work have become particularly interested in the effects of the fumigant, ethylene oxide. The use of this substance provides a good example of how varied the effects of one chemical can be on artifacts as well as demonstrating toxicity to the humans who use it or come into contact with it in one way or another.

Ethylene oxide is used industrially to increase the wet strength of paper by reacting with the cellulose in paper to create another, stronger molecule. Thus conservators should be aware that using ethylene oxide on cellulosic materials may produce similar molecular changes. The long-term effects of such changes are not yet known, but ethylene oxide *is* known, however, to have other undesirable effects, including loss of adhesiveness in gum arabic and animal glues, increased solubility of some paints and pigments, and a cross-linking reaction with proteinaceous materials which prematurely ages and embrittles them. Once exposed to ethylene oxide, the carbon-dating characteristics of some artifacts may be altered slightly. This happens because small amounts of carbon-containing polyethylene glycol can be produced in artifacts fumigated in the presence of moisture (in turn, polyethylene glycol is associated with corrosion of lead, zinc, iron, and aluminium). Other ethylene oxide reactions may threaten a conservator's health, or the health of other museum employees. Fatty substances, for instance, such as those found in bones, horns, skins, and many other vegetable and animal products, absorb ethylene oxide during fumigation and afterwards release it very slowly. Certain types of artifacts and some tightly packed or crated materials have been found to give off ethylene oxide in amounts significant to threaten health for days, weeks, or even months after fumigation.

Inorganic chlorides, present in some artifacts, pose another threat to conservators after artifacts containing them are fumigated with ethylene oxide. An artifact might contain chlorides as a result of being exposed to seawater or marine environments, or being handled often, or from contact with some soils, cell protoplasm and blood, or from the presence of corroded metal. Ethylene oxide reacts with chlorides to form ethylene chlorohydrin, which is highly toxic but less volatile than water, and tends to remain in the artifact. If a conservator (or anyone else) then handles the artifact, he or she can absorb this highly toxic ethylene chlorohydrin through the skin. Systematic research into the effects of ethylene oxide and other fumigants and pesticides is long overdue, as is use of safer alternative methods. Some non-chemical alternatives—freezing, exposure to carbon dioxide, and subjecting artifacts to ultra-high-frequency sound, for example, are showing promise, but adopting them is as yet premature. At the moment, a museum pest control program should combine using the best proven pest-killing methods, isolation of new artifacts, and excellent housekeeping. Together they should provide a good overall means of controlling pests.

Other Toxic Chemicals

In addition to highly toxic pesticides and fumigants, many other very toxic chemicals find uses in museums.

1. Solvents. If the museum does some or all of its own preservation or conservation work it is likely to employ highly toxic solvents. In some cases, museum conservators use solvents such as carbon tetrachloride, which are banned in ordinary consumer products, or which are tightly regulated in industrial use (benzene or carbon disulfide are two such solvents). Conservators, however, can without restriction purchase these solvents through chemical reagent suppliers. Those who do so should discontinue this practice and substitute safer solvents. Even in museums where such solvents are no longer used, old stocks are often discovered when industrial hygiene surveys are carried out. Less toxic but still very dangerous solvents abound in museums for the conservation, cleaning, and dilution of many products. It is common also to find these chemicals either used in ways which pose hazards to museum personnel or stored in amounts which pose safety and fire hazards.

2. Preservatives. Museum personnel often treat objects in their collections with highly

Table 1. Hazards of Fumigants

Registered Name	Carbon disulfide	Carbon tetrachloride	Dichlorvos	Ethylene oxide
Synonyms	Carbon bisulfide	carbon-tet tetracloromethane	dimethyldichlorovinylphos-phate	ETO, epoxyethane
Trade Names		Dowfume 75	AI-20, Vapona strips, 738 Vapona strips, no-pest strips, DDVP, Vaponite, Nuvan	carboxide, Oxyfume, Penn-gas, Oxirane
Appearance & Warning Properties	Colorless to faint yellow liquid; strong (slight sweet) odor at less than 1ppm. Good warning properties	Colorless liquid with ether-like odor, poor warning properties, irritating to the eyes.	Colorless-mild amber liquid, mild chemical odor. Poor warning properties. Not known to be an eye irritant.	Poor warning properties. Odor threshold not precisely known but very high.
Standards * OSHA PEL ACGIH TLV NIOSH Recommendations	20 ppm (30 ppm ceiling) 10 ppm (30 ppm STEL) 1 ppm (10 ppm ceiling)	10 ppm (25 ppm ceiling.) 5 ppm (20 ppm STEL) 2 ppm (1 ppm ceiling)	1 mg/m^3 1mg/m^3 or 0.1 ppm (0.3 ppm STEL)	50 ppm; proposed 1 ppm 10 ppm; proposed 1 ppm
Routes of Entry	Skin absorption, inhalation, ingestion	Skin absorption, inhalation, ingestion	Skin absorption, inhalation, ingestion	Inhalation, ingestion
Signal Word **	WARNING	DANGER	CAUTION	DANGER (pure) WARNING (mixture)
Acute Health Effects	Narcosis (dizziness, nausea, headache, fatigue, loss of co-ordination, unconsciousness) severe skin & eye irritation, nerve damage, psychosis & possible death	Acute exposure has resulted in many fatalities, particularly when used in combination with drinking alcoholic beverages during or after exposure. Symptoms of overexposure resulting in toxic hepatitis include nausea, vomiting, abdominal pain, diarrhea, enlarged & tender liver, & jaundice. Diminished urinary volume, red & white blood cells in the urine, albumin in the urine, coma, & death may be consequences of acute kidney failure.	Symptoms can be mild, moderately severe or severe, depending on exposure. Mild symptoms can include: inability to walk, chest discomfort, construction of pupils of eyes, & muscular twitching. Severe symptoms include unconsciousness & seizures.	Skin, eye, nose & throat irritation. Possible chemical pneumonia. Can cause depression of central nervous system, resulting in dizziness, delayed onset of nausea.
Chronic Health Effects	May affect nervous system, kidneys, liver, heart and eyes. Symptoms include severe behavioral & psychological effects, tremors, memory loss & impotence. Skin allergies.	Dermatitis from repeated skin contact. Other chronic effects include liver & kidney damage, central nervous system depression, & gastrointestinal symptoms.	Possible central nervous system effects such as slowness of thinking, memory defects, irritability & delayed reaction times.	Headaches, burning eyes, swelling of eyelids, nausea, drowsiness, fatigue, chest pain, sinus congestion, dermatitis of exposed areas of head, neck & hands. May also cause allergies.
Carcinogenic Effects	unknown	Suspected human carcinogen; causes liver cancer in animals.	National Cancer Institute tests are negative.	Human carcinogen-causes leukemia
Reproductive Effects	Reproductive damage in humans. Suspect human teratogen; causes birth defects & fetal death in rats.	Animal studies show damage to reproductive system in males & females; may be fetotoxic.	Suspect human teratogen; causes birth defects & fetal death in rats.	Causes reproductive damage in men & women; causes mutations in animals.
Reactivity	Tarnishes metals	Dissolves lacquers, waxes & rubbers. In presence of water it corrodes, while as a vapor it can soften lacquers, waxes & rubber.	In humid conditions, vapona pest strips may act as an acid. May blend onto materials and corrode metals. Can cause tackiness in resins & glues and dissolve polystyrene plastics.	Loss of adhesiveness to some glues, reacts with proteins to cause premature aging of protein materials. Settles in fatty substances. Reacts with salt, cellulose & other materials.
Comments	Registered for general use, although not registered for use in museums or other allied public institutions. Extremely flammable & explosive. *Do not use.*	Registered for restricted use in museums as Dowfume 75 only by certified exterminator. N.B. Dowfume 75 is 70% ethylene dichloride & 30% carbon tetrachloride.	Registered for non-restricted use in public institutions. Use in display cases and in storage areas. *NB* Only pest strips should be used.	Registered for restricted use in fumigation chambers by certified exterminators. Because of flammability do not use pure ethylene oxide but mix with freon or carbon dioxide. *Avoid when possible.*

* *Standards*

The OSHA Permissible Exposure Limit (PEL) is the 8-hour time-weighted average legally enforceable standard. Ceiling limits are maximum values not to be exceeded.

The ACGIH Threshold Limit Value (TLV) is the 8-hour time-weighted average exposure recommended by the American Conference of Governmental Industrial Hygienists.

The Short Term Exposure Limit (STEL) of the ACGIH is the maximum exposure for a period up to 15 minutes.

NIOSH recommended standards are recommendations of the National Institute for Occupational Safety and Health

Table 1. Hazards of Fumigants (contd.)

Hydrogen cyanide	Methyl bromide	Naphthalene	Para-dichlorobenzene	Sulfuryl fluoride
HCN, hydrocyanic acid	Bromomethane, MeBr	Naphthalin	p-dichlorobenzene paradichlorbenzene, PDB	
Aeor Discoids, Cyanogas Cyclon prussic acid, Formonitrite	Brom-O-Gas Brozone, Methogas, Terr-O-Gas	White tar, Moth Flakes, Moth balls	Di-Chloricide Para, Para-Di Paracide, Paradow	Vikane
Colorless-pale blue liquid, gas with bitter almond odor. Poor warning properties.	Colorless liquid or gas which at high concentrations has a chloroform like odor. Poor warning properties.	Colorless-brown solid, moth ball-like odor. Good warning properties.	Colorless & solid; mothball like odor. Good warning properties	Colorless & odorless gas. Poor warning properties.
10 ppm or 11 mg/m^3 10 ppm^3 ceiling 5 mg/m^3, 10 minute ceiling	20 ppm 5 ppm (15 ppm STEL)	10 ppm 10ppm (15 ppm STEL)	75 ppm 75 ppm (110 ppm STEL)	5 ppm 5 ppm (10 ppm STEL)
Skin absorption, inhalation, ingestion	Skin absorption, inhalation, ingestion	Skin absorption, inhalation, ingestion	Inhalation, ingestion	Inhalation, ingestion
DANGER	DANGER	CAUTION	WARNING	WARNING
Mild skin & upper respiratory irritation & chemical asphyxiation which inactivates the cell respiratory system. Large doses can cause rapid loss of consciousness, respiratory failure and death. Lower doses may cause weakness, headache, confusion, nausea & vomiting, possibly followed by unconsciousness & death. Note that the greatest number of occupational poisonings have resulted from its use as a fumigant.	Irritation to skin, eyes & upper respiratory system. Acute effects usually 30 minutes to 6 hours after exposure, & include malaise, visual disturbances, headaches, nausea, vomiting, vertigo, & hand tremors. The tremors may become more severe & widespread, developing, into epileptic-type convulsions followed by coma & death due to pulmonary &/or circulatory failure.	Direct eye contact with dust has produced irritation & cataracts. Inhalation of high concentrations may cause hemolysis (destruction) of red blood cells. Individuals with Glucose-6-phosphate dehyrogenase deficiency (a genetic disease found mainly in blacks & Mediterraneans) may develop severe hemolytic anemia at low levels of exposure. Other effects included profuse sweating, nausea, abdominal pain, bladder, & acute kidney failure.	Narcosis (dizziness, drowsiness, headaches, nausea, loss of coordination), skin & respiratory system irritation.	Conjuctivitis, rhinitis ("hay fever"), nausea, vomiting, abdominal pain. In animals, tremors, convlusions, & chemical pneumonia have been documented.
Possible skin rash and symptoms of itching of throat & nose, burning & reddening of eyes, metallic taste in mouth with burning of tongue, pressure in head, & a feeling of apprehension	Usually limited to central nervous system, with symptoms of lethargy, muscular pains, visual, speech & sensory disturbances, & mental confusion.	Dermatitis & skin allergies.	Dermatitis, liver & kidney damage, loss of appetite, nausea, vomiting, jaundice & liver cirrhosis.	Fluorosis (bone & teeth defects). In animals, lung & kidney damage has been found.
unknown	unknown	unknown	under EPA investigation	unknown
unknown	Mutagenic in bacteria	unknown	unknown	unknown
Slight odor retained on ethnographic materials	Do not use with rubber, furs, feathers, & leather, woolens and other hair fibers.	Can recrystallize on specimens. Softens some resins and corrodes some metals.	Known to soften some plastics (especially styrofoam & styrene), some resins, and damages feathers, leather, dyes and bronze. Forms chlorine gas in closed containers that may bleach specimens.	Unknown; liquid possibly reacts with metals.
Registered for restricted use only. *Do not use.*	Registered for restricted use by certified applicator in *approved* fumigation chamber.	Registered for non-restricted use in museums. Naphthalene is a repellant not a fumigant & its effectiveness is questionable.	Registered as general use pesticide. Not classified as fumigant. Not registered for use in museums. Use only in closed cases etc, not in open.	Registered as restricted use fumigant for chamber use by certified pest applicator. Not approved for museums. When heated sulfuryl fluoride produces highly toxic gases.

** *Signal Word*

The signal word on a pesticide label indicates its relative toxicity. Pesticides have four Toxicity Categories: I (signal word DANGER); II (signal word WARNING); III (signal word CAUTION); and IV (Signal word CAUTION). If a Toxicity Category I pesticide is in Category I because of ingestion, inhalation or skin contact, the label shall also carry a skull and crossbones.

toxic preservatives, most of which are actually pesticides in a form which can be applied directly to artifacts. For instance, a number of leather preservatives contain pentachlorophenol (PCP) or its derivatives. In the case of pentachlorophenol and its salts, US agencies consider them restricted-use pesticides, and unlicensed users are violating the regulations. Museum personnel, however, often unwittingly use them because they still can order such products from foreign manufacturers who do not label their products.

Other toxic preservatives commonly used by museum personnel include formaldehyde phenol, thymol, o-phenyl, and copper and zinc naphthanates.

3. Dangerously Outdated Stocks. Some chemicals when stored overlong become highly hazardous. Some can even become shock-sensitive explosives. Polyester resin curing agents and other organic peroxides, ethyl ether, certain perchlorates and other oxidizers, and picric acid are a few of the chemicals which become hazardous when stored too long (except for picric acid, the present author has found outdated supplies of all these types of chemicals during surveys). It is important for museums to keep complete inventories of supplies to prevent serious accidents from outdated stocks.

4. Unidentified Chemicals. Unless a museum keeps a complete inventory of chemicals, it is likely that numbers of unidentified or misidentified chemicals will be found on its shelves. One reason for this may be inherent to the nature of those who work in museums—that is, their desire to preserve and keep. When this urge extends to chemicals, however, it can be dangerous. For instance, the present author has found pigments and conservation chemicals handed from teacher to students, or passed from generation to generation of successive employees. These 30–50-year-old pigments and chemicals are often identified by old common names and may indeed be mislabelled. All unidentified chemicals pose threats to workers as well as to artifacts, and they should be either discarded, or analyzed and relabelled if still usable and useful. It should be noted also that disposal of unidentified chemicals can prove costly, if the procedures are to comply with waste disposal regulations.

5. Polychlorinated Biphenyls. There are several sources of polychlorinated biphenyls (PCBs) in museums. Often these are first discovered by waste-disposal companies that pick up a museum's hazardous refuse. Disposal companies usually analyze solvent, paint, and other hydrocarbon wastes because disposal of PCB-contaminated material is vastly more complex and expensive than disposal of ordinary wastes. In some cases, museum waste has been contaminated by fluids leaking from transformers or fluorescent light ballasts, both of which are common sources of PCBs. However, on two occasions of which the present author is aware, the contamination was from Arochor slide-mounting medium (a material which contains PCBs and polychlorinated triphenyls) and/or PCB-contaminated pigments such as phthalocyanine blue and green, and diarylide (benzidine) yellow.

6. Nitrate Film. Stocks of old cellulose nitrate film and photographs can become highly flammable and have been responsible for some spectacular fires. Fortunately, most museum personnel are now aware of nitrate film hazards, but occasionally old nitrate materials are still to be found unvaulted or unrefrigerated. Also, many people are not aware that workers can experience respiratory distress while handling cellulose nitrate-based materials. Good ventilation and cool environments are prerequisites for working safely with nitrate film and photographs.

Emergency Evacuation Plans

All museums and public buildings need written general emergency procedures with which all workers must be familiar. These plans typically establish procedures for dealing with accidents, fires, medical emergencies, chemical spills, bomb threats, and the like. Especially important for museums, however, is development of detailed evacuation procedures in response to emergencies which take into considerations both protection of people and collections. Obviously, protection of employees and the public must take priority over protection of property, however valuable. Nevertheless, one particular problem observed all too often in museums is inadequate planning for evacuation of the handicapped, since efforts to provide *access* for the handicapped have not been balanced by equal efforts to provide for their safe and rapid *egress*.

Special plans for evacuating the disabled must include not only the obvious categories, such as people in wheelchairs and those with impaired sight and hearing, but also people with less obvious impairments such as severe emphysema, heart problems, or advanced age. Such people might not be able to move quickly enough on their own to leave a building rapidly. Procedures for the evacuation of disabled persons might include a means of identifying their disabilities when they enter a museum, tracking their locations while they are in the museum, training security guards in how to move people in wheelchairs, providing safe areas where the disabled can wait for evacuation assistance, etc. Special procedures to suit individual museums must be developed if groups of disabled visitors are accommodated.

Once a plan has been developed, regular practice drills should be held. These obviously should be scheduled when the museum is open to the public, as only when the public are present do a plan's inadequacies become obvious, and only during such drills can staff members develop the skills necessary to carry out a successful evacuation during a real emergency. For further information, see the COH data sheet 'Emergency Plans for Museum Conservation Laboratories', cited in the chapter bibliography.

Hazards in Maintenance or Renovation of Museum Buildings

A museum's health and safety program will be taxed especially hard during building maintenance and renovation work, and off the premises when historic site preservation is carried out. Especially hazardous procedures include removal of asbestos and the renovation of old paintwork.

1. Asbestos Identification, Control, or Abatement. Museums and historic buildings should be checked for asbestos in connection with renovation and restoration work. Asbestos-based materials are present in most buildings built between 1945 and 1975, and in older buildings repaired or renovated in the mid-20th century. Asbestos will be found in many types of materials, including:

(a) Surfacing materials, i.e. those trowelled or sprayed on walls or ceilings; and scratch and finishing coats of stuccos, ornamental plaster, and cement surfaces.
(b) Pipe and boiler insulation around hot and cold pipes, boilers, ducts, and tanks. Such insulation is often wrapped with canvas outer layers. (In the USA, where during the Great Depression the government subsidized artists under the Works Progress Administration, the unsold paintings of those subsidized artists often found their ultimate use as such wrappings!)
(c) Miscellaneous materials, including wallboard or partitions, ceiling and floor tiles,

acoustical tiles and boards, decorative plaster panels, asphalt roofing shingles and tile, vinyl tiles, fireproof textiles, wallpapers and sealers, grouts and caulking compounds, etc.

All suspect materials should be analyzed for asbestos content by a reputable laboratory (in the USA, those certified by the American Industrial Hygiene Association). Museum personnel should not conduct these analyses themselves even if they know how and have the proper facilities. (It should be noted that in the USA, the OSHA Asbestos Standard does not differentiate between blue, brown, and white asbestos, applying to all three a Permissible Exposure Level of 0.2 fibers per cubic centimeter. If the new OSHA Standard's partial stay is lifted, tremolite, actinolite, and anthophyllite will be similarly regulated.)

If asbestos is found in the museum, experts should be consulted and it is essential to follow all national, state, and local regulations. Asbestos abatement (its encapsulation, removal, or containment) and the disposal of asbestos waste must be carried out by trained professionals. If abatement is undertaken, then a program to monitor the museum's air constantly during the procedures will need to be undertaken. In many cases in the USA, penalties for violating asbestos regulations are high: in New York City, penalties can cost tens of thousands of dollars per day. If asbestos contamination of a site occurs, cleanup costs and other damages can be astronomical. Administrators also must be aware that asbestos regulations are in flux, so they must keep abreast of the rapid changes in these laws.

2. *Maintenance or Removal of Old Paint.* A number of museums have problems related to the renovation of old painted surfaces. In two cases the present author has been involved with health effects and maintenance problems related to earlier paint renovation which were still evident after several years. In one of these museums, further renovation was necessary to correct the first renovation problem. Whenever museum repair or renovation involves old painted surfaces, the existing paint should first be tested for lead and other toxic metal pigments. Both indoor and outdoor paints manufactured before 1976 are likely to contain lead. Metal-primer, boat, automobile, and artists' paints *may still contain lead legally*, and many in fact do. The backing for murals and the gesso under oil-paintings are also likely to contain some lead.

Other toxic pigments which are found in old paints may contain:

1. toxic metals (such as arsenic, cadmium, manganese, or chromium);
2. organic chemical pigments which (a) are inherently toxic (such as toluidine red, which can cause cyanosis), (b) contain highly toxic impurities (such as phthalocyanine blues and greens containing PCBs), or (c) break down into highly toxic or carcinogenic chemicals (such as benzidine pigments).

It is therefore important to learn as much as possible about paint pigments before choosing removal methods. If lead is present, there are national, state, and/or local laws regulating its maintenance or removal. In the USA, some of these laws require procedures similar to the strict asbestos abatement rules. These procedures include isolating the work area with taped plastic walls, providing negative pressure ventilation, wearing protective clothing and respirators, and the like. Removal of lead-containing paint waste may be regulated also. You must select removal methods for paints containing other toxic pigments just as carefully as you select ways to remove lead-bearing paints. For example, acid or alkaline removal methods could result in the release of highly toxic arsine gas from paints containing arsenic pigments and preservatives. Instances of arsine exposure among conservators have been documented recently (see Williams and Spain, 1982). When choosing paint removal methods, it is necessary to consider both health and safety, and the need to protect the integrity of the historic artifact. The choice is often difficult, since all methods have their hazards. Some methods and their hazards are:

(i) *Torching or burning methods.* These methods should be used rarely, if ever, because of the large volumes of lead, cadmium, and other toxic fumes and vapors they create. These methods are also known to cause fires, and they are destructive of the surfaces under the paint.

(ii) *Heat gun and plate methods.* Studies now show that lead fumes can be created by heat guns. Although the amounts of lead fumes are smaller than those produced by torches, cases of lead poisoning from heat gun use have been documented. Lead fumes are particularly hazardous because they remain in work areas as a fine dust for workers to inhale or ingest long after the work which created the fumes has been completed. If heat gun or plate methods are used, one must adhere strictly to all the provisions required for isolating the workplace and for ventilation, respiratory protection, and a scrupulous cleanup.

(iii) *Mechanical sanding and abrasive blasting methods.* Power sanding and blasting of painted surfaces generates great amounts of dust. Accordingly, some localities have forbidden such treatment of lead-painted surfaces. Indeed these methods are often too hazardous and destructive for preservation and conservation work.

(iv) *Hand scraping methods.* Although these methods generate less dust than power-tool sanding, hazardous amounts may still be created if the paints contain lead or other toxic pigments. All the necessary precautions should be followed for isolation of the work area, respiratory protection, and cleanup.

(v) *Acid and alkaline methods.* Workers who use these methods must be equipped with protective clothing, goggles, gloves, boots, and all other safeguards against acid or alkaline burns. If toxic pigments such as those containing arsenic are involved, workers may have to use air-supplied respirators.

(vi) *Solvent-based stripping methods.* Paint-strippers usually contain some of the most toxic common solvents, including suspect carcinogens like methylene chloride. All necessary precautions, especially ventilation, should be taken when using solvents with these materials (see the COH data sheet, 'Solvents Used in Conservation', listed in the bibliography). If the paint waste contains lead or other toxic substances, it is essential to adhere to the relevant regulations when disposing of it.

Medical Surveillance

Pesticides, solvents, highly toxic or explosive chemicals, asbestos, and lead paint are just a few of the many hazards which museum personnel may encounter. Investigating products, planning for emergencies, and providing protective equipment are only some of the ways in which museum personnel can protect themselves and their institutions' visitors. Protective measures like these should be combined with a health monitoring or medical surveillance program in order to maintain the good health of museum personnel. Medical surveillance should include a pre-employment physical checkup and periodic re-examinations. In the USA, OSHA regulations actually *require* medical surveillance and the retention of medical records about exposures to specific substances, including lead and asbestos. Usually a specialist in medical surveillance, or a doctor who is board-certified in occupational medicine, will need to be consulted on such examinations. United States museum administrators often remark that such surveillance plans are expensive, but they actually may be cost-effective when pre-employment physical examinations find pre-existing medical problems (which allow workers to avoid jobs for which they are at higher risk), or when occupational illnesses are diagnosed at very early stages. In any case, conscience dictates that the highest priority in a museum's budget goes always not to the museum's collections, but to the care and preservation of its personnel.

Acknowledgements

My special thanks to Karan Yager, conservator and writer of COH's 'Historic Preservation Structures' sheet, for sharing her knowledge about asbestos and lead paint hazards. The table from COH Data Sheet 'Safe Pest Control Procedures for Museum Collections' is reproduced with permission.

Bibliography

COH Data Sheets—Write for a Publications List and order form to The Center for Occupational Hazards, 5 Beekman Street, New York NY 10038, USA.

A Health and Safety Program for Conservation Labs;
Emergency Plans for Museum Conservation Laboratories;
Fire Safety in the Conservation Laboratory;
Hazards of Dyes and Pigments for Museum Personnel;
Health and Safety for Historic Structures Preservation;
Historic Preservation Hazards;
Ionizing Radiation Protection for Conservation Laboratories;
Respirator Use in Conservation Laboratories;
Safe Pest Control Procedures for Museum Collections;
Solvents in Conservation Labs;
Storage and Disposal of Conservation Chemicals;
Thymol and O-Phenyl: Safe Work Practices;
Ventilation for Conservation Laboratories.

Construction Industry Occupational Safety and Health Standards, US Department of Labor (OSHA), 29 CFR 1926/1910, Federal Register (1986).

Federal Hazardous Substances Act Regulations, US Consumer Products Safety Commission, Federal Register (September, 1973).

Fischbein, A. et al. 'Lead Poisoning from "Do-It-Yourself" Heat Guns for Removing Lead-Based Paint: Report of Two Cases', *Environmental Research*, *24*, pp. 425–431 (1981).

General Industry Occupational Safety and Health Standards, US Department of Labor (OSHA), 29CFR 1910, Federal Register (1986).

Lead-Based Paint Hazard Elimination: Final Rule and Proposed Rule, 24 CFR, Part 35 et al., Department of Housing and Urban Development, Federal Register (August, 1986).

Occupational Exposure to Asbestos, Tremolite, Anthophyllite, and Actinolite; Final Rules, 29 CFR Parts 1910 and 1926, Department of Labor (OSHA), Federal Register (June, 1986).

Pest Control in Museums: A Status Report, 1980, The Association of Systematic Collections, USA (1981).

'Removal of Lead Paint from Old Housing: The Need for a New Approach,' *American Journal of Public Health*, *76*, No. 3 (1986).

TLVs, American Conference of Governmental Industrial Hygienists, Cincinnati, Ohio (1986–7).

Ventilation: A Manual of Recommended Practice, American Conference of Governmental Hygienists, Cincinnati, Ohio (1986).

Ventilation: A Practical Guide, Center for Occupational Hazards, New York (1984).

Williams, P. L. and Spain, W. H. 'Industrial Hygiene and the Arts: Restoring the Battle of Atlanta.' *Occupational Health and Safety*, April, pp. 34–38, 58 (1982).

2.2 Museums and Safety: Trends and Developments

F. M. P. Howie

Within the United Kingdom, the application of industrial occupational hygiene principles and the operation of defined safe systems of work in museums are both recent developments. Before the commencement of the Health and Safety at Work Etc. Act (HASAWA) in 1974, few museums were required to take notice of workplace safety legislation under either the Factories Act, 1964 or the Offices Shops and Railway Premises Act, 1963 and, in common with most types of educational establishment, the last decade has come as something of a shock. The past decade, especially the last few years, has seen some attempts directed at a rapid, and on occasion over-hasty, adoption of safer practices across a range of activities in museums, including research, conservation, visitor welfare and fieldwork—all areas in which health and safety should be prime considerations.

It is, perhaps, pertinent at this stage to pose a few questions: Just how safe are museums for both the people who work in them and those who visit them? What is the safety record of museums as a specific class of employment? How many major accidents have there been? How many fatalities which are entirely due to occupational causes have occurred in museums? To answer the last questions first, no one really knows, though museum and gallery staff and others have from time to time been killed in fires.[1,2] There are rumours and reports in the literature about museum staff dying from the effects of pesticide use[3] and craftsmen dying from exposure to chemicals.[4] The numbers of major accidents and fatalities are, however, not really the best yardstick by which to measure the current degree of safety enjoyed in museums. Data on both minor, everyday accidents and the extent of work-related health problems are very scant and far more worthy of investigation. In the first part of this chapter an attempt is made to demonstrate how to assess a museum's safety record with the view to using it as the starting-point for safety planning. Without a firm foundation of specific accident and safety performance data it is difficult to see how accident prevention, improvements to safety performance, and the development of safe systems of work can be achieved.

Much of the health and safety literature which has been directed towards museum workers has tended to be informative and preventative[5,6] Published lists of chemical and physical agents, together with the effects of exposure to them, are informative but, without additional information concerning both the manner in which agents are used and the feasibility of control measures which *can* be used, they are not a great help, even to the specialist. In addition, without clearly set-out objectives which are *achievable by the specialists concerned* and well-planned work programmes, little overall progress will be made. Excuses which are often heard, such as 'management ignores the safety problems because of the costs entailed' are, on analysis, usually without foundation. Most improvements can be achieved at little or no cost. A major problem, however, is often to persuade the specialist that a risk exists at all.

The activities of conservation, taxidermy and display technology have received relatively little attention from occupational hygienists and safety practitioners in the past. Traditionally, the practice of these museum activities is rooted in the use of some fairly hazardous materials and techniques, and customs which are today still maintained by many. A brief and necessarily incomplete review of some of the more contentious safety issues with which the profession has been faced for many decades is attempted in the second half of the chapter.

Accident Recording and Prevention in Museums

There can be no doubt that systematic collection and analysis of data on accidents, occupational diseases and dangerous occurrences in museums would be a reasonably effective means of identifying those work activities and, possibly, aspects of visitor safety (see the following section) which would benefit from detailed investigation and improvement. At the time of writing, however, little of such information, even if available, has been published. But, with effect from April 1986, all United Kingdom organizations are required to report specified accidents and occupational diseases to staff, and dangerous occurrences in the workplace to the relevant enforcing authorities under the Reporting of Injuries, Diseases and Dangerous Occurrences Regulations 1985 (RIDDOR)[8] and these data will in due course be available for analysis. The majority of accidents are not serious enough to be reported under RIDDOR, and responsible museums will need therefore to keep adequate records of these lesser accidents and 'near misses' if they wish to try to improve their safety record. Figure 1 illustrates the type of report form used in one large United Kingdom museum.

To date few professional organizations have published surveys of accident rates amongst their members, and the only source of hard data on industrial or commercial groups in the United Kingdom has been the statistics provided by the *Chief Factory Inspector's Annual Report on Health and Safety.* This document reports only the fatalities and major accidents in 'Standard Industrial Classifications'. Of relevance to the museum profession, which constitutes a group far too small to figure in the Standard Classification, are the health and safety statistics published for the years 1981–1984

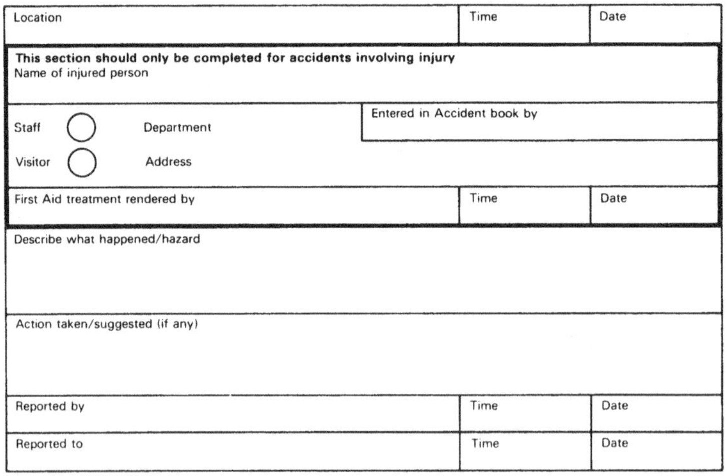
Location | Time | Date
This section should only be completed for accidents involving injury
Name of injured person
Entered in Accident book by
Staff ◯ Department
Visitor ◯ Address
First Aid treatment rendered by | Time | Date
Describe what happened/hazard
Action taken/suggested (if any)
Reported by | Time | Date
Reported to | Time | Date

1. Example of an accident/hazard report form.

Table 1. Fatal and Major Injuries at Work, 1981–1984: Selected Groupings from the Chief Factory Inspector's Annual Reports

Standard Industrial Classification	Fatal[1]/major injury incidence per 100 000 employees			
	1981	1982	1983	1984
XXIV. Insurance, business, etc.	1.1	0.9	1.4	1.3
XXV. Professional and Scientific Services	36.4	30.3	27.3	27.1
XXVII. Public administration, etc.	78.0	71.3	87.7	81.6
Average for manufacturing industries	70.8	74.6	79.3	87.4
XX. Construction Industry	164.0	204.0	220.7	232.6
Average for all industries	60.3	62.1	62.4	60.7

concerning fatal and major injuries occurring in related work sectors (see Table 1). It would seem reasonable to locate museum workers in Grouping XXV where the expected incidence rate of major injury per 100 000 employed would be around 30. How does this figure compare to the limited data available on museum accident rates in the United Kingdom? Direct comparison can be made because there were in 1984 at least two major injuries sustained by staff employed in the United Kingdom national museums 'group' (employing about 6500 people). Crudely put, this represents a major injury rate of 30.8 per 100 000 employees. This figure is of course statistically difficult to interpret because of the small sample size, but it probably represents fairly accurately the general position of museums in the serious accident stakes, i.e. neither very good nor very bad.

Table 2 shows the accident rates of a sample of museum staff employed in the national museums in London during 1985–1986, together with some data on types of accident, and the number of notifiable injuries and dangerous occurrences. (The number of reportable accidents is significantly higher than for 1984 because the new 1986 reporting regulations include several types of accidents which went unreported in previous years). Significantly, a large proportion of accidents were attributable to handling and lifting problems, and the number of accidents due to chemical and physical agents is fairly small. Direct comparison of the percentages of various types of accidents can be made between this sample of staff in museums and those working in universities.

Table 2. Accidents to Staff in Some of the National Museums (London) 1985–1986

National Museums (London)	1985	1986
Total staff employed	2500 (approx.)	2500 (approx.)
Total accidents all types	150	220
No. of RIDDOR accidents[a]	–	8
No. of RIDDOR dangerous occurrences[a]	–	3
No. of handling/lifting accidents[b]	23+	30+
No. of accidents due to hazardous agents, e.g. chemicals, scalds, electricity etc.	14+	18+
No. of accidents due to falls, etc.	28+	60+
No. of accidents due to cuts, etc.[b]	48+	60+

[a]Reports limited to post-April 1986 in half the museums sampled.
[b]Underestimated because some museums (representing 600 staff) did not report this type of accident.

Similarly, Table 3 indicates that, as might be expected, fairly close correlation can be established between different activities involving manual handling. The significantly higher percentage of falls in museums may be due to the nature of the buildings occupied by curators and their collections. In addition, the incidence of handling and lifting accidents is relatively high, presumably because both objects and furniture are in a state of perpetual flux, often in restricted storage areas. On the other hand, the percentage of accidents caused by exposure to chemicals, spillages, electric shocks, etc., is much smaller in museums than in the universities. This last figure is significant for two reasons: firstly, it might suggest that the great emphasis placed upon chemical and physical hazards in the specialized museum literature, particularly conservation publications, is misplaced. Secondly, it might be asked whether the data on acute incidents involving such agents are the best means of determining the extent of chemical and physical hazards in the museum. Certainly, acute accidents with chemicals or electricity can be much more serious than simple cuts and sprains, but what about the effects of occasional or prolonged exposure to chemical and physical hazards, and how are they related to the occurrence of chronic occupational ill-health?

Today, one can make only a rough estimate of the extent of occupational ill-health in most industries, with the notable exception of those involving asbestos and agriculture.[9] The extensive use of chemicals in research, display and conservation activities in museums has been responsible for the occasional acute injury. However, the types of materials used, and the pattern of exposure to them, all too often in poorly equipped studios and workshops, have given rise to concern for the long-term health of conservators and restorers.[10,11] This aspect is examined in some detail elsewhere in this volume[12] and it suffices to note here that there is a considerable mythology or mystique associated with the use of chemicals and proprietory materials in museums. In many technical disciplines—notably taxidermy, picture restoration and paper conservation—a degree of 'professional' secrecy was maintained during the 18th and 19th centuries with regard to the precise recipes for preparations in use. Vestiges of this approach still linger on today and, compounded by the poor standard of information available concerning the potential hazards of many proprietory substances, it is not too uncommon to discover highly toxic materials in regular use with little in the way of precautions to control exposure.

There are, in the United Kingdom, about 450 deaths per year resulting directly from accidents at work, with a further 900 deaths per year from prescribed industrial diseases and, at present, an 'unknown' number of deaths due to cancers of occupational origin. This unknown number is considered to lie at present somewhere between 1400 and 7500

Table 3. Comparison of Accidents by Type Between Museums and Universities, 1985–1986

Percentage of accidents in:	University laboratories[a] (%)	Involving technicians[b] (%)	Museums[c] (%)
Handling glassware, knives, etc.	30.5	23.5	34
Handling/lifting	7	10.5	19
Spills/release of agents	19.5	8	6
Equipment	–	13.5	–
Falls	–	9	18
Struck by an object	10	6.5	6

[a]Kibblewhite (1984);[13] [b]Bowes (1985);[14] [c]Author's data.[15]

deaths per year in the United Kingdom, and thus the total annual number of deaths resulting from all occupational causes is much higher than we like to think and probably far exceeds the yearly number of road fatalities. Under-reporting of both accidents and, more importantly, ill-health at work is considerable. Estimates of the ratio of reported major accidents to unreported minor accidents and to minor incidents, including near misses, are a staggering 1:10:600.[16] Near misses are rarely reported, unless covered by RIDDOR in the context of an aware management, and minor accidents, as well as near misses, are not usually investigated. A good accident-prevention scheme necessitates the investigation of not only the occasional major accident but all accidents, near misses and cases of ill-health at work.

Visitor Safety

Griffith[17] and Malaro[18] highlight the need for museums to exercise a duty of care to their public. Failure to do so, in the United States of America at least, may lead rapidly to a costly lawsuit. Most museum administrations of course take particular care to ensure that access to exhibits and galleries is not impeded and that fire exits and evacuation systems are provided, in many cases to satisfy specific insurance requirements. Accidents involving visitors do occur, however (see Table 4), although the incidence rate for major injuries is thankfully extremely low. The limited survey used as the basis for Table 4

Table 4. Visitor Accidents in Some of the National Museums (London), 1985–1986

Approx. total visitors in period assessed		Total accidents	Accident rate per 100 000 visitors	Falls and trips (% of total)	Accidents caused by structures in display areas, etc. (% of total)
1985	9 000 000	175	1.9	35	35
1986	9 000 000	195	2.0	35	38

covered a sample of London national museums during 1985 and 1986. Of the total of 370 accidents reported only 8 resulted in serious injuries, such as broken limbs. In this sample a number of injuries were actually caused by the exhibits, either by the objects themselves or their display cases. Poor lighting, steps and inadequate maintenance of flooring were significant factors in a sizeable minority of accidents in galleries. Areas where people tend to congregate, such as those near entrances, eating areas and museum shops, are particular danger points. The poor siting of temporary barriers, which severely restrict passageways, is all too often a feature during the renewal of displays, and the museum designer has a degree of responsibility in ensuring that the exhibits and their settings are so constructed as to minimize the hazards to which the visitor is exposed.

The trend towards allowing the visitor free access to objects requires even more careful planning; not only should overt hazards such as splintered wood, chipped glazing and exposed sharp projections on objects be avoided but some classes of objects may well, for example, present a physical, mechanical or toxic hazard for children. Engineering and similar exhibits pose many safety problems, and one major United Kingdom museum recently proposed to exhibit objects composed of metallic lead at levels just perfect for young children to chew! Arsenic-impregnated natural history specimens may too present a toxic hazard in 'hands on' educational sessions. Signs warning the public to 'keep off' or 'do not touch' are in themselves not usually adequate. The museum visitor should have no choice when it comes to safety; all hazards should be removed from public areas. Contractors working in or above galleries pose particular problems. Quite often there is pressure to carry out repairs or modifications to the displays or building fabric as quickly as possible. Hastily erected scaffolding, ladders used improperly and work being undertaken on stairs have all on occasion resulted in injuries to the visiting public.

Suitable facilities are essential wherever children and/or handicapped visitors are especially encouraged to visit and participate in museum activities. Sufficient numbers of adults, either teachers or museum-based guides, should accompany children in groups. The handicapped require adequate access and, more important, adequate emergency exit routes. Museum attendant staff have been injured when helping to move wheelchairs up and down stairs; it is therefore most important that handicapped visitors should find the routes available to them easily passable using only their own resources.

Some Old and Some New Safety Problems

From the earliest times the production of art objects has been associated with a degree of risk to both the artists and the suppliers or manufacturers of their materials. Lead and mercury were amongst the earliest substances to be recognized as toxic[19] to both the slaves who mined their ores and the artisans who made use of the crudely refined substances as pigments and for gilding, etc. The writings of Pliny the Younger and several of his contemporaries suggest that many of the major hazards stemming from toxic substances had been identified during ancient times. Thus, amongst the metals, mercury, lead, antimony and arsenic were known by the Ancient Egyptians to possess lethal properties, both as fumes (or dusts) and by ingestion. Lung diseases were known by the Greeks and the Romans to be caused by exposure to the dust of minerals such as asbestos and silica (in the form of flint),[20] but not that of lime, alabaster or gypsum.[21] Little, however, was known about the way in which these materials acted upon the body, and although murderers from Nero to the Borgias had brought the art of poisoning to an almost scientific exactitude, precise data on doses and the antidotes to a large number of organic and inorganic toxins were available only a little before 1500 AD. During the 16th century one Phillipus Aureolus Theophrastus Bombastus von Hohenheim—better known as Paracelsus (died 1541)—first postulated that toxic agents were chemical entities and that, depending upon the dose, they would in some cases have therapeutic or toxic effects.[22] He also recognized that although a degree of specificity between the therapeutic and toxic effects of chemicals was predictable, it was not always possible to distinguish between these properties. Paracelsus thus discovered the 'dose–response' relationship, which is the essence of the modern study of pharmacology as well as toxicology, and this empiricism is widely used nowadays to correlate the effect on a sample of an organism of steadily increasing quantities of a toxic substance.

Ramazzini (died 1714) was amongst the first to define the dangerous occupations.[23] Of relevance to the arts and museums are the following categories: chemists, potters, glass and mirror makers, painters, sculptors, stone-cutters, textile-workers, porters, those who strain their eyes over fine work, printers, carpenters and metalsmiths. Not only did he recognize that exposure to physical and chemical agents produced both acute and chronic illnesses, but that environmental conditions, including the provision of fresh air, physical exercise, proper working posture and cleanliness, were all of fundamental importance to the well-being of the worker. Three hundred years later, we are still very little ahead of Ramazzini or even, in some regards, Pliny. We still experience lead and mercury poisoning, although both are now much less common, whilst asbestosis, silicosis and mesothelioma are the mid-20th century legacy of progress. It is looking more than likely that a host of 'modern' diseases, including many types of cancer, may well be one of the results of the mushrooming growth in the production and use of organic compounds, ranging from solvents to plastics, that has taken place during the past 65 years.

It is at this stage that the artist and restorer again figure. Mallary[24] drew attention in the early 1960s to the fact that many of the organic materials used by artists could cause liver and kidney damage. In 1985, *The Wall St Journal*[25] became concerned that the hazardous materials used by modern artists had on occasion resulted in the deterioration of their health. Two recent statistical reports on mortality[26] and cancer[27] rates amongst artists indicate that incidences of heart disease, leukemia, arteriosclerotic conditions and cancer were substantially higher for painters and that the incidence of other cancers was higher for sculptors. To date, the present author is not aware of any similar surveys which have been carried out on sample populations of museum and gallery staff, such as conservators, restorers and museum designers and display technicians, who are also regularly exposed to many of the materials used by artists. Exposure to organic solvents, resins and synthetic adhesives is probably characteristic of more museum activities than exposure to other hazardous agents and thus they would be worthy of detailed surveillance. Other specialized activities, working with archives, furniture, and natural history and ethnographical collections, as well as textile conservation, share a much discussed hazard in the use of pest control agents. Since before the 17th century attempts have been made to slow or stop the decay of organic materials using a variety of substances. Weiss and Carruthers[28] have reviewed, in an annotated bibliography covering over 2000 years, many of the early methods of attempting to control insect pests attacking paper and bindings. Most notable was the early use of cedar oil, saffron and protective sleeves to preserve scrolls and papers during the Roman period. The use of such insect-repellent chemicals continued up to the end of the 17th century, when arsenic- and mercury-based treatments became the vogue, not only for books but for natural history specimens as well. Hawkes,[29] in an excellent review of the use of arsenic in natural history collections, notes that both arsenic and mercury compounds are still in use, although in much reduced quantities, as fixatives and insecticides in museums and by taxidermists.

Amongst the earliest reports of arsenic poisoning amongst museum workers must be that of Charles Wilson Peale who, as a young naturalist in the 1760s, regularly used a hot concoction of arsenious oxide to prepare bird and mammal skins in his garden. Even so, the fumes were strong enough to cause him acute arsenic poisoning.[30] By the latter part of the 18th century serious doubts were being expressed as to the widespread use of arsenic and mercury compounds as book preservatives,[31] and by 1821, no less an organization that the Comité Consultatif des Arts et Manufactures in Paris effectively banned the use of arsenic on paper.[32] During the mid- to late 19th century there was an epidemic of chronic arsenic poisoning in the United Kingdom due to the use of the pigments Scheeles Green ($CuHAsO_3$) and Paris Green ($3Cu(AsO_2)_2 \cdot Cu(CH_3COO)$) in just about every type of fancy paper used at the time, including sweet-wrappers, book covers, wallpaper and card boxes. The pigments were even used in foods.[33] Even so, it was not until 1902 that arsenic-based colouring agents were prohibited in the United Kingdom. During the 1830s mercury-based preservatives became widely used in

European museums, particularly in herbaria. The use of arsenic and mercury compounds in natural history technology and taxidermy has actually been actively encouraged over the past century with the inclusion of countless recipes for fixatives based on mercuric chloride, arsenious oxide and other compounds.

Over the past decade a number of reports have appeared which indicate that the previous use of these materials constitutes a potentially high health risk still for some museum workers. A case of a taxidermist severely poisoned by arsenic was reported in 1982.[34] Muir[35] had reported (in 1981) that arsenic levels were very high during an occupational hygiene survey in one large natural history collection in the United Kingdom, and Briggs[36] reported (in 1983) extremely high levels of mercury vapour in a major British herbarium. Table 5 illustrates the levels of contaminants found in the latter surveys. Several other highly toxic materials have been used in conservation but, because of their toxicity, they have been phased out. For example, DDT was used extensively to dust mounted animal skins, and asbestos was a common fine-powder filler, during the period *c.* 1930–1970, for the adhesive used in filling gaps in fossil material.[37] Other materials used in geological conservation and specimen preparation pose severe hazards, and some of the minerals found in collections can themselves constitute a moderate risk.[38]

Table 5. Arsenic and Mercury Levels Recorded in Some National History Collections

Location	Contaminant levels	
Cambridge University, Herbarium:[a]	Mercury,[c] airborne concentrations:	
	(a) Breathing zone	(b) Cabinet interior
before ventilation improvements (1974)	10–20 μgm^{-3}	40–700 μgm^{-3}
after ventilation improvements (1981)	8–10 μgm^{-3}	15–400 μgm^{-3}
Bristol Museum, storage areas[b]	Mercury,[c] airborne concentrations: $0.4 \times 10^{-3}\ \mu gm^{-3}$	
Bristol Museum, skin collections[b]	Arsenic levels of 77 to 10 000 ppm recorded Mercury levels of up to 200 ppm recorded	

[a]See Briggs et al. (Note 36).
[b]See Muir et al. (Note 35).
[c]The recommended short-term exposure limit (10 minutes duration) for mercury vapour is 150 μgm^{-3}.

In the late 19th century pest control by fumigation became widespread in the protection of archive[39] and museum material: benzene, carbon disulphide, formaldehyde, hydrogen cyanide, chloropicrin, ozone, sulphur dioxide, carbon tetrachloride, chlorine and, eventually, ethylene oxide, and various mixtures of this gas with carbon dioxide or carbon tetrachloride were the main compounds used. The very serious hazards experienced as a consequence of fumigation with many of these compounds, for both the operator and the object, were soon recognized, and by the 1930s the range of fumigants had been reduced to mainly hydrogen cyanide, ethylene oxide and carbon disulphide,[40] although carbon tetrachloride was used as the basis of Dowfume 75 up to the early 1980s in the United States of America. Fumigation technology has moved forward a little over the past half-century, with the introduction of methyl bromide, phosphine and 'Vikane' (sulphuryl fluoride) and all of these, together with ethylene oxide, are still commonly in use on museum material. However, more recently, because of renewed concern about both the toxic effects on operatives and the likelihood of damage to objects from fumigants, their use is being re-evaluated, particularly in the United States of America.[41,42]

Monitoring Hazards and Controlling Exposure to Hazardous Agents in the Museum

At the present time, the exposure of people at work to chemical hazards is controlled by reference to the limits set by safety authorities, i.e. the occupational exposure limits set by the Health and Safety Executive in the UK and threshold limit values set by the Occupational Safety and Health Association in the USA. In the UK two types of limits are currently in operation: recommended limits and control limits.

Recommended limits are the exposure limits advised by the Health and Safety Commission's Advisory Body on Toxic Substances, whose remit is to establish standards of good practice and 'realistic criteria for the control of exposure, plant design, engineering controls and, if necessary, the selection and use of personal protective equipment'. Failure to observe these exposure limits, whilst not automatically constituting a breach of the Health and Safety at Work Act, could form part of a Health and Safety Executive Inspector's criteria for assessing compliance with the law, and would be taken into consideration in a tribunal or court of law. Some 500 chemicals are listed in EH40[43] with their 8 hour TWA (time weighted average concentrations) and STEL (short-term exposure limit = 10 minute TWA) values in ppm or mg m^{-1}. Similarly, in the USA some 700 substances have listed threshold limit values.

Control limits are based on Regulations, Approved Codes of Practice, European Community directives, or Health and Safety Commission instructions, and are limits which should not be exceeded. Failure to comply with a control limit may result in enforcement action by a Health and Safety Executive Inspector. With some controlled substances (i.e. those with no minimum threshold below which adverse effects do not occur, or where short exposure to high concentrations cause injury) exposures may need to be reduced to the lowest levels justifiable on a cost/risk basis. The present strategy behind the application of control limits for exposure to relatively few substances, some of which are not highly toxic, is based on the recognition that these substances are very commonly used at work. Until a few years ago, a great many were used without any real control of exposure (e.g. asbestos, vinyl chloride and lead compounds). Some, such as methylene chloride, formaldehyde and styrene, have been shown more recently to be potentially very harmful, in both the short and the long term, at levels of exposure just above the limits set, and they are included because of their widespread use at work.

Prolonged exposure to a number of the controlled substances (and, of course, other toxic materials) may occur in the laboratory, workshop or elsewhere. Styrene, glass fibre, isocyanates and chlorinated solvents are amongst the substances most frequently used in conservation workshops. Exposures to levels above the control limit can occur where there is insufficient containment. In the laboratory or workshop the use of local exhaust ventilation or a fume cupboard will reduce the risk, but outside the laboratory, however, the use of polyurethane foam, epoxies, styrene and fibreglass may lead to problems.

Familiarity with the materials and/or lack of knowledge of the risks involved can lead to complacency. Figure 2 illustrates the use of portable extraction equipment for the removal of styrene fumes during work with polyester resins in a gallery situation. The operators are also using filtered-air supply hoods for the removal of dust and nuisance

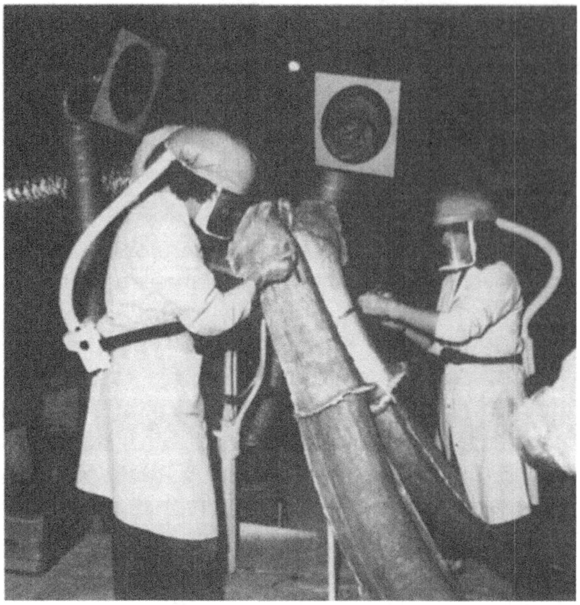

2. Portable fume extraction equipment used to exhaust styrene from a gallery area during work with polyester resin.

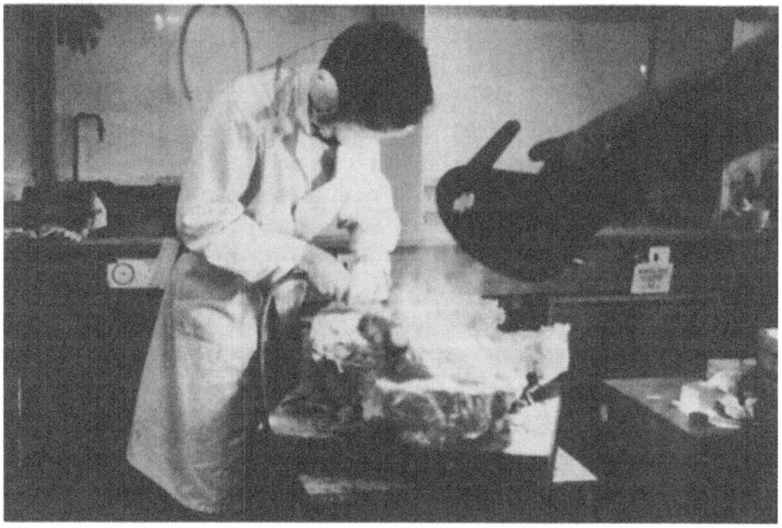

3. Mobile local exhaust ventilation system used for the removal of rock dust during mechanical preparation.

odours (not styrene). The localized removal of styrene is achieved by the use of a flexible ducting and hood system; the styrene fumes are collected and ducted to atmosphere via a nearby window. Using this type of approach it was possible to undertake the job without closing off more than a small section of the gallery to the public. Past experience in carrying out this type of work in public areas, without some form of containment, caused problems for staff and public alike through the buildup of fumes. This type of problem is frequently encountered when building contractors operate in museum premises. Adequate control under these circumstances is often more difficult to achieve because it generally involves the museum in controlling the activities of outside contractors and subcontractors. These outside agencies, however, have precisely the same responsibilities, under the HASAW Act, to themselves, museum staff and visitors as do the museum authorities.

4. 'Push–pull' exhaust ventilation system for removal of acetic acid fumes from preparation tanks in the British Museum (Natural History) Palaeontology Department.

5. Canopy hood arrangement in the British Museum (Natural History) Palaeontology Department.

Reduction of the risk of harm from exposure to hazardous agents is best approached systematically. The following criteria represent a basic strategy for workplace hygiene and, to a great extent, could be adopted in all aspects of laboratory, workshop or studio work:

1. Assess any hazards before commencing work.
2. Eliminate the hazardous element if possible, otherwise try to substitute a safer substance or process.
3. Control exposure where necessary.
4. Ensure that control measures are used effectively.
5. Maintain the control measures adequately.
6. Monitor exposure regularly.
7. Adopt health surveillance where necessary.
8. Inform, instruct and train staff in safe systems of work.

1. Assessing the Hazards This is usually straightforward unless a new substance is being used. Manufacturers or suppliers are now bound to display hazard data and other information on the package, and many supply more detailed information in the form of hazard data sheets. The latter vary considerably in standard at present, and it is prudent to obtain supplies from the most reputable dealers. In cases of doubt you can obtain guidance from the Health and Safety Executive, an occupational hygienist or, but not always, a chemist.

2. Elimination or Substitution. This can be extremely difficult, especially when traditional approaches and well-tried and tested techniques are involved, or when utilizing particularly noxious substances.

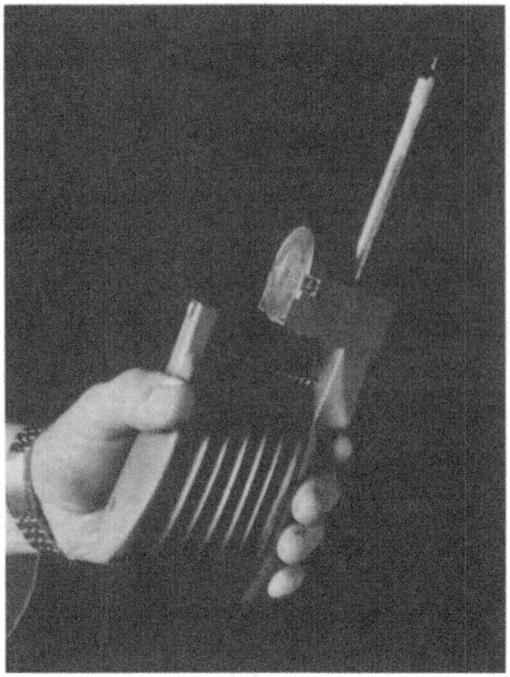

6. Combination hand-operated bellows pump and gas detector tube.

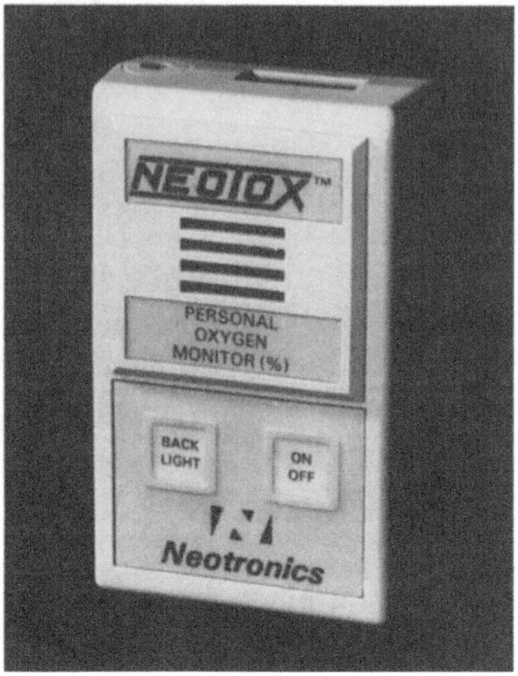

7. Personal monitor for measuring exposure to hazardous atmospheres.

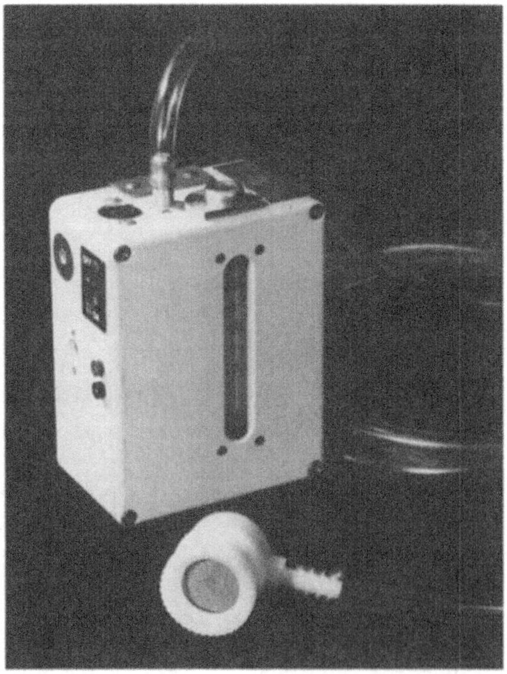

8. Sampling pump with sampling head.

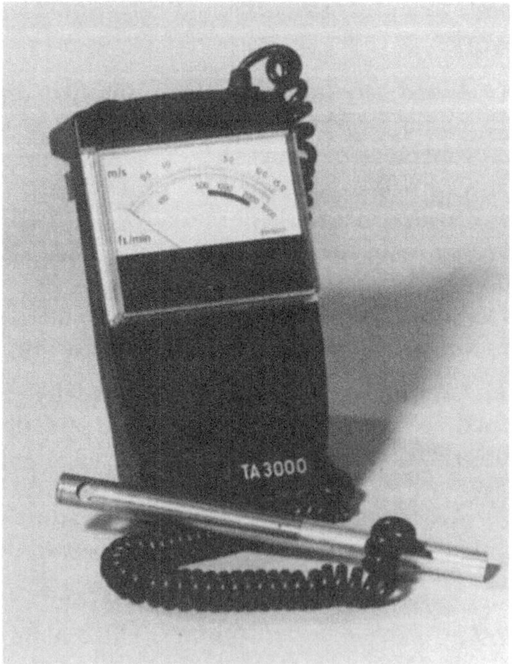

9. Thermal anenometer.

3. The Control of Exposure. This should be achieved primarily by engineering means and extraction, i.e. containment (see Figures 3, 4 and 5: use of three types of local exhaust ventilation systems). The use of protective clothing and personal protective equipment (see Figures 2 and 3: use of gloves, eye and ear protection, respirators and laboratory coats) is very much a secondary option, which, however, often becomes the preferred course of action in the workplace.

4. The Duty to Ensure That Control Measures Are Used. This lies with both staff and management. Management has to provide the measures, whether mechanical systems or protective clothing, and the staff must ensure that they are used effectively.

5. Maintaining the Control Measures. The maintenance of mechanical protective equipment is a management responsibility, but the maintenance of protective clothing is the responsibility of the operator (see Bartlett's chapter).

6. Monitoring of Both Atmospheric Hazards and the Efficiency of Some Control Measures. This may be carried out on site by laboratory or workshop staff. Figure 6 illustrates a simple vapour detection system, and the hand pump draws air through a colorimetric tube selected to react with the particular chemical contaminant present. This method is not accurate for a number of reasons, but in a preliminary survey it will often give an indication as to whether or not a serious problem exists. Figure 7 depicts a simple, personal, electronic detection system which the operators carry about with them. Several types are now available, which cover exposure to gases such as sulphur dioxide, carbon monoxide and formaldehyde. This type of device is relatively inexpensive and sufficiently accurate to give a warning of hazardous situations. Figure 8 shows a basic personal or static air-sampling pump and sampling head of the type used in a detailed survey by an occupational hygienist. Very accurate exposure measurements can be carried out using this equipment, but it is not suitable for use by untrained staff. Ventilation rates can be monitored using a variety of methods, and it is not enough merely to use a piece of tissue or paper to gauge airflow across the face of a fumecupboard or fumehood. Figure 9 depicts a simple anemometer which provides accurate air velocity measurements. For most extraction systems minimum airflow rates of $0.5–1.0\,m\,s^{-1}$ are essential to collect and entrain vapours. Fumecupboard face velocities, when the sash is open, should never fall below $0.5\,m\,s^{-1}$.

7. Health Surveillance. This may be required for some work, and it is usually sensible to consult an occupational health physician when exposure to highly toxic or controlled substances is involved. There is also some merit in obtaining pre-employment screening for certain types of laboratory work (e.g. with epoxy resins and other sensitizers). Furthermore, it is generally recommended that pregnant women should avoid contact with all laboratory chemicals, etc., and here again an occupational health specialist should be consulted. The integrated occupational hygiene approach to laboratory and workshop safety is likely to become standard in the United Kingdom following the introduction of legislation in 1987–1988, i.e. the Control of Substances Hazardous to Health Regulations (Health and Safety Commission, 1984). The main thrust of these regulations is to ensure that exposure of individuals to hazardous substances is reduced to the minimum, and that such exposures are monitored and recorded. Some types of work will need to be closely monitored, and it may be necessary to employ an occupational hygienist to carry out some or all of the monitoring aspects required.

Acknowledgements

Photographic credits: Figures 1, 2 and 6–9, courtesy of Frank Howie; Figure 3, courtesy of the London School of Hygiene and Tropical Medicine; Figures 4 and 5, copyright the Trustees of the British Museum (Natural History).

Notes

1. *Recommended Practice for the Protection of Museums and Museum Collections NFPA911, 1985* (National Fire Protection Association, Quincy, Mass., 1985).
2. 'Hampton Court Palace Fire', *BRE News of Fire Research*, September 1986 (front page).
3. *Museums Association Working Party on Natural Science Collections: Draft Report of Biological Collections Survey Pt 2* (London, 1985).
4. M. McCann, *Artist Beware: The Hazards and Precautions in Working with Art and Craft Materials*, (New York, 1979), pp. 3–4.
5. A. Clydesdale, *Chemicals in Conservation: A Guide to Possible Hazards and Safe Use* (Edinburgh, 1982).
6. N. S. Baer, 'Risk Assessment as Applied to the Setting of Solvent Toxicity Limits', in *Adhesives and Consolidants* (London, 1984), pp. 26–31.
7. M. Pascoe, 'Toxic Hazards from Solvents in Conservation', *The Conservator, 4*, 1980, pp. 25–28.
8. *Reporting of Injuries, Diseases and Dangerous Occurrences Regulations* 1985 (London, HMSO, 1986). The regulations replaced the earlier Notification of Accidents and Dangerous Occurrences Regulations 1980; the new regulations contain a very much enlarged list of reportable injuries, together with the requirement to report all accidents at work which result in more than 3 days' absence.
9. M. Alderton, *Occupational Cancer* (London, Butterworths, 1986), pp. 24–30.
10. See Monona Rossol's chapter, this issue.
11. The Center for Occupational Hazards (New York) publishes a range of literature on hazards and their control in several branches of the arts and crafts as well as on museum disciplines such as conservation, fire safety and natural history.
12. See Monona Rossol's chapter, this issue.
13. J. F. Kibblewhite, 'Analysis of University Accidents', *Safety Practitioner, 2* (12), 1984, pp. 12–21.
14. C. M. Bowes, 'Academic Accidents', *Occupational Safety and Health, 2* (12), 1985, pp. 12–21.
15. Data on accidents were obtained from several sources, including the British Museum, Science Museum, British Museum (Natural History) and National Maritime Museum.
16. H. W. Heinrich, D. Petersen and N. Ross, *Industrial Accident Prevention* (New York, McGraw Hill, 1980), pp. 62–92.
17. See Elizabeth Griffith's chapter, this issue.
18. M. C. Malaro, 'Visitor and Employee Safety as It Relates to Collections', *A Legal Primer on Managing Museum Collections* (Smithsonian Institution, Washington DC, 1985), pp. 301–307.
19. D. Hunter, *Diseases of Occupations* (London, Hodder & Stoughton, 1980), p. 251.
20. D. Hunter, op. cit. Note 19, pp. 936, 990.
21. Ibid., pp. 934–935.
22. L. J. Casarett and M. C. Bruce, 'Origin and Scope of Toxicology', *Casarett and Doulls Toxicology* (New York, 1980), p. 6.
23. B. Ramazzini, *De Morbis Artificum Diatriba* (Modena, 1700).
24. R. Mallary, 'The Air of Art is Poisoned', *Art News*, 1963.
25. *Wall Street Journal* (New York), 14 January 1985.
26. B. A. Miller, A. Blair and M. McCann, 'Mortality Patterns Among Professional Artists: A Preliminary Report', *Journal of Environmental Pathology, Toxicology and Oncology, 6*, 1985, pp. 303–313.
27. B. A. Miller, D. T. Silverman, R. Hoover and A. Blair, 'Cancer Risk Among Artistic Painters', *American Journal of Industrial Medicine, 9*, 1986, pp. 281–287.
28. H. Weiss and R. Carruthers, *Insect Enemies of Books* (New York, 1937), pp. 21–57.
29. C. Hawkes and S. Williams, 'Arsenic in Natural History Collections', *Leather Conservation News, 2*, 1986, pp. 1–4.
30. C. Sellers, *Charles Wilson Peale*, Vol. 1 (American Philosophical Society, Philadelphia, 1947).

31. C. Arthand, *Dissertation sur le papier, dans laquelle on a rassemblé tous les essais qui out été examinés par le Cercle de Philadelphes sur le moyen de préserver le papier de la piqûre des insectes* (Port-au-Prince, 1788).
32. Comité consultatif des Arts et Manufactures, 'Note sur les moyens de préserver le papier des insectes . . .', *Société d'encouragement pour l'industrie nationale: Bulletin, 20,* 1821 (Paris), pp. 290–292.
33. D. Hunter, op. cit. Note 19, pp. 348–349.
34. B. Gombos et al., 'Severe Accidental Poisoning by Arsenic', *Pracovni Lekarstri, 34,* 1982, pp. 28–31.
35. D. Muir et al., 'Health Hazards in Natural History Museum Work', *Museum Journal, 80,* 1981, pp. 205–206.
36. D. Briggs et al., 'Mercury Vapour: A Health Hazard in Herbaria', *New Phytologist, 94,* 1983, pp. 453–457.
37. F. Howie, 'Materials Used for Preserving Fossil Specimens Since 1930: A Review', *Adhesives and Consolidants* (London, 1984), pp. 92–97.
38. F. Howie, 'Safety Considerations for the Geological Conservator', *Geological Curator, 4,* 1987, pp. 379–401.
39. J. Westwood, 'On the Insects Which Injure Books', *Meeting Reports of the British Association for the Advancement of Science, 49,* 1879, pp. 371–372.
40. C. Weber et al., 'Effects of Fumigants on Paper', *United States National Bureau of Standards Journal of Research, 15,* 1935, pp. 271–275.
41. M. W. Ballard and S. Baer, 'Is Fumigation Possible?', *The International Journal of Museum Management and Curatorship, 6,* 1987, pp. 83–86.
42. S. Edwards et al., *Pest Control in Museums: A Status Report* (Lawrence, Kansas, 1980).
43. *Guidance Notes, Environmental Hygiene EH40, Occupational Exposure Limits 1987* (HMSO, 1987).

2.3 Occupational Health in Museums

Peter Constable

One could search in vain in the published lists of hazardous occupations for data on museum work, and therefore it may appear something of a luxury for the national museums and art galleries to have an occupational health service. This is particularly so when one considers the overall situation in the United Kingdom where about 40 per cent of those employed have no direct access to occupational health advice other than that arising from first aid or statutory regulations. Even so, the provision of occupational health care within museums is not unnecessarily lavish. Although no excess mortality or morbidity has been demonstrated in those so employed, there exists within museums—in galleries, workshops, laboratories, as well as in the field—a wide range of potential hazards which require assessment. This context is one in which an occupational health service can make an important contribution to the development of safe working practices.

As in other areas of employment, the occupational health service provides three distinct categories of advice:

1. advice on the medical aspects of recruitment;
2. guidance on fitness for work and rehabilitation at work after illness or injury;
3. advice on environmental problems.

It is interesting that all the national museums and galleries use the Civil Service Occupational Health Services (CSOHS) for the first two categories, but there are wide variations in the frequency with which establishments seek advice on problems arising from their working environment. Does this indicate that some establishments have such a safe working environment, without particular occupational health hazards, that they have no need for an occupational health service? Or, does it reflect the level of commitment, training and enthusiasm of the safety officer and the support he receives from departmental heads and governing bodies? On the other hand perhaps it indicates only that they have never heard of the CSOHS, and obtain occupational health and hygiene services from elsewhere. One suspects that all these factors may play a part, but possibly the principal underlying cause is a lack of understanding of the true functions of an occupational health service.

Not all museum managers appreciate the contribution that an occupational hygienist or an experienced occupational nurse or physician can make to a working environment. To some extent this situation is understandable as museum staff are a heterogeneous collection of workers who fall into three broad occupational categories. By far the largest group consists of gallery and security warders, whilst two smaller categories are formed from the curatorial grades, and the conservation staff together with research scientists. Museum administrators most frequently face staff health problems that relate to the monitoring and interpretation of sickness absence, rather than prevention and identification of work-related hazards. Here it is the common diseases of Western industrialized society which contribute largely to the burden of sickness absence, and which exercise personnel departments in providing the necessary security for their exhibits. Given this background, the problem of educating personnel departments is not altogether surprising—not unique to museums, this situation is common to other enterprises without high-risk occupations. However, it has been repeatedly demonstrated that regular contact between occupational health service staff and personnel departments can educate and alter attitudes towards the preventive aspects of occupational health.

Although museum administrations react appropriately to specific environmental problems when they arise, there is still an unfortunate tendency to rely on this reactive approach rather than use the resources of an occupational health service in a preventive role. The paternalistic approach which physicians adopted earlier this century is now no longer appropriate, either in general or in occupational medicine. Today, overt occupational illness is a clinical rarity, and occupational health is no longer the sole prerogative of doctors. It is tackled far more effectively, using a multidisciplinary approach, by a team which will include the safety officer, the occupational hygienist, an occupational health nurse and an occupational health physician, who may call on other skills and disciplines as required. The need for such an approach exists within museums just as much as in manufacturing industry, and two examples of problems arising in museums discussed here clearly demonstrate this requirement.

Problems of Restoration

A national museum has a large collection of Greek and Roman mosaics, some weighing as much as 1 or 2 tonnes, which were mounted in the Victorian era onto a backing of concrete and slate. Many of these mosaics required conservation, and it was planned to remount the collection on a lighter backing so as to render their display more flexible as well as to remove critical loads from certain areas of the museum's structure. The work was initially planned to occupy four staff for about seven years, with the possibility that other collections might subsequently wish to use the facilities.

The selected technique consisted of a combination of lengthy, repetitive tasks, combined with a need for manipulative skills which required considerable experience. First the mosaic is inverted and the backing of 19th century concrete and slate, together with any remaining Greek or Roman plaster, is removed using power tools driven by air-compressors. (Initially a small compressor was placed within the workshop, but this was later replaced by a much larger machine installed outside the workshop, with the benefit of considerable noise reduction.) Once the tessellate is fixed and cleaned it is stabilized with varnish, then backed with a thin separating layer of Plaster of Paris, and finally supported with a thicker matrix of vermiculite and resin.

A separate workshop, put aside for this project, was equipped to deal with the environmental hazards which had been identified previously, but this made the procedure unexpectedly lengthy and costly. Among the principal problems encountered was the need to handle bulky and heavy objects. In order to cope with them a mechanical hoist was installed. Another potential hazard, identified long before the project started, stemmed from the use of solvents over large surface areas of work. The principal solvent used was styrene, and the design of the workshop included the construction of a separate 'curing' booth with integral exhaust ventilation. Dust, too, was recognized early in the project as an inevitable problem. Although dust was likely to be a nuisance, the presence of slate alerted us to the possibility of a more serious hazard. Local exhaust ventilation proved adequate for the small-scale work, but was unable to cope satisfactorily with larger tasks. As a result, a combination of local exhaust ventilation and the use of lightweight 'Airstream' helmets was adopted with success.

A survey confirmed the presence of a noise hazard, mainly from the use of the first air-compressor, and ambient sound levels of 95 dB(A) being reached, sometimes rising to over 100 dB(A) when pneumatic tools were in use. High noise levels were also produced by the pneumatic needle gun and a pneumatic chisel. Alternative methods of removing the concrete backing from these mosaics were considered and thought to be either harmful to the personnel or ineffective in freeing the mosaic. No method could be found of reducing the noise level arising from the tools, but provision of ear-defenders and the subsequent installation of a large compressor outside the workshop reduced the noise hazard to a general level of 75 dB(A).

In order to remove the backing from the tessellate, the conservators used a variety of tools, ranging from percussion hammers for the coarse work to needle guns and engraving pens for the more delicate tasks. Use of these tools exposes the workforce to the possible risks of 'Vibration White Finger'. After lengthy use all operators noticed altered sensations in their fingers, and general tingling of the hands, extending as far as the wrists. Although these symptoms disappeared within two minutes of ceasing work, clearly the use of these vibrating tools could put the workers at risk. After the pilot study was completed, it was recommended that the work programme be modified so that no individual conservator be required to handle vibration tools for longer than 4 hours per day. The conservation staff involved in this work were medically examined before starting on the project, and thereafter at 3-monthly intervals to ensure that there was no progression in their symptoms. The limitation of working with these tools for only 4 hours a day had the added advantage of reducing the operator's exposure to noise.

This project stemmed from an academic and managerial decision taken, one suspects, without a clear understanding at the time of the financial implications and technical resources needed to provide a safe working environment. That an acceptable working environment has been achieved is a tribute to good cooperation between the conservation staff and the occupational health nursing adviser, who between them alerted the safety officer and medical adviser to the problems. Advice was sought in turn from an occupational hygienist and a ventilation engineer, thereby neatly demonstrating the teamwork which is required to resolve such complex tasks.

Procedures and Substances in the Fumigation Process

The second example of an apparently straightforward project which became surprisingly complex developed rather differently. As far as the Occupational Health Service was concerned it started as a relatively innocent question on anthrax risks. In a particular museum ethnography store the facility exists for fumigating organic materials by exposure to ethylene oxide, the plant having been installed some 15 years ago. In 1979 advice was sought from the Public Health Laboratory service concerning the level of risk from anthrax, and although immunization of personnel was considered at that time it was rejected for a number of reasons. Principal among these was the infrequent and intermittent exposure of staff who handled hides, furs and wool; and second was the apparently low level of risk in contracting the disease, based on the notifications of anthrax in England and Wales. Some years later the Health and Safety Executive questioned this policy and as a result the situation was reassessed with the objective of ensuring a safe working environment for staff.

The plant consists essentially of a fumigation chamber approximately 2 × 2 × 4.5 metres installed in a fumigation room about twice this size. The chamber is connected to a reciprocating vacuum pump and a stainless steel ethylene oxide vaporizer with manual control valves which are all enclosed in a separate control room. The plant room is ventilated by an inlet air grid high above the floor level and an air-extraction grid in the outside wall at floor level. The fumigation chamber vent, which is controlled from the plant room, extends 20 metres up an outside wall, well above the roof level. The fumigation room is extracted by a solitary extractor fan in the window.

The museum's potentially contaminated specimens are laid on trays and packed into boxes which are stacked in the fumigation chamber. At the end of the fumigation and venting period the chamber door is opened and the boxes are dragged out by operators. The fumigation process consists of passing measured quantities of ethylene oxide into the dosing vessel, from where it is dropped into the stainless steel evaporator. The fumigation chamber is evacuated and the ethylene oxide introduced until the pressure stabilizes at 75 mm Hg^{-1}. The ethylene oxide is then held in the chamber for 4 hours after which it is repeatedly purged with fresh air before the door is opened.

The concentration of ethylene oxide, measured at various sites during the process, showed the distribution pattern exhibited in Table 1. Following their inspection the

Table 1. Distribution Pattern of Ethylene Oxide Concentrations during the Fumigation Process

Site	Ethylene oxide (ppm)
Plant room	0.5
Fumigation room (a)	Faint trace
Fumigation chamber—door open	200–270
Fumigation room (b)	100 falling to 15
Specimen boxes	270
Previously fumigated boxes	10–35

Health and Safety Executive voiced concern over the possibility of contamination with anthrax spores and the hazards for staff exposed to ethylene oxide. The HSE identified the need for a change in working procedures, and in particular the system of purging was considered unsatisfactory and in need of modification. Observations on ethylene oxide concentrations suggested that the degassing process was quite slow, and raised the possibility that ethylene oxide might be adsorbed onto some fabrics thereby inadvertently exposing subsequent handlers to the gas. The need was established for workers to wear respiratory protection when entering the chamber, but it was also felt desirable to confirm the validity of ethylene oxide as a sterilizing agent for anthrax spores.

The authorities at CAMR Porton Down were approached for an opinion, and they confirmed that ethylene oxide was lethal to anthrax spores, though only sublethal to the vegetative forms of the anthrax bacillus. The efficacy of the treatment was tested by using a non-pathogenic spore tracer which gave comparable results to anthrax spores. In the initial tests not all the spores were killed; but when the quantity of ethylene oxide used for fumigation was increased the test results became satisfactory. As this work was under way a number of other factors became apparent. Firstly, the increased quantities of ethylene oxide that were being used and exhausted into the atmosphere alerted the museum to its responsibilities to its neighbours. At the same time there was increasing evidence, derived from animal experiments, of the neurotoxicity of ethylene oxide and its role as a carcinogen. This led to a meeting of interested parties representing the museum's management, the museum safety officer, the Health and Safety Executive Inspectorate, ventilation engineers and an adviser on atmospheric pollution, as well as the Occupational Health Service.

The team, for that is what it may now be called, reviewed the problem in the light of basic principles of occupational hygiene: was the process necessary; and could the hazards be eliminated? It soon became apparent that some method of fumigation was necessary, in order to assist in the conservation of objects, and to remove the potential health hazard of anthrax. Consideration was given to whether fumigation could be carried out by substituting a less toxic agent. Alternative methods of fumigation were reviewed, but each in turn was rejected as being less satisfactory. Thus it was concluded that while ethylene oxide fumigation remained technically the most satisfactory method, its use should be continued provided that a satisfactory safe working practice could be developed. Arising from this it was decided to adopt several procedures in order to protect the staff and comply with the recommendations from the Health and Safety Executive. Immunization with anthrax vaccine would be offered to those museum staff liable to come into contact with untreated hides and suspect animal products from overseas. The decision was also taken to install automatic monitoring equipment to check the concentration of ethylene oxide within the fumigation chamber and thus remove the need for manual sampling. Furthermore, the respiratory protective equipment previously in use was found to be ineffective against ethylene oxide, and was replaced by airline masks. Finally, a change in working procedures would be brought about with the objective of reducing any environmental contamination by ethylene oxide within the building to levels below 2 ppm.

Discussions were held with engineers on possible modifications to the exhaust and flushing systems during which it became apparent that the initial exhaust after fumigation resulted in a concentrated cloud of ethylene oxide being expelled into the atmosphere. This museum store and workshop are situated alongside a canal in a residential area, and the roof of the museum building is overlooked by a nearby block of flats. It became apparent that to conduct a survey of ethylene oxide levels in the neighbourhood would prove prohibitively expensive and likely to arouse needless anxiety. Most important of all, such a study would be of doubtful validity. Instead, alternative systems were considered which included: construction of a higher exhaust stack; a slower rate of discharge of ethylene oxide in order to obtain a more effective dilution; passing gas through filters or a scrubber; or moving the process to a greenfield site. The possibility was explored of building a new extraction system for the fumigation chamber, incorporating an oxidation plant in which the gas passes over a platinum catalyst heated by gas burners. This expensive but attractive proposition has the advantage of breaking down the ethylene oxide to carbon dioxide and water vapour so that there is no discharge of hazardous materials to the atmosphere.

This example demonstrates yet another situation where in order to provide a safe working environment a representative team drawn from different disciplines is required. After the first look at this problem, a series of unsuspected secondary hazards became apparent, thereby increasing the level of resources required.

Conclusions

Both examples illustrate situations which occur fairly regularly in the specialized field of conservation. That is, the decision to undertake a particular project will be taken on professional and technical grounds, and only subsequent evaluation uncovers unsuspected occupational hazards which inevitably cause delays to the project and additional expense. Frequently, the potential hazards, though representing only low levels of risk, are in fact quite complex, and necessitate consultation with a variety of disciplines. This suggests that it is necessary to develop, as part of the museum safety policy, clear guidelines for departments. Consequently, when the issues appear to be growing in complexity, a team administrator can be nominated who will bring together and coordinate the various disciplines whose expertise now contributes to occupational health.

Section 3. Hazards and Their Control

Museums draw upon divers types of expertise in their daily work. Display technicians are often expected to be 'jacks-of-all-trades' and cope with woodworking and metalworking one minute, airbrush spraying or glass-fibre reinforced resin fabrication the next, and so on. Conservators and museum researchers will often work with a variety of toxic materials in basements, corridors or attics with little in the way of safety facilities. There are of course some excellent facilities available for the handling of hazardous materials, but these are all too often found only in the better-endowed museums. Gallery guards and other security staff are in the front line when it comes to fire safety precautions and, sometimes, controlling unruly visitors! Curators can be

Recent Fire Damage to Collections

Location and date of fire	Injury and loss of life	Collections lost	Damage estimate (1985 prices)	How the fire started
Museum of Modern Art, New York City (April 1958)	1 death, 33 injured	2 major paintings	$2 million	Flammable materials plus smoking by contractors
Engineering Library, University of Toronto (February 1977)			$10 million	Cause unknown
Aerospace Museum, San Diego (February 1978)	None	Library, archives and 40 planes	$30 million	Arson
George Eastman House, Rochester, New York (May 1978)	None	3000 reels original films	–	Spontaneous combustion of cellulose nitrate film
Museum of Modern Art, Rio de Janeiro (July 1978)	None	900 paintings	–	Electrical fault or cigarette
Benešov and Ploudnici (1980)		Complete Czech reserve collection of oriental works of art		Fire spread from area used by local authority for receptions
Royal Ulster Museum (1980)	None	Textile Reserve Collections		Terrorists
Hampton Court Palace (1986)	1 death	Paintings; architectural structures	£5+ million	Lighted candle in private quarters

found working as often in their stores as in their offices, and the safety aspects of handling objects which are bulky or awkward vies with the equally immediate problems posed by air-conditioning systems for both objects and personnel.

Ever present, and perhaps the greatest hazard to museum staff and visitor alike, is the danger of fire. Of all the likely causes of death, injury and loss in the museum and gallery fire has time and again taken its toll. Just a few of the more recent museum, gallery and library fires and their cost in terms of human suffering and loss of cultural heritage, are tabulated on p. 73. A large number of minor fires in museums have been caused by electrical wiring faults both in building conduits and exhibition cases. However, unsupervised contractors using welding torches, the spillage and ignition of inflammable liquids, and smoking, together with the careless use of electrical equipment, explosions due to the escape of flammable gas, and arsonists have been responsible for the majority of the fires. In nearly every case the institution of a safe operating system to control the hazard would have prevented the disaster.

The following subject areas are considered in this section:

- Toxic materials—how the body handles them
- Toxic effects of solvents—acute and chronic
- Toxic metals
- Fumigants and pesticides
- Protection and monitoring
- Occupational exposure limits
- Control by ventilation
- General dilution ventilation
- Local exhaust ventilation
- Partial enclosures
- Fume cupboards
- Extract and air-supply systems
- Assessing laboratory and workshop hazards
- Organizing and applying hazard data in the workshop or laboratory
- Fire legislation
- Fire prevention in museums
- Fire drills and training
- Infection hazards in museum work
- Allergy and sensitization
- Infection hazards in museum buildings
- Workshop machinery hazards
- Risk assessment
- Safeguarding machinery
- Electrical hazards
- Scaffolding
- Radiation, non-ionizing and ionizing
- Choosing protective clothing
- Achieving protection using protective clothing
- Eye protection, hearing protection, gloves and respirators

3.1 The Toxicology of Materials Used in Restoration and Conservation

H. A. WALDRON

In a single chapter it would be impossible to give a complete account of all the chemicals which may be encountered by restorers and conservators. What is provided instead is a discussion of the basic principles of the metabolism and toxicology of the different classes of potentially toxic substances, and some guidelines for the protection and monitoring of those exposed to them.

Handling of Toxic Materials by the Body

Absorption

Toxic materials may enter the body by one of three routes: inhalation, ingestion or through the skin.

1. Inhalation. The uptake of substances through the lung depends upon their physical state and their solubility in body fluids. Gases and vapours penetrate readily to the deepest parts of the lung and are generally absorbed completely. They may also be absorbed from the upper airways if they are soluble in water. In order for solid materials to be available for absorption, however, they must be of a sufficiently small size to penetrate into the terminal airways (the alveoli). As a general rule, only particles less than 7 μm in diameter can penetrate the alveoli; fibres or other particles of a non-uniform shape will enter the alveoli if they behave aerodynamically as though they were spheres of 7 μm or less. Larger particles are filtered out in the upper airways and cleared by special mechanisms. Particles which enter the alveoli are seldom completely absorbed into the blood stream; at best 40 per cent will be taken up, the remainder being cleared from the alveoli into the lymph vessels. The actual rate of uptake will vary as a function of solubility, and when considering the toxicity of chemical compounds it is important to bear this in mind. Lead chromate, for example, is highly insoluble in body fluids and is relatively non-toxic, whereas lead oxide, which is highly soluble, is extremely toxic on this account.

2. Ingestion. The absorption of swallowed materials is a complex phenomenon and during the course of evolution elaborate systems have developed to control the uptake of substances from the gut, principally the so-called essential trace elements which are themselves toxic if their concentration in the blood exceeds certain limits. There are thus a number of specific transport mechanisms for the transfer of essential metals across the gut wall, and some toxic metals, such as lead and cadmium, can take advantage of these to gain access to the body. Even so, it is necessary for the metals to be in the correct chemical state for absorption to take place. Highly soluble metal compounds may cross the gut wall by simple diffusion, and organic compounds which are fat soluble can also pass into the bloodstream with great facility. As a general rule, however, the uptake of inorganic compounds is less efficient than from the lung, and usually not more than about 10 per cent of a swallowed dose will gain entry to the blood.

3. Skin absorption. Most inorganic compounds are unable to cross the skin in sufficient quantities to render them harmful; one important exception is mercury and its compounds. It is not generally realized that metallic mercury is readily absorbed through the skin and should therefore be handled with much more care than is customary. Many organic compounds, by contrast, including many of the commonly used solvents, cross the skin with ease and this may add considerably to the risk posed by inhalation.

Distribution and Biotransformation

Having gained access, foreign substances are distributed throughout the body in a manner which is largely determined by their solubility in water or in fat. Water-soluble compounds tend to be the most widely distributed because they are able to gain access to any organ of the body which contains water, whereas fat-soluble compounds tend to accumulate in organs rich in fat. The latter group are of great importance, however, since they include the brain and the peripheral nerves. Some toxic substances show a predilection for certain organs of the body and exert their principal toxic effects there; these are then referred to as target organs. Many of the heavy metals, such as cadmium, lead and mercury, accumulate in and cause damage to the kidney. Lead has an unusual pattern of distribution in that it accumulates in the bone where it remains for very many years without causing any damage (unless absorbed in large amounts during the period of active growth).

The majority of foreign organic compounds present in the body undergo a series of reactions which take place predominantly in the liver in order to render them in a form which makes them suitable for elimination. This process, which is sometimes referred to as detoxification, is more correctly called biotransformation. This distinction is important since in some cases it is the products of the biotransformation which are toxic, not the original parent compound. The products of biotransformation are known as metabolites and appear predominantly in the urine. Some organic compounds—1,1,1-trichloroethane, the solvent used in a number of typewriter correcting fluids, is an example—do not undergo biotransformation but are excreted unchanged. A knowledge of the metabolites of organic compounds may be of importance for the purpose of monitoring exposed individuals, and these are referred to again later. Inorganic chemicals do not undergo biotransformation unless they are bound to an organic group, in which case the organic moiety is split off from the molecule, after which it may be further metabolized.

Elimination

There are three major routes for the elimination of foreign compounds: the urine, exhaled breath and the faeces. Compounds which enter the body and are then eliminated (in their original form or as their metabolites) are said to be excreted. Elimination also takes account of the voiding of materials which have been swallowed but not absorbed. For example, the faeces contain varying amounts of metals and their compounds which have been ingested but never absorbed—this represents the 90 per cent of the ingested dose which has not been taken up from the gut. The faecal concentration of some potentially toxic metals can therefore be used as an indication of the total amount in the diet but not as a measure of the amount in the body.

For the majority of inorganic compounds the most important route of excretion is via the urine, and urinary concentrations may be used to monitor exposure. Some metals (manganese is an example) are excreted predominantly into the bile and then excreted into the gut to appear finally in the faeces. Toxicologists seldom rely on faecal analysis to monitor exposure, for reasons which should be apparent to all.

The metabolites of the organic compounds which undergo biotransformation are also excreted in the urine. Sometimes small amounts of the parent compound also appear in the urine, and both parent compound and metabolites may appear in the exhaled breath. Exhaled breath is the most important route for the excretion of those organic compounds which are not biotransformed.

Toxic Effects of Classes of Compounds

The toxicity of the principal classes of toxic compounds is considered here in general terms; for more detailed information the reader should refer to the texts listed at the end of the chapter.

Solvents

Solvents comprise almost certainly the largest single class of compounds with which museum workers will be brought into contact as the result of their work. They are very far from being a homogeneous group in terms of their chemical structure, but they do, nevertheless, share a number of toxicological features which can be classified either as acute or chronic.

Acute Effects. All solvents produce a vapour to a greater or lesser extent and this vapour exerts an effect which is most analogous to that produced by an anaesthetic. Indeed, some compounds which are, or have been, used as solvents have also been used as anaesthetics: chloroform and trichloroethylene are cases in point. The effects produced are non-specific and include symptoms such as lassitude, depression of mood, irritability, headaches and sometimes giddiness. The likelihood of these symptoms appearing increases as the degree of exposure increases, but they are completely reversible and have no long-lasting effects. The time taken for their reversal is also a function of exposure but it would be somewhat unusual for them to persist for more than a few days after the cessation of exposure. Workers exposed to solvents may also perform less well in psychometric tests than non-exposed workers. Again, however, this is evidence of an acute rather than a chronic effect, although there have been some claims that there may be long-lasting effects on the central nervous system—an assertion which is touched on again later. The most consistent finding has been that exposure to solvents prolongs the reaction time, but this is a small effect which is of academic rather than practical importance. It does not seem to be related to an increase in accidents at work, for example, and recovery to normal can be noted when exposure ceases, although this may take many weeks.

Chronic Effects on Body Organs. Many organs of the body may be adversely affected by solvents, the most important being the liver and the peripheral and central nervous systems. Benzene is unique amongst the solvents in adversely affecting the bone marrow.

1. The liver. In the days when exposure to solvents was much less well controlled than it is now, liver damage was one of the most severe forms of intoxication with solvents. The most toxic of the liver poisons were chloroform (which was the reason for it falling out of favour as an anaesthetic) and carbon tetrachloride. Carbon tetrachloride produces liver damage in such a predictable manner that it is usually used in studies of liver toxicity as a 'positive' control, that is as a means of showing that the livers of the unfortunate animals in the experiment behave to liver toxins as they should. Neither of these compounds should be in general use nowadays, although it is still possible to buy proprietory cleaning fluids which are based on carbon tetrachloride.

As a general rule, solvents which contain chlorine atoms are the most toxic to the liver, but their toxicity decreases as the ratio of chlorine atoms to other atoms decreases. Chlorinated solvents in common use, such as trichloroethylene, 1,1,1-trichloroethane, perchloroethylene and methylene chloride, are not significantly toxic to the liver even in much larger doses than would be encountered in normal working practice. Using extremely sensitive techniques it has been found that toluene and styrene may induce changes in the normal concentrations of bile acids in the serum, but these changes are slight and their significance for long-term health is obscure.

2. The peripheral nervous system. Only a small number of solvents produce an adverse effect of the peripheral nervous system: these include n-hexane, methyl butyl ketone (MBK) and carbon disulphide. None is likely to be encountered commonly in the laboratory, but n-hexane and MBK may be constituents of glues, and damage may follow the abuse of these materials. The most distant parts of the peripheral nerves are first affected by these solvents and the first indication of harm is a symmetrical alteration of sensation in the hands and feet. This may progress up the arms and legs and be followed by a weakness in the muscles of the hands and feet. With cessation of the exposure, an almost complete recovery should be expected.

There have been some reports of a peripheral neuropathy following exposure to trichloroethylene, but, in this case, sensation is first impaired around the mouth and then spreads out to involve other areas of the face. The muscles involved in swallowing may become paralysed, but this is a most uncommon manifestation of intoxication by this solvent. There is no good evidence that any of the other solvents in common use is capable of producing peripheral neuropathy, but it is known that solvents of rather low toxicity may interact with others in a mixture and either have their neurotoxicity enhanced (methyl ethyl ketone with MBK, for example) or diminished (MBK with toluene).

3. The central nervous system. Several solvents can markedly affect the mental state if they are inhaled in excess. They may induce a pleasant state of euphoria and have been abused in order to achieve this result. Trichloroethylene and toluene are the most notorious in this respect and there is a good deal of anecdotal evidence about 'sniffers' in industry; the abuse of glues containing toluene is probably well known to everyone. The abuse of these solvents, however, can have the most unfortunate results as, for example, when the sniffers suffer from the delusion that they can fly and take off from a height. Solvents are often inhaled to the point of unconsciousness; should the victims then vomit (as it not uncommonly the case) there is a grave danger that they may inhale the vomit and die from immediate suffocation or from an aspiration pneumonia. Occasionally the change in the mental state is so bizarre and relatively long-lasting that a misdiagnosis of schizophrenia is made and the person recovers in a psychiatric hospital. A serious consequence of long-term abuse of toluene is the development of irreversible damage to the cerebellum and to the cerebral cortex, resulting either in profound disturbance of balance or in dementia.

The changes in mental state may sometimes be disturbing and frightening and lead to extremes of behaviour as the victims try to escape the terrifying influence. Carbon disulphide was particularly notable in this respect, and the early literature contains graphic accounts of the bizarre effects which it had on those who worked with it under extremely poor conditions. These effects will usually be seen only in those who are deliberate abusers; but there has been some recent evidence which suggests that exposure to solvents at concentrations which may be encountered in the workplace can lead to the development of long-term and presumably irreversible effects. The condition produced is characterized by a deterioration in memory, with lassitude and an inability to concentrate—all non-specific symptoms and somewhat reminiscent of the acute effects. The evidence that this condition exists at all is by no means unequivocal; almost all the reports have emanated from Scandinavian countries, and to date no cases have been recognized in the United Kingdom. It seems likely that a minimum of 10 years' exposure to relatively high concentrations is required before the condition develops, and then it affects only a small number of those exposed.

4. The bone marrow. Benzene is unique amonst solvents in that it is able to suppress the bone marrow and hence the normal production of red blood cells. In its most extreme form the bone marrow may be damaged to such an extent that there are not sufficient red blood cells to sustain life, a condition known as aplastic anaemia. There is also enough evidence from case reports, and from epidemiological studies, to support the view that benzene is capable of inducing some forms of leukaemia. On this account, this solvent should never be found in general use.

Other Chronic Effects. Those solvents which are able to dissolve fats may cause dermatitis if there is prolonged skin contact, and those who handle solvents frequently should bear this in mind. The potential carcinogenicity of solvents is a matter about which concern is sometimes expressed, as are their possible reproductive effects. There is some rather poor evidence from animal experiments which purports to show that trichloroethylene is carcinogenic, but this has never been confirmed so far as human exposure is concerned. Some solvents can be shown to have mutagenic properties in laboratory tests but, again, there is no evidence which would lead one to believe that any of the solvents in common use can cause cancer.

There have been a number of epidemiological studies which show that women who are exposed to solvents are more likely to have an adverse outcome of pregnancy as compared with those not so exposed. The increased risk is of a low order and should not engender a too great concern, but the results underline the fact that during the early months of pregnancy, when the foetal organs are being formed, care should be taken to avoid undue exposure to any noxious substance, including cigarette smoke and alcohol.

One rare but extremely serious manifestation of solvent poisoning should perhaps be mentioned in conclusion. A small number of sudden deaths have occurred, predominantly in young people who have been exposed, either deliberately or accidentally, to high concentrations of solvents and who have then immediately engaged in some vigorous physical activity. A typical case might be a young man who had been cleaning out a tank which had contained solvents used for degreasing metal parts, without wearing any respiratory protection, and who then ran across the factory floor or up a flight of stairs. It seems that some solvents may sensitize the heart muscle to the effects of adrenaline so that, on exertion, instead of the heart responding by beating more quickly it is sent into a state of ventricular fibrillation.

Toxic Metals

There are toxic metals of which lead, cadmium and mercury are the most important. In museum practice, however, lead is the only one which is likely to be a potential hazard because it was formerly used as a pigment in paints. Lead may have adverse effects on the blood, the central and peripheral nervous systems and the kidneys, and it may also adversely affect the foetus. Almost all these effects require prolonged and heavy exposure. Its effect on the blood is principally to interfere with the synthesis of haem, part of the haemoglobin molecule which gives the red blood cells their colour and which carries oxygen from the lungs to the other tissues. The synthesis of haem is a multi-stage process, each stage being dependent upon the proper functioning of a specific enzyme. Lead interferes with several of these enzymes with the result that the formation of haem is diminished. Several of the intermediates in the synthetic pathway are formed to excess (because their further metabolism is partially prevented) and may appear in the urine or in the red blood cells. The concentration of some of these intermediates in the urine can be used as a means of monitoring exposure to lead.

Although interference with haem synthesis can be demonstrated at relatively modest blood lead concentrations, there is a considerable reserve capacity in the system so that the haemoglobin level remains normal and the individual suffers no harm. The first indications of lead poisoning are usually undue tiredness, headaches, abdominal pain and constipation. More severe effects should never be seen in those who are occupationally exposed to lead and have regular medical surveillance. The monitoring of lead workers is based upon estimations of the blood lead concentration which, for men, and for women who are not of child-bearing age, should be kept below $70\,\mu g\,dl^{-1}$ of blood. Because of the susceptibility of the foetus, the blood lead of women of child-bearing age should remain below $40\,\mu g\,dl^{-1}$ of blood. Anyone who is found with a blood lead concentration in excess of the appropriate upper limit should have the test repeated immediately; if it is still high, then the worker *must* be removed from exposure until the blood lead has fallen to an acceptable limit and his or her medical adviser is satisfied that it is safe to resume the work which exposed them to lead.

Fumigants and Pesticides

Fumigants. Materials brought into a museum may be fumigated before they are handled further, and it is not uncommon for display cases to contain pesticides. The most important fumigants are formaldehyde and ethylene oxide, although the former has largely been superseded by the latter. Both are powerful irritants and may affect the eyes, the upper respiratory tract and the lungs. These effects are so unpleasant that anyone who comes into contact with these gases will quickly remove themselves from exposure. Very rarely, individuals may become sensitized to formaldehyde and develop bronchial asthma which can be brought on by exposure to extremely low concentrations of the gas. Both formaldehyde and ethylene oxide have been suspected of being carcinogens on the basis of animal experiments. There has been no convincing evidence at all that formaldehyde is a human carcinogen, and that implicating ethylene oxide is equivocal.

Pesticides. There are four major classes of pesticides, the organo-chlorines, the organo-phosphorus compounds, the carbamates and a class based on pyrethrins, chemicals which occur naturally in plants. The organo-chlorine pesticides, of which DDT is the best-known, are no longer in use because of their adverse environmental effects. They are not markedly toxic to humans but some, such as dieldrin, may produce neurological symptoms. The organo-phosphorus pesticides inhibit the enzyme acetyl cholinesterase which is essential for the normal functioning of the nervous system. Acute poisoning with these compounds produces increased sweating and lachrymation, nausea and vomiting, diarrhoea and involuntary urination and tightness of the chest. In addition, there may be muscular fatigue and weakness, and central effects such as anxiety, restlessness and insomnia. In the most extreme cases these symptoms may be followed by coma and death from respiratory paralysis. The inhibitory effect on acetyl cholinesterase is slowly reversible and, in cases of acute poisoning, the treatment is with specific antidotes. Carbamates are also cholinesterase inhibitors, but the inhibition which they induce is rapidly reversible, and hence they are not nearly as toxic as the organo-phosphorus compounds.

Dust and Fibres

During the course of work with museum artifacts, some contact with dusts and fibres is inevitable. Although these substances may be a nuisance, for the most part they will be non-toxic. Dusts of metal compounds may be encountered, and of these lead is by far the most important, as mentioned earlier. Increasing use is being made of glass fibre in museum work, whilst the hazards relating to the styrene which is evolved have also been mentioned previously. The glass fibres themselves are an irritant to the skin, and to the respiratory tract if they are inhaled, but almost certainly they have no other harmful effects.

There is a great deal of concern about asbestos wherever it is encountered. Staff in some museums may come across it in stored objects and it would be surprising if some asbestos products were not in their environment. A due sense of proportion is required when discussing the hazards of asbestos. White asbestos (chrysotile) is the form most commonly found in buildings and, even if asbestos fibres are being liberated into the atmosphere from asbestos ceiling tiles or defective lagging, the risks from such exposure are trivial. It is not the case that lung cancer can be caused by a single fibre of white asbestos as some maintain; prolonged and heavy exposure is required before the effects on the lung are noted. With blue asbestos (crocidolite), on the other hand, things are different and there is quite good evidence that mesotheliomas (tumours of the pleura or peritoneum) have developed in those whose exposure to blue asbestos has been slight. Blue asbestos is not commonly found in buildings, but when it is, great care should be taken to keep exposure to the minimum whilst it is being eliminated.

Protection and Monitoring of Workers Exposed to Toxic Materials

Protection

The most important means of protecting workers exposed to potentially toxic materials is the development of a safe code of practice, as has been emphasized elsewhere in this volume. It should be an accepted part of any code of practice that exposures will be kept as low as is reasonably practicable. Wherever possible, exposure should be limited by the provision of adequate ventilation, but if this is impossible because of the nature of the work, then proper protective equipment must be available. It is unwise to eat or drink in areas where potentially toxic materials are handled, and if lead is a known hazard, eating and drinking should under no circumstances be allowed in the areas where exposure may occur. Attention to personal hygiene is obviously important, particularly if there is a possibility that materials may be transferred from hand to mouth. Smoking should be actively discouraged, since solvent vapours inhaled through a cigarette may be thermally decomposed into extremely toxic compounds. Cigarettes may also become contaminated by toxic substances which may then be inhaled; lead workers who smoke, for example, have higher blood lead concentrations than those who do not.

It is of great importance that workers who come into contact with toxic materials are given adequate instruction on the potential hazards of the materials and on how to handle them safely. They should also be able to have access to an informed, and preferably independent, source of advice if they have any anxieties about their work. One of the greatest hazards to those who are exposed to chemicals is the ill-informed opinion of those with little expert knowledge or experience of clinical toxicology. Much anxiety is engendered by the exaggeration of the risks of chemicals in the workplace, and, conversely, much needless exposure may be allowed by those who are willing to take unacceptable risks on behalf of those whose interests they are supposed to protect.

Monitoring

Some form of monitoring programme for those exposed to chemicals is usually desirable and sometimes mandatory. It may be environmental, biological or a mixture of both. With environmental monitoring, the airborne concentrations of chemicals are measured at regular intervals using static samplers (to determine the concentration level of the workplace as a whole) or personal samplers attached to individuals to give a more accurate indication of their own exposure. The Health and Safety Executive publishes lists of currently acceptable limits for airborne contaminants in the United Kingdom.

The basis of biological monitoring is to measure the actual amount of compound (or compounds) which has been taken up from the environment, or the effect which this absorption might be having on the individual. This can be done directly by measuring the concentration of chemical in the blood or exhaled breath or, indirectly, by measuring the concentration of metabolites in the urine. For many of the common solvents, estimation of metabolites in the urine is a very good measure of uptake whilst, as has already been mentioned, measurement of the blood lead concentration is an important method for monitoring lead exposure. Measurement of the excretion of some of the intermediates of haem synthesis in the urine or blood can also be used as an index of the biochemical effect of lead within the body.

In any programme of biological monitoring there should be well-defined action levels: that is, levels above which exposure is reduced or discontinued altogether. Some action levels are generally agreed upon and can be found in the book by Lauwerys (1983—see the bibliography below for details). When deciding on an action level, it may be necessary to consider the effects of multiple exposures, and the effects which any exposure might have on staff who are taking medication, particularly psychotropic drugs or antihistamines in the case of solvents.

Conclusion

Although staff engaged in restoration and conservation may come into contact with a wide range of chemicals which are potentially toxic, the risks which this poses to their health are generally small because the nature of their work tends to vary and their exposures are neither prolonged nor heavy. It is a sound toxicological principle, however, to limit exposure to any chemical as far as possible, and this should be the aim of all those with a responsibility for the health and safety of those working in museums.

Bibliography

More information about the toxicology of the chemicals discussed here can be found in the third edition of the present author's *Lecture Notes on Occupational Medicine* (Blackwell, Oxford, 1985). Those wishing for a much more detailed account should consult *Casarett and Doull's Toxicology* (second edition) edited by J. Doull, C. D. Klaassen and M. O. Amdur (Bailliere Tindall, London, 1980). *Industrial Chemical Exposure: Guidelines for Biological Monitoring* by R. R. Lauwerys (Biomedical Publications, Davis, California, 1983) contains a synopsis of the toxicology of a number of chemicals and gives currently agreed action levels. *Art Hazard News* is published ten times a year (Center for Occupational Hazards, 5 Beekman Street, New York NY 10038), and gives information on any chemical likely to present a hazard to those working in the visual arts, performing arts and museums. Written specifically with an American audience in mind, it presents up-to-date information which is, however, not always objectively interpreted.

3.2 The Containment and Ventilation of Hazardous Fumes in Laboratories, Workshops and Studios

D. Hughes

Occupational Exposure Limits

There is a need to contain and ventilate fumes in the workplace because they are or may be toxic, radiotoxic, carcinogenic, teratogenic, mutagenic, narcotic, lachrymatory or just objectionable. The indices used for many years for the control of toxic fumes were the threshold limit values published by the American Conference of Governmental Industrial Hygienists.[1] These limiting values for the concentration of fumes in the workplace are presented as: the time-weighted averages (twa), relating to the average concentration calculated over an 8-hour period; the short-term exposure limits (stel), relating to a prescribed number of short-duration excursions to higher concentrations; and ceiling limits, which must not be exceeded at any time. Threshold limit values were replaced in the United Kingdom in 1984 by occupational exposure limits published by the Health and Safety Executive;[2] these limits are presented as: control limits, which should not be exceeded; and recommended limits, which are further divided into long-term limits (relating to average concentrations taken over 8 hours), and short-term limits (relating to exposures of 10 minutes duration). In addition to their response to the toxic effects of contaminants, persons who have become sensitized to an allergen may subsequently react to substances at concentrations well below the occupational exposure limits listed.[3]

Control Procedures

Methods available for dealing with a fume problem may include non-ventilation and ventilation techniques.[4,5,6]

1. Non-ventilation
   (a) Elimination of the substance or process;
   (b) Substitution of an alternative, less hazardous, substance or process (e.g. replacing benzene by toluene or xylene).
2. Ventilation
   (a) General dilution;
   (b) Local exhaust;
   (c) Partial enclosure (e.g. fumecupboards or fumehoods);
   (d) Special enclosures;
   (e) Total enclosures (e.g. glove-boxes).

General Dilution Ventilation

In general dilution ventilation, uncontaminated air is introduced continuously into the workplace, mixed with the contaminant and extracted.[7] The relative positions of the source of the contaminant, the person, the extract point and the air-supply configuration, and the degree of mixing of the contaminant with the fresh air are important. In Figure 1, arrangement (a) is obviously poor, with the contaminant being blown into the breathing zone of the person. Arrangement (b) is good, and arrangement (c), with a large-area air-supply grille, is even better because a large proportion of the volume of the room is being swept by the fresh air. When estimating the concentration in the air resulting from a known evaporation rate of a given contaminant, the degree of mixing can be allowed for by introducing a distribution factor into the calculation.[7] General dilution ventilation should never be used as the sole method of controlling highly toxic contaminants, but it is often an adjunct to some other method, such as the use of a fumecupboard or other means of partial enclosure.

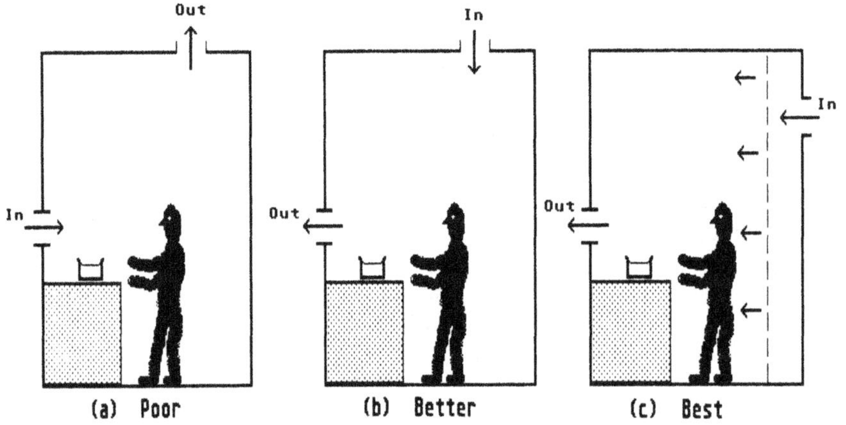

1. General dilution ventilation: relative positions of source of contaminant, person and air-supply grilles. (a) = poor arrangement; (b) = better arrangement; (c) = best arrangement.

Local Exhaust Ventilation

With local exhaust ventilation, the aim is to capture the contaminant near its point of release before it has dispersed into the workplace. In principle, the contaminant is sucked into a pipe whose open end is placed near the source. The detailed design depends on the application and, in particular, on the rate at which the contaminant is being released. For example, where there is quiet evaporation of a liquid, a comparatively low air velocity of 0.5 metres per second would be required at the point of release to capture the vapours reasonably efficiently.[6] A higher velocity of, perhaps, $2.5\,m\,s^{-1}$ would be required to capture vapours from a process which generates rapid air movements, such as those produced as a liquid is discharged quickly into a large vessel.

Sucking into a pipe is not an efficient way of capturing fumes, especially if the source is far from the end of the pipe. For example, with a circular opening to the pipe, the air velocity reduces to approximately 10 per cent at a distance from the opening equal to the diameter. The efficiency of capture can be improved by adding a flange to the opening so that more air is drawn in from in front of the pipe and less from behind the opening.[8] The design of local exhaust ventilation can be developed to quite high degrees of

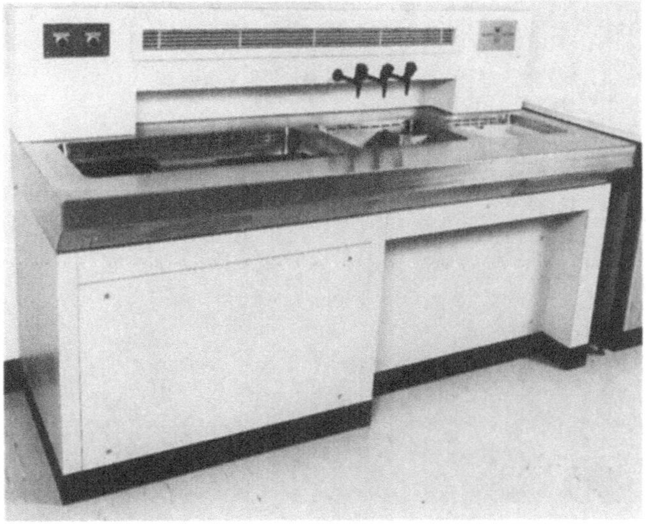

2. A workcentre providing local exhaust ventilation. (Photo: courtesy of Holliday, Fielding & Hocking Ltd[9])

sophistication, and Figure 2 shows a ventilated workcentre with sink and cut-up area designed to protect the worker from formaldehyde vapour when preparing specimens for histological examinations.[9] The workcentre could have other applications where articles are giving off fumes as they are being manipulated. Local exhaust ventilation can also be improved by adding side-screens to nullify the effects of cross-draughts, and a canopy to deal with thermal rises from hot processes. Even so, the efficiency of capture is not as high as that achieved by a properly designed and installed fumecupboard or fumehood.

Partial Enclosures

The principal form of partial enclosure is the fumecupboard or, in American parlance, the fumehood.[10,11] Regrettably, and alarmingly, there are still fumecupboards in use today which are real 'museum pieces'! In the event of an accident to a worker using such a facility, there would be little defence to offer. However, a fumecupboard and its associated ventilation systems can be considered under the following headings:

1. The fumecupboard itself:
   (a) containment;
   (b) other safety features;
   (c) chemical resistance of surfaces;
   (d) working temperature of surfaces;
   (e) siting in the laboratory.
2. The extract system (see later section)
   (a) rate of extraction;
   (b) duct construction;
   (c) noise;
   (d) efficiency of dispersal.
3. The air-supply system (see later section)
   (a) adequacy;
   (b) siting of supply grilles;
   (c) degree of conditioning;
   (d) noise.

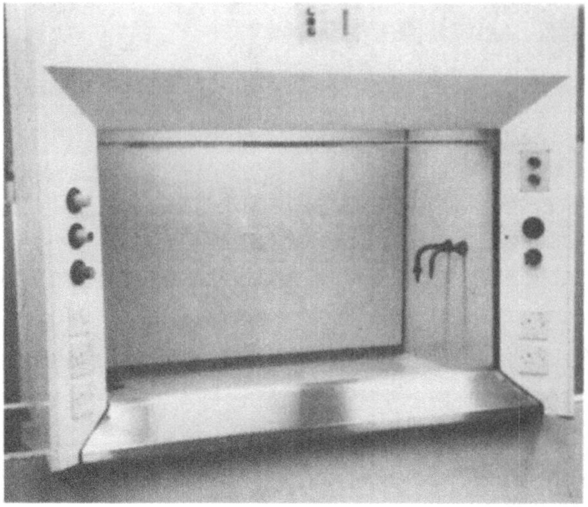

3. An aerodynamic fumecupboard. (Photo: courtesy of Holliday, Fielding & Hocking Ltd[9])

Modern fumecupboards are expected to have aerodynamic features such as angled fascias and rear baffles (Figure 3). To contain fumes, an adequate air velocity is required through the working aperture: this is usually in the range of 0.5–1.0 $m\,s^{-1}$ (100–200 feet per minute) and an air bypass or other device is usually fitted to prevent the velocity rising to dangerously excessive values as the sash is lowered.[10,12] The importance of detail in the design is not always apparent from visual inspection. 'Aerodynamic' sill sections and bypass grilles have been known to perform unsatisfactorily[11] and designs have to be tested to demonstrate satisfactory performance.

Fumecupboards are devices of *partial* containment and not of total containment, such as a glove-box. Informative tests of the efficiency of a fumecupboard can be performed by observing the flow patterns of smoke. Such a procedure is quite widespread and can have considerable impact when demonstrating fumecupboard performance to a potential purchaser. However, it provides only a qualitative assessment, and there have been various proposals advanced for the development of a numerical index to describe quantitatively the performance of a fumecupboard, both in an ideal situation and when it has been installed in the workplace.[11,13,14] Other safety features of note relating to the physical arrangements are:

(a) Faucets which can be reached by the user without the necessity of placing head and shoulders inside the fumecupboard;
(b) Absence of maintenance service panels on the inside surfaces;
(c) Rear baffles that are readily demountable for ease of cleaning behind them;
(d) Sashes with fail-to-safe mechanisms which would prevent them from falling on the user's arms if the sash-supporting device failed.

Adequate resistance to attack from a wide range of chemicals is usually sought of the materials of construction for the working surface and for the linings of the working chamber of the fumecupboard, unless its use (now and in the future) can be restricted to a few specified chemicals. Among the traditional materials are:

(a) coated mild steel;
(b) stainless steel;
(c) vitrified ceramic slab;

(d) plastics materials (e.g. polypropylene);
(e) lithium aluminium silicate glass ceramic;
(f) sheet lead;
(g) man-made stone;
(h) toughened glass;
(i) solid epoxy resin.

The choice is also affected by the methods available for jointing the linings and working surface, and by the working temperatures involved.

The siting of the fumecupboard in the laboratory is also of considerable importance. Among the points to consider, in addition to the working patterns of the users, are that it should not obstruct an escape route, and should be located away from doors, circulation paths, obstructions such as pillars, and air-supply grilles.

Special Enclosures

On occasion the present author has been called upon to assist in the design of other ventilated enclosures for special purposes, such as fumecupboards with water washdowns for perchloric acid, cabinets with restricted access through a hole in the sash, cabinets for exposing rodents to various test substances, and pilot-plant scale enclosures for industrial laboratories.[9,10,11] Furthermore, under the heading of special enclosures, we can also consider the open-fronted Class I and Class II safety cabinets used for microbiological work.[14]

Total Enclosures

Total enclosures include glove-boxes and Class III microbiological safety cabinets. Here there is a physical barrier in the form of a rubber glove and a high-efficiency filter between the interior of the enclosure and the operator and workplace. Such enclosures are for work involving very hazardous substances or requiring special atmospheres to protect the specimens being handled.

The Extract System

The extract system from a fumecupboard or other ventilated enclosure has to be carefully designed. Among the particular points to be considered are:

(a) rate of extraction;
(b) negative pressure within building;
(c) noise levels/silencers;
(d) route/fire compartments;
(e) avoidance of horizontal sections;
(f) drainage connexions;
(g) filtration (baggable)/automatic dampers;
(h) water washdown;
(i) fire dampers;
(j) fire extinguishers;
(k) running indicator (fail-to-safe);
(l) failure alarm/muting;
(m) duct materials (corrosion, fire, temperature);

(n) encasing for additional fire or ultraviolet radiation protection;
(o) inspection covers (not in bottom surface of duct);
(p) fan type (preferably centrifugal driven by two belts);
(q) fan material (corrosion, sparking);
(r) lockable setting-up dampers;
(s) non-return dampers (if available);
(t) labels describing the hazard.

After capturing the contaminant in the enclosure and safely conveying it through ducts to the outside of the building, it must be discharged in such a manner that it disperses and does not re-enter any building. Examples of badly designed discharge terminations are legion:[10,11] some deflect the fumes downwards, many are too low and discharge onto walkways, especially on flat roofs, whilst there is often a high probability of recirculation into the building via air intakes or open windows.

Of particular concern to engineers and to architects is the height to which a discharge stack has to rise above a building in order to ensure adequate dispersal. Recommendations[10] that fumes should be discharged from points at heights of two-and-a-half or one-and-a-half times the height of the building have been made at various times. Such heights are unnecessary and obviously impracticable on tall buildings. Also, the airflow patterns which govern dispersal are very complex when the laboratory is not a simple cuboid in shape but a group of buildings of various heights with deep intervening courtyards. Practical experience provides some guidance, and smoke tests on site and on scale models can be of value, but it must be recognized that combinations of building geometry, land contours and meteorological conditions can make it difficult if not impossible to achieve complete dispersal at all times.

For single-storey, isolated buildings our experience has been that stacks rising 2 metres above the roof have proved inadequate but that a height of 3–3.5 metres above the roof level [with a vertical efflux velocity, usually of 15–20 $m\,s^{-1}$ (3000–4000 feet per minute] has proved acceptable in many instances.[10,11] The draft British Standard[12] recommends, for an isolated rectangular building of low plan ratio in flat open territory, a discharge height above ground of 1.5 times the height of the building or 3 metres above the highest point, whichever is the higher. It also recommends efflux velocities of not less than 7 $m\,s^{-1}$ and preferably 10 $m\,s^{-1}$, and recognizes that greater heights and velocities are sometimes necessary.

The School of Chemistry at the University of Leeds provides a good example[10,11,13] of an investigation of a large building complex which required drastic upgrading of the fume-dispersal system because of re-entry of fumes into buildings. During the 1960s, smoke tests were performed on site and on a scale model of that part of the campus using a wind-tunnel. The results showed the inadequacy of a discharge stack rising 0.76 metres above the highest roof of the six-storey building [efflux velocity 12 $m\,s^{-1}$ (2400 feet per minute) vertically; windspeed 6.7 $m\,s^{-1}$ (15 miles per hour)], whilst a stack rising 9 metres was acceptable.

The Air Supply System

Fumecupboards and other partial enclosures are devices through which large quantities of air are discharged to atmosphere. In small installations with, perhaps, only one fumecupboard, some designers have been tempted to save capital expenditure by omitting air supply plant and hoping that an adequate flow of air will be induced through the doorways, free-transfer grilles to adjacent areas such as corridors, or even through the windows. Such a situation gives rise to uncontrolled conditions with possible ingress of dirt, draughts which adversely affect the performance of the enclosure, discomfort for the users, and impaired smoke barriers to the adjacent areas in fire emergencies.

In the United Kingdom, very many systems have been installed without any attempt being made to recover the heat carried away by the extracted air. Recently some of the larger installations have been built with 'run around' heat-interchanger pipes[15] or heat pipes. For a fumecupboard with an average air velocity of $0.5\,m\,s^{-1}$ and a working aperture 650 mm high, the power needed to heat the air supplied to the room, assuming a difference of 10 °C between the temperature of the air outside the building and that required inside, is 4.2 kW for every metre of fumecupboard width. A large laboratory complex containing many fumecupboards or experiencing greater temperature differentials can therefore be very demanding on energy resources for heating (or cooling) the quantity of air required.

Various methods of limiting the air required by a fumecupboard have been proposed[10,11] but not all are acceptable because of possible adverse effects on performance. For example, there appears to be little to commend designs which incorporate an auxiliary ventilation system to supply unconditioned or partially conditioned air either directly into or near the face of a fumecupboard, thereby reducing the demand for the fully conditioned air supplied to the main area of the laboratory. The draft British Standard,[12] reflecting requirements in the United Kingdom, states that air drawn from outside the building has to be warmed in cold weather to avoid adverse effects on the work, prevent undue condensation of aggressive substances and avoid severe discomfort to the users. To install additional fans and ductwork to provide auxiliary air of quality similar to that of the air supplied to the main area of the laboratory appears to involve unnecessary expense, and little energy saving can be expected. Concern for the very marked adverse effects of supply air on the efficiency of a fumecupboard, when the supply grilles are positioned too near, is expressed in the requirement for adequate spacing of grilles from the working faces of fumecupboards.[12,16]

References

1. *Threshold Limit Values for Chemical Substances in Workroom Air,* American Conference of Governmental Industrial Hygienists, PO Box 1937, Cincinnati OH 45201, USA (updated periodically).
2. *Occupational Exposure Limits,* Guidance Note EH40, Health and Safety Executive, Her Majesty's Stationery Office, London (1987, updated periodically).
3. G. W. Cambridge and B. F. J. Goodwin, *Allergy to Chemicals and Organic Substances in the Workplace,* Occupational Hygiene Monograph No. 12, Science Reviews Ltd, PO Box MT27, Leeds LS17 8QP, UK (1984).
4. M. Piney et al., *Controlling Airborne Contaminants in the Workplace,* British Occupational Hygiene Society Technical Guide Series No. 7, Science Reviews Ltd (1987). See Note 3 for address.
5. N. Clark, T. Cutter and J.-A. McGrance, *Ventilation: A Practical Guide,* Centre for Occupational Hazards Inc., 5 Beekman Street, New York NY 10038, USA (1984).
6. *Industrial Ventilation: A Manual of Recommended Practice,* American Conference of Governmental Industrial Hygienists, 6500 Glenways Avenue, Bldg D-5, Cincinnati OH 45211, USA (1984, 18th ed.).
7. N. I. Sax, *Dangerous Properties of Industrial Materials,* Van Nostrand Reinhold, New York (1984, 6th ed.).

8. B. Fletcher, 'Effects of Flanges on the Velocity in Front of Exhaust Ventilation Hoods', *Annals of Occupational Hygiene, 21,* 1978, pp. 265–269.
9. Courtesy of Holliday, Fielding and Hocking Ltd, Wesley Works, Greenfield Road, Leeds LS9 8DB, UK (Tel: 0532 487755).
10. D. Hughes, *A Literature Survey and Design Study of Fumecupboards and Fume-Dispersal Systems,* Occupational Hygiene Monograph No. 4, Science Reviews Ltd (1987). (See note 3 for address.)
11. J. D. Cook and D. Hughes, *Fumecupboards Revisited,* HHSC Handbook No. 2, H. and H. Scientific Consultants Ltd, PO Box MT27, Leeds LS17 8QP, UK (1986).
12. *Laboratory Fume Cupboards,* Draft for Development, DD80: Parts 1, 2 and 3, British Standards Institution (1982).
13. D. Hughes, 'Laboratory Fumehoods and Fume-dispersal Systems', in H. D. Goodfellow, Ed., *Ventilation '85,* Proceedings of 1st International Symposium on Ventilation for Contaminant Control (October, 1985, Toronto), pp. 53–63; Chemical Engineering Monograph No. 24, Elsevier Science Publishers (1986).
14. R. P. Clark, *The Performance, Installation, Testing and Limitations of Microbiological Safety Cabinets,* Occupational Hygiene Monograph No. 9, Science Reviews Ltd (1983). (See Note 3 for address.)
15. R. Lees and A. F. Smith, Eds, *Design, Construction and Refurbishment of Laboratories,* Ellis Horwood, Chichester (1984).
16. K. J. Caplan and G. W. Knutson, 'Laboratory Fumehoods: Influence of Room Air Supply', *Transactions of the American Society of Heating, Refrigerating and Air-conditioning Engineers ASHRAE 9, 84* (1), 1978, 522–537.

3.3 Managing Safety in the Laboratory and Workshop

JAKE BHARIER

Objectives and Priorities

An earlier chapter has described the importance of safety policies. While, in the United Kingdom and some other countries, there are legal reasons for employers to commit their safety policies to paper, the value of these policies lies in how they can be applied as an effective means of managing safety. This chapter examines some ways in which a formal policy document can become a useful and practical tool for laboratories and workshops.

Policy statements usually set out broad, and some might say pious, aims. They are, though, very public documents, and whatever reservations might be expressed within them, it is reasonable for any employee to strive to match the reality of the workplace to the intent in the policy. It is particularly important for managers to do this. The policy statement is, after all, a description of what is expected of managers. Inevitably, there will be some differences between reality and intent, but those differences should be analysed in detail. Usually, they will amount to a few large and expensive items and a much larger number of smaller items that may need little money or may simply be matters of organization. To take an example, a museum safety policy may say something about providing and maintaining safe working conditions, and within the workshop, the problems could range from a floor in a poor state, or grossly inadequate ventilation, to making sure that fire-escape routes are kept clear. The cost of improvement will similarly range from many thousands of pounds to a technician sore at receiving a telling off.

Once the problems are listed, it is relatively easy to prepare solutions. A list of solutions can then become a list of tasks, and names and target dates should be put against each task. The result is a set of specific safety objectives. In this way a large and nebulous problem can be broken down into manageable chunks, the chunks can be assigned to people to deal with, and a time can be expected when all the jobs are completed. Would that it were quite so easy! The constraints on this are money, time and people, and part of the skill of management must be to make the best use of these resources. It is often helpful not just to set objectives, but to set priorities as well. Within a museum, as in any other organization, the first priority should be the safety of people, whether employees, researchers, contractors, volunteer helpers, or the visitors for whom the museum exists; next comes the safety of the artifacts, the objects to be preserved; and finally, comes the safety of the building. There may be some people in museums who handle irreplaceable or extremely valuable items, and who may not agree that their own safety comes before that of the specimens. They may need to be persuaded.

Assessing the Hazards of Workshop and Laboratory

The general statements of the safety policy give superficial guidance on the assessment of hazards in the workplace. More detail is normally needed, with a deeper analysis of the potential hazards. An important method of examining detail is by inspecting the workplace. This is not quite as straightforward as it sounds. Familiarity with an obvious hazard becomes a camouflage. The hazard may not be obvious because the inspector may have had no experience of it. Preoccupation with one type of hazard may obscure others. The hazard may be transient, arising from a particular work practice.

The commonest way to introduce order into safety inspection is to use checklists, and there are many examples—most textbooks on safety contain at least one. Although the examples can be used as models, the best checklists are those constructed for a particular workplace. The basis for them all, though, is much the same. They comprise a list of types of hazard, together with a list of how hazards could manifest themselves. Within a museum workshop, the main types of hazard are likely to be fire, chemicals, electricity, radiation, machinery, handling equipment, micro-organisms and the general work layout. Most of these are self-evident from a quick inspection of the workplace.

On the other hand, the sources and the extent of hazards may be more difficult to assess. There are in effect two sets of raw materials in the workshop: the objects being treated, and the materials used to treat them. The object to be treated could present a chemical, biological or mechanical hazard. In some cases, it will be in the laboratory so that more can be learned of its composition or structure. It may, then, be necessary to impute the worst possible hazards to the object until it has been shown to be safe. This is particularly important for some types of biological specimen if there is a history of infection. An example was the archaeological investigation of a graveyard in the City of London in 1985 where it was thought that those interred had died of smallpox. A check was carried out before work started, but no active smallpox was identified.

The hazards stemming from the raw materials used in the process should, at least in theory, be simple to assess. The suppliers should be able to provide safety data sheets on their products. In practice, though, a number of problems are encountered. Some suppliers think that they will suffer commercial damage if they give too much information about their products. This is, so far as health and safety is concerned, nonsense. If the risk is to be assessed then the constituents of proprietary products must be known, and if a supplier will not give this information the possible courses of action are to analyse the product and ask the supplier to confirm the analysis, or else to stop buying it. Analysis in these cases is usually easy and cheap. Next, the information from the supplier may be inadequate. The test to apply is to assess how much is fact, how much opinion and how much is vague. The fact may be, for instance, that the principal component is acetone; the opinion would be that 'acetone has a low order of toxicity'; and the vagueness, 'use with good ventilation'. If a judgement is made in the data sheet, or is required to be made by the user, then the data sheet should give the facts on which the judgement is based. To judge whether ventilation is good, one needs to know the identity of the chemical concerned, and the occupational exposure limit recommended for it. Chemical safety data sheets have often been of poor quality, but perhaps pressure from customers will persuade suppliers to do better.

Equipment is the next source of hazard to consider. The tools and machines used in the workshop should be suitable for the job, and should be maintained in good condition, whilst the system or pattern of work could itself present a threat to health or safety, especially if it has been adapted for a 'one-off' job, without forethought. Finally, the services, such as steam, electricity or gas, need to be considered.

With such a list of types and sources of hazard, a more detailed checklist can be prepared. The workplace manager and safety representatives should look at each part of their area in turn, and identify the specific hazards. The checklist can then be used for regular inspections, but while checklists are a valuable way of assessing the state of the workplace, they do have weaknesses. First, regular use of a checklist may cause the user to look at the amount of change since the last inspection, rather than the actual condition. If, for instance, a piece of equipment was thought to be worn but serviceable on one inspection, the next time it is looked at it may be judged to be a *little more* worn, whereas it may have become a *lot less* serviceable. Next, a checklist may inhibit a more imaginative look at conditions, which could reveal hazards not seen when the checklist was prepared. The answer to these points is to review and to revise the checklist regularly. Most important, though, is that a checklist will not normally help assess the effectiveness of safety management. For this a safety audit is required (described in St John Holt, Chapter 1.3). In essence, they are examinations of the way safety and health matters are organized, and are the mechanism for matching policy to reality, as described earlier in this chapter. Audits are generally more effective when they are carried out by people a little divorced from the area being audited, who can give a more distanced view.

Organizing Information

This chapter has already hinted strongly at the need for information. If people are to work safely then, obviously, they need to know not just what hazards are present, but how to avoid them. For this, there has to be a body of knowledge which can be disseminated effectively. One source of information has already been described: *product safety data sheets.* For all their faults, they are usually the basis of any data bank on chemical hazards. A practical problem is that few suppliers use the same format. It may, therefore, be helpful for laboratory or workshop managers to prepare internal data sheets, in a common format, for local use. Just as with the suppliers' data sheets, these should concentrate on fact and avoid opinion. If, though, some chemicals are thought to be particularly dangerous, then the opportunity to highlight them should be taken.

Suppliers' data sheets, together with user manuals, are equally important for plant, machinery and tools. The habit of many people of unpacking the whizzmodge and playing with it before reading the instructions is not an aid to safety.

The third main source is the huge quantity of *general information* available on health and safety. The main problem with this is the difficulty of identifying the parts that are relevant. Computer databases, such as HSELINE, CISDOC (see the bibliography) and Laboratory Hazards Bulletin, are a great help, but there will remain a need for some standard reference works to be on bookshelves. Some of these too are suggested in the bibliography. Publications from the health and safety bodies such as the National Institute for Occupational Safety and Health (NIOSH) and the Health and Safety Executive (HSE) are very valuable: their catalogues should be reviewed regularly.

The fourth and most approachable source (normally) is the *staff* of the laboratory or workshop. The skills, knowledge and experience for which people are employed will, inevitably, include aspects of safety, and have a more direct bearing on the work than most of the published information. The divides between art, craft and science can become blurred, especially in the museum environment. This may mean that the information is not as precise as the scientist might like, but it should not be ignored.

Normally, there already exist, within and between museums, mechanisms for people to exchange information and experience. The mechanism can be extended easily to cover

GENERAL PERMIT

36174

COURTAULDS GROUP To .... Department ....

Company/Division .... Works: ....

EVERY ITEM MUST BE FILLED IN OR DELETED AS APPROPRIATE **PLEASE WRITE CLEARLY**

A. JOB DETAILS | Department | Supervisor

1. Area or equipment to which this Permit applies:

2. Work to be done:

B. ISOLATIONS (specify where necessary)

	YES	NO	Intls.
1. Circuit breaker locked out/fuses withdrawn/isolator locked off			
2. Circuit tested and found to be dead			
3. Mechanical or physical isolation.			
4. Valves closed/locked off/spades inserted			
5. Pipelines drained/purged/disconnected/vented to atmosphere			
6. Attached isolation procedure			
7. Other			

C. PRECAUTIONS (to be taken as indicated. Additional to those specified on other permits).

	YES	NO			YES	NO	
1. Protective clothing			Type........	3. Non sparking tools			Type........
			Type........	4. Protected electrical equip.			Type........
2. Respiratory equipment			Type........	5. Standard operating procedure			Number ....

6. **State additional precautions required (if none state none)** ....

....

....

....

....

....

....

7. Atmosphere tests are not/are required at intervals of........ ....and results must be recorded overleaf.

D. ADDITIONAL PERMITS AND SIGNATURES REQUIRED BEFORE WORK STARTS

1. Confined Spaces Entry No...............................
2. H.V. Electrical No...............................
3. Hot Work No...............................
4. Excavation No...............................
5. CS2 Unusual Circumstances No...............................
6. Other (specify)... No...............................

7. In my opinion the engineering precautions are adequate.

Signed Engineer.. Date ....

8. In my opinion the precautions against chemical hazards are adequate

Signed Technical .... Date ....

9. In my opinion the precautions against.. hazards are adequate.

Signed ....Position .... Date ....

E. ISSUE AND RECEIPT BEFORE WORK

1. **Issue**
I have examined the area specified and permission is given for the work to start, subject to the conditions hereon, under the control of

....

Signed .... Date ....

2. **Receipt**
I have read and understand the conditions of this Permit. (see notes overleaf).

Signed .... Date ....

3. This Permit is valid from: (max. one day) Hrs. to Hrs. on

For extensions see overleaf.

F. CLEARANCE AND CANCELLATION AFTER WORK

1. **Clearance**
All men under my charge have been withdrawn. The permitted work is/is not complete.

Signed ....

Time ....Date..............................

2. **Cancellation**

	YES	NO
Work complete		
Isolations removed		
Area/Equipment safe to use		

I have notified the supervisor specified.
This permit is cancelled.

Signed ....

Date ....

Time ....

101-547 (Revised 1981)

1. Example of a permit to work.

health and safety matters. There may be a case in larger establishments for setting up a hazard bulletin, to highlight particular areas of concern or to tell people about common accidents, whilst someone in the workplace should be made responsible for collecting and collating information. If a library facility already exists this makes matters easier, but if not, then the manager or safety officer should have the job. The information must be readily and openly available to everyone.

Applying the Information

A library or database is a passive source of information. It depends on people realizing that they need to find out something. Hazard bulletins and safety meetings are useful to improve people's awareness of hazards, but the manager of a laboratory or workshop has, nevertheless, a responsibility to make sure that staff understand the particular hazards, and know how to avoid them. The body of collected information must, therefore, be rearranged and edited to meet two needs: for general guidance within the workshops and for guidance on specific tasks.

Generally guidance will tend to take the form of a workshop or laboratory safety manual. Topics covered in the manual could include, among many other things, the procedures in case of fire or accident, the functions of the safety committee, purchasing policy (to make sure that what is bought is safe and supplied with adequate information), and rules for the use of mechanical handling equipment. If ionizing radiation is used then the manual should contain the local rules for protecting people. All safety manuals should be revised regularly, and all staff should have easy and open access to the manuals, with any changes well publicized. Safety information for specific tasks should be integrated with all the other information needed for the purpose, in 'standard operating procedures' (SOPs). An SOP should set out, in some detail, the correct way of doing the task. It should explain the general hazards, and highlight particular safety points. An SOP is not the same as the set of instructions for using a machine, although those instructions may be incorporated into the SOP. Consequently, SOPs are not easy to write. They will be an amalgam of information from instruction manuals and data sheets, experience gained by people doing the job, and knowledge derived from the safety adviser or workshop manager. Draft SOPs must be discussed thoroughly with the people who are expected to follow them. The result, though, should be a document describing the best and safest way to do the job, and thus the SOP should state the limits of its application.

Of course, not every task lends itself to SOPs. Many jobs, especially in laboratories and workshops, will be singular, or may need to be done only occasionally. In these cases, there should be a mechanism for reviewing the proposed system of work before the job starts. One such mechanism is the permit to work. This is, essentially, a checklist of hazards, together with a system of authorization, to show that each hazard has been given proper consideration, and that appropriate counter-measures have been taken. An example of a permit is shown in Figure 1. Although this example was designed mainly for use in factories, it is used successfully by research laboratories, and forms a model which could be adapted easily for museum use.

If a task requires deviation from an SOP, but does not warrant a permit to work, a review mechanism is still needed, with a system of authorization. For example, an SOP could be written for the cleaning of paintings. This might be appropriate for canvases up to 1 metre square, and the limit might be set because of restrictions imposed by space, equipment or ventilation. The basic method of work will be the same for larger canvases, but special arrangements would be needed to overcome the limitations. Any deviations from the SOP should be reviewed and authorized by the manager responsible for safety.

Of course, all these systems for safe working are useless unless staff are trained to follow them. New employees, researchers or volunteers should not be allowed to do anything until they have received basic safety training. The safety manual will, to a large extent, provide the syllabus for this. The SOPs can then be used as the basis for specific job training, whilst existing employees may also need training or retraining in procedures and systems. Once systems are in place, and people are trained to follow them, they must be monitored. The safety audit, described earlier, will give a general view of compliance with systems, but day-to-day supervision is also important. This may be touchy, especially where people are employed for their special and rare skills. Nonetheless, a degree of discipline, or better, self-discipline, is needed. Many accidents happen because people depart from established safe systems of work. In nearly all cases, their motives were good, but they did not understand the consequences.

Summary

A strategy for safety requires assessment of risk, collection of information, safe systems of work, self-assessment and auditing, and, above all, a commitment to ensuring the safety of people. Throughout the chapter there has been a strong emphasis on written systems and procedures. The establishment and retention of a corporate safety memory is the backbone of safety management. Museums, with their *raison d'être* of preserving the past, are uniquely placed to manage health and safety effectively.

Bibliography

There are many books on general safety management, and quite a few on laboratory management directed mainly towards chemists. These include the *Code of Practice for Chemical Laboratories* (The Royal Institute of Chemistry, London) and *Hazards in the Chemical Laboratory*, by G. D. Muir (Chemical Society, London). The best review of chemical safety data sheets is *Chemical Risk*, by Maurice Frankel (Pluto Press, London). *The Handbook of Reactive Chemical Hazards*, by L. Bretherick (Butterworths, London) is a very useful compendium of chemicals which do not mix well or need careful treatment.

The most important databases for health and safety information are CISDOC, produced by the International Labour Office, Geneva; HSELINE, from the UK Health and Safety Executive; and RTECS (the Registry of Toxic Effects of Chemical Substances) from the National Institute for Occupational Safety and Health (NIOSH) in the United States. CISDOC and HSELINE are available through the ESA set of databases. RTECS is also available in hard copy, from NIOSH agents.

Both NIOSH and HSE publish catalogues of their own publications. There is advice available from these sources on specific hazards or occupations.

3.4 Fire Safety

R. C. Slade

Introduction

Of all workplace hazards fire is probably the most universal. It causes death and severe injury to persons and, in the United Kingdom, results in financial losses of between £400 and £500 million each year. In museums a fire, unlike other hazards, does not distinguish between employee and visitor, or between priceless artifacts of antiquity and modern reproductions: all are at risk. Consequently, fire precautions must assume a central position in the safety management of museums, and fire prevention should be the concern of curators, safety officers and all other grades of staff.

The functions of a museum include the collection, conservation and preservation of natural and man-made objects. Much of this work is carried out in laboratories and workshops, away from public galleries, by skilled scientists and technicians using modern instruments and techniques. Such workplaces, with a variety of easily combustible fuels and ignition sources, are generally high-risk areas in relation to fire hazards. In the United Kingdom during 1983 there were 2209 fires in workshops and 167 in laboratories, with a total of 12 fatalities and 176 other casualties. Why do these fires occur? Can we do anything to reduce the numbers? Is money spent on fire safety cost-effective?

In this chapter we are concerned primarily with the fire risks attendant upon laboratory and workshop activities and processes, with the means of preventing those fires and the means of protection should they occur. Fire-prevention procedures require an expert knowledge of the workplace and its activities, and an understanding of the fire hazards of these activities. The cleaning and restoration of paintings involves the use of solvents and solvent mixtures, including acetone, 2-ethoxyethanol, propanol and white spirit, all of which are highly flammable. Where are these solvents stored? How are they dispensed? Radiation-induced resin polymerization, employed to conserve wooden or other organic artifacts retrieved from waterlogged sites, involves large-scale use of the highly flammable solvent methanol. Many materials commonly found in general workshops are equally flammable, including cellulose paint thinners, solvent-based adhesives, liquefied petroleum gases (butane and propane) and town gas. Add to this list an equal number of potential ignition sources: electrical equipment and installations, open flames, heating and drying appliances, the surreptitious smoker, etc., and the high fire-risk rating is undeniable.

Our approach to fire safety is twofold: *to prevent* fires occurring; and *to protect* the building, its contents and inhabitants if fire does occur. The protection of human life is the primary objective of fire legislation, whereas the protection of property is the concern of fire insurance companies. Legislative and insurance standards and requirements may differ in emphasis, but museum management should consider prevention and protection in the context of life safety *and* property loss. Thus museum management should be aware of all relevent fire safety legislation, and not only because of the general duties imposed, in the United Kingdom, by the Health and Safety at Work Etc. Act 1974 and the recent trend towards more self-regulation. Fire safety in laboratories and workshops cannot be divorced entirely from the requirements for the whole building of which they are a part. Consequently, the next section summarizes general fire legislation for museums as places of work and as public buildings; whilst the other five following sections investigate the more specific problems of workplace activities.

Fire Legislation in Buildings

Fire safety legislation exists primarily to protect life. It aims to do this by reducing the risk of fires developing and getting out of control, by requiring the provision of means of escape, fire-detection systems, and emergency fire-fighting equipment and systems to enable safe and orderly evacuation of a burning building. *Passive* fire safety measures, including adequate means of escape, the compartmentalization of the building into fire-resisting subunits and the fire resistance of load-bearing and load-separating structural elements, are required in the United Kingdom by the Building Regulations 1985. These regulations apply to new buildings and to those involving a material change of use, with the exception of the inner London area where the London Building Acts (Amendment) Act 1939 applies, and Scotland and Northern Ireland which both have their own building regulations. The 1985 Regulations prescribe fire-resistant structures and compartmentalization as the means to limit or control the internal and external spread of fire, and detailed guidance is given in the 'Approved Document: Part B 2/3/4 Fire Spread' for museums as 'a place of assembly'. Although these regulations do not specify what constitutes an adequate means of escape from a place of assembly, the overriding requirement is contained in the Public Health Act 1936, Section 59, and County and District Councils, as the appropriate planning authorities, are required to consult with the fire authority regarding the provision of means of escape from certain public buildings. Where adequate ingress and egress are not provided or maintained then the local authority can require the defect to be remedied.

It is important that the activities of the museum, whether in the public galleries or workrooms, etc., do not lower the standard of passive fire protection. Fire exits and escape routes are liable to be obstructed by temporary displays and exhibitions, subdued lighting may enhance the displays but can also reduce the ability of visitors to recognize emergency routes and exits, and large wall-hung tapestries, carpets, etc., may significantly reduce the resistance of the wall surface to the spread of flame. Staff responsible for public galleries and the mounting of displays and exhibitions should be aware of structural fire safety needs and their responsibilities to visitors.

Legislation may also impose *active* fire safety requirements, including systems for the detection and extinguishing of fires using manual or automatic equipment, and for the training of staff. These measures are largely enacted through the Fire Precautions Act 1971 as extended to workplaces by the Health and Safety at Work Act 1974, although the workplaces thus incorporated are those covered by various sections of the Factories Act 1961 and the Offices, Shops and Railway Premises Act 1963, and not to the 'new entries' to health and safety legislation. Museums have not been designated under the Fire Precautions Act and so do require fire certificates. However, management should be aware of the standards which might be expected of museums as workplaces under this

Act by reference to the relevant Home Office and British Standards guides and codes.

The principles of passive and active fire safety apply just as strongly to the ancillary and workplace activities of the museum as to those of the public areas. Laboratories and workshops may be located in basement or other areas remote from the public galleries, and it may be necessary to consider additional escape routes and exits to avoid 'dead end' situations. There may be also certain structural requirements associated with workplace activities involving highly flammable or otherwise hazardous substances.

Fire Legislation and Workplace Activities

Fire-related legislation dealing with the work activities of museums is concerned largely with the control of highly flammable materials. Prevention involves the control of potential ignition sources in storage and work areas, whereas protection is achieved by restricting the quantities in use and by the provision of fire-fighting apparatus. Museums are subject to the statutory requirements of the Petroleum (Consolidation) Act 1928 which regulates the use of petroleum and certain other highly inflammable liquids. Under Section 1 of the Act a licence is required if petroleum spirit (which is defined as either a petroleum spirit, or a petroleum derivative—being any liquid made or extracted from petroleum—or a petroleum mixture with any other substance having a flash-point below 73 °F (23 °C) when tested in the prescribed manner) is to be kept in quantities exceeding 3 gallons. Local and County Councils as the licensing authorities may attach such conditions to the licence to ensure safe storage, dispensing and use throughout the premises. The provisions of the Act, either in whole or in part, are extended to many other liquids with flash-points below 73 °F (23 °C) by a series of orders and regulations. Many solvents found in museum laboratories and workshops are by definition 'petroleum spirit' and subject to control by licensing, e.g. toluene, xylene and n-hexane, whereas many other solvents are covered by certain restricted sections, including Section 16, which empowers government inspectors to enter and inspect premises where these substances are kept.

The Factories Act 1961 and its associated regulations apply only to factory premises as defined, and so do not necessarily impose direct statutory requirements on museums. However, Health and Safety Executive inspectors will use the Act and its detailed regulations to set appropriate standards in meeting the general duties of the Health and Safety at Work Act, particularly where the museum workplace activities are broadly similar to factory activities. Museum management should be aware of the fire safety standards promulgated through these regulations where similar activities, processes and materials are handled in their workshops, studios and laboratories.

Thus the Factories Act contains general fire safety requirements covering adequate means of escape, the provision, maintenance and testing of fire-fighting equipment, and the instruction of staff, whereas statutory regulations deal with more specific processes and materials. The most important of these in the present context are The Highly Flammable Liquids and Liquefied Petroleum Gases Regulations 1972. These regulations apply to solvent and liquid preparations having a flash-point of less than 32 °C, an extensive range, including many not covered by the more restrictive petroleum regulations, and to the liquid gas fuels butane and propane. Highly flammable liquids and the stores and workplaces where they are used are subject to controls over storage, the marking of storage facilities and vessels, fire prevention, the provision of fire-fighting apparatus and means of escape, whereas liquefied petroleum gases are subject to storage restrictions. An important requirement, Regulation 5(1), affecting workroom activities is the need to limit the aggregate quantity to no more than 50 litres kept in suitable bins or cupboards of fire-resisting structure. Note that the terms 'flammable' and 'inflammable' are used in the same sense in the HFL and LPG regulations and in the petroleum regulations, respectively.

The disposal or removal of flammable liquids and residues involves both protection against fires when onsite incineration is undertaken [HFL and LPG Regulation 15(2)], and against pollution of the environment. Substances having a flash-point of 21 °C or less are 'special waste' for the purpose of The Control of Pollution (Special Waste) Regulations 1980, and museums that produce such waste have duties under Section 4 of the Regulations.

Fire Prevention in Museum Workplaces

Prevention of fires requires a knowledge of the basic elements and conditions which must coexist for a fire to occur. The 'fire triangle' is a convenient schematic representation of the conditions under which combustion reactions occur, and therefore the key to preventing such reactions. Fire is a chemical reaction in which a substance (the fuel) combines with oxygen in the evolution of heat. Under normal circumstances fuels and

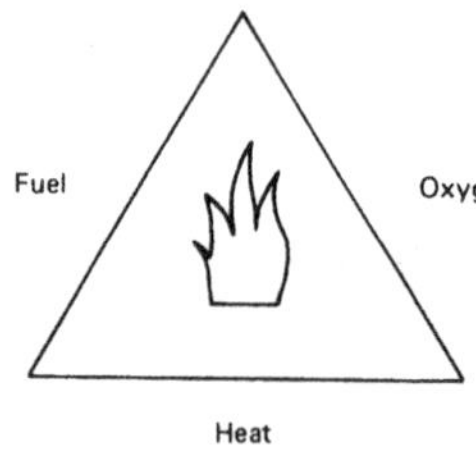

1. The fire triangle.

oxygen are in contact with one another, since the air contains some 21 per cent by volume of oxygen, without a fire occurring. Initiation of a fire is associated with the application of a source of ignition to a flammable fuel–air mixture. As with chemical reactions generally, the reactant molecules must be excited to a sufficiently activated or reactive state for the reaction to take place. The external application of energy, usually in the form of heat, raises the temperature and hence energy of the reactants so that combustion occurs. Once the reaction has started, sufficient heat is generated to maintain or increase the temperature of the reactants (the fuel) so that combustion is self-sustaining and an external heat source is no longer required. Combustion reactions usually occur in the vapour phase, i.e. are reactions between two or more vapours or gases, one of which is oxygen. Combustible gases and highly flammable liquids can be ignited easily with a small flame because at ambient temperatures a flammable vapour–air mixture exists, whereas liquids with high flash-points and most solids need to be heated before flammable vapours are formed. A further requirement for combustion is that the proportion of vapour to air in a mixture must be within the 'flammable limits' for ignition to occur. The lower flammable limit is the percentage of vapour in air at which a flame will be propagated when a test flame is applied to the mixture. Vapour–air mixtures may be too lean or too rich to burn, but in relation to fire prevention the lower limit is the more important.

This simple understanding of the nature of combustion reactions can be used beneficially, to prevent fires occurring, by the informed exercise of appropriate controls over the fuel, ignition sources and fuel–ignition source interactions.

Control of Fuels

1. Storage. The quantities of flammable materials, especially highly flammable liquids in the laboratory or workshop, should be kept to the minimum compatible with daily needs and should never exceed 50 litres. Highly flammable liquids should be kept in suitable containers, and these containers in a cabinet, cupboard or bin of sufficient fire resistance to allow persons to escape from the room should the liquids be involved in any fire. The storage cabinets should be equipped with sills to retain spillages, and they should be located away from ignition sources, exits and other combustible materials. Special safety containers for flammable liquids are available for a variety of purposes. Quantities greater than 50 litres should be kept either in a store detached from the main building (which may be required also for petroleum spirit storage) or an internal store-room. Adequate ventilation of a solvent store is necessary and, in the case of internal rooms, adequately fire-resistant walls are essential. Liquid petroleum (LPG) cylinders should be stored, wherever possible, in a secure place, in the open air, away from drains and the entries to basements and cellars.

2. Dispensing. Highly flammable liquids may be purchased in containers up to a 45 gallon capacity and thus facilities for dispensing from bulk to workroom containers may be necessary. The bulk solvent store is generally unsuitable for dispensing; preferably, a small section of the adequately ventilated workroom, where spillages can be contained, should be set aside for this purpose. Alternatively, dispensing should be carried out in the open air.

3. Workroom use. Working practices in laboratories and workshops should be designed around a sound knowledge of the fire hazard properties of the specific substances involved. In general, procedures should minimize the quantities in use, segregate flammable vapours and materials from potential ignition sources, prevent the unplanned escape or leakage of ignitable vapours and reduce the atmospheric concentration of vapours to well below the lower flammable limit. Ventilation is probably the most effective means of controlling fuels so that flammable vapours are diluted and removed from the workplace environment. The subject of laboratory ventilation is treated elsewhere, but the basic requirements for handling highly flammable liquids and vapours are to maintain the concentration to below one-quarter of the lower flammable limit and to provide extractors at both high and low levels, since most vapours are more dense than air and will settle and flow at floor level. Mains gas and liquefied petroleum gases are used as fuels for fixed or portable burners, heaters, etc. Installations of mains gas must comply with The Gas Act 1972 and the Gas Safety Regulations 1972. Non-return valves should be fitted in the gas main and to gas-burning ovens and furnaces. Flame-protective devices should be provided for fixed gas equipment, whilst portable appliances should have bayonet-type connectors, with flexible tubing kept to the minimum length. Liquid petroleum gas-supplied equipment should be fitted with flame failure devices and shut-off valves, and the supply protected by a main shut-off valve, regulator and non-return valve.

Consideration should also be given to waste fuels and material such as swabs, cloths and rags that may be impregnated with highly flammable liquids. Safety containers are available both for flammable liquid waste and for rags, etc. Flammable waste material should be removed from the workplace at frequent intervals and kept in a safe area until final disposal can be arranged.

Control of Ignition Sources

In most laboratories and workshops where highly flammable liquids or combustible gases are used there is a strong probability that a vapour–air mixture within the flammable limits will persist for some period of time. Whether a fire results will depend upon whether this transient flammable mixture contacts an ignition source. All workplaces contain a variety of potential ignition sources, ranging from the obvious open flames, electrical equipment and installations, and heating appliances which are necessary for the work activities, to the surreptitious smoker who is a hazard to the work activities.

The major direct cause of fires in occupied buildings is electricity, and particular attention should be given to equipment such as thermostatic constant-temperature baths and refrigerators incorporating make-and-break contacts which spark under normal operating conditions. Faulty electrical equipment may short-circuit and cause arcing, or may produce small earth leakage currents which can cause fires. The surfaces of electric furnaces and ovens can be hot enough to ignite flammable vapours or to cause wood to smoulder, should they be stood directly on wooden surfaces with insufficient air-gaps. Lack of maintenance of electric motors results in overheated bearings through loss of lubrication or because the ventilation slots are encrusted with dust or debris. Electrical installations and wiring will overheat when currents in excess of the design rating are carried for any length of time. Appropriate fuses, circuit-breakers and residual current detectors will reduce this risk. Static electricity has also been implicated in several laboratory fires, and for this reason overalls and coats made of synthetic fibres are not recommended where highly flammable liquids are used in dry, low-humidity conditions.

Space-heating appliances should be both safe and effective. Hot-water radiators or ducted hot-air systems are best for workrooms because they do not attain sufficient temperatures to ignite flammable vapours. Whatever system is used must be capable of maintaining an adequate temperature, since otherwise there is a tendency towards uncontrolled introduction of portable items, such as radiant electric fires, oil-filled radiators and gas heaters.

Prohibition of smoking in all laboratory, workshop and storage areas must be strictly enforced by management and supervisors, and the rule must apply to all grades of staff and to all visitors. 'No Smoking' signs should be prominently displayed to enforce the verbal instructions.

Control of Fuel–Ignition Source Interactions

This is frequently the most expensive, inconvenient and least effective means of preventing fires. Flame-proof lighting, spark-proof switches and flame-arrestor devices, etc., may be appropriate where large volumes of highly flammable materials are stored or used, but the scale of most museum workplace activities probably does not justify such preventive measures.

Fire Protection of Museum Workplaces

The need for fire protection is a prudent admission that fires will occur whatever preventive measures have been taken. In general, fire protection involves the provision of appropriate measures to restrict injury to persons and structural damage to property by detecting, containing and extinguishing fires. Passive measures incorporated into the building at design and construction stages to meet insurance and building regulation requirements have been discussed earlier, so this section is concerned with the active measures by which fires may be detected and extinguished. The statutory requirements for detection and extinguishing systems extend only to those premises which have been designated under the Fire Precautions Act, and for those which are not designated the general duties imposed by the Health and Safety at Work Act, insurance requirements and common law liabilities together make a compelling case. The planning authority, when approving the building plans, may also make certain stipulations regarding fire-extinguishing systems. Advice on the choice of fire-protection systems is available from insurance companies, fire risk surveyors, the Fire Offices' Committee of the insurance companies, and from the published codes of practice and specifications of the British Standards Institution.

Provision for Giving Warning

Early warning of fire allows the maximum time for evacuation of the building, time for the emergency services to arrive on the scene and, if circumstances permit, the safest opportunity for staff to tackle the fire. Detection of fire may involve automatic sensors which respond to the combustion products (smoke, heat or radiation) and are connected directly to an alarm system. Alternatively the system may be manual, relying on the occupants to set off an alarm. The size of the building and its rooms, the nature of the contents and activities carried out, are all factors involved in determining which system is appropriate. Modern microchip technology allows automated fire alarm systems to be integral with security alarms or a range of optional responses if combustion products are detected.

The most common type of sensor is the ion-chamber smoke detector which is activated, when smoke particles enter the chamber, by a change in the minute electric current passing through it. Where such equipment is installed in laboratories and workrooms, consideration should be given to the consequences of false alarms caused by normal workplace activities and other environmental factors, such as draughts, flying insects, dusts, which may activate the detectors. The choice of detector, its siting, and the responses of associated control and indicating equipment are all a matter for expert opinion. Requirements for the protection of property and those for life safety may be different; whilst rooms or areas which are unoccupied for long periods of time may have different needs from those where staff are always present or patrol at frequent intervals. Detailed advice is available in *British Standard BS 5839:Part 1, 1980 Fire Detection and Alarm Systems in Buildings*, or from fire insurers. Whichever system is installed, a responsible person within the museum staff must be given the task of supervising, testing and arranging for maintenance, and subsequent alterations to the building, whether temporary or permanent, should be reviewed for their impact on the alarm system.

Whether detection of fire is by automatic sensors or by people, the system must have the means to transmit a clear warning when it has been activated. Usually this is in the form of fire-alarm sounders which are located throughout the building, and which are all activated from a control panel on receipt of a signal from any one of the automatic detectors or manual 'break glass' call-points. The alarm may be single-stage, indicating the need for immediate evacuation of the whole building, or two-stage, with evacuation of the area immediately at risk, or restricted and recognizable to staff only, in order to avoid distress and panic in the public areas. Since the fire-alarm sounders are provided for life safety, the fire authority should be consulted on the most appropriate equipment.

The usefulness of an alarm system sounding, for the protection of property and the limiting of damage and loss, depends on the provision of appropriate fire-fighting equipment, not least if the Fire Brigade is unlikely to attend within 10 minutes.

Provision for Fighting Fires

The means of fighting fires will generally involve both fixed installations and portable, or hand-held, extinguishers. Fixed installations, provided in response to planning or insurance requirements, include fire hydrants, dry or wet rising mains, and hose-reels connected directly to a mains water supply. In addition, fixed sprinkler or drench systems capable of delivering water spray, foam, inertial vapour, carbon dioxide or dry powder are available, but their use in laboratory or workshop areas is not common because of the damage caused by false alarms and the difficulty of selecting a suitable extinguishing agent for a multi-activity workroom. On the other hand, automatic sprinklers are the most effective form of fire protection and are widely encouraged by insurance companies.

Portable fire-extinguishers are commonly found in workrooms, with a variety of types, colours, sizes and operating mechanisms. Selection of the most appropriate type of extinguisher is dictated largely by the type of fire anticipated, but other factors, such as ease of maintenance and effectiveness together with the general environmental conditions, need careful consideration. Whatever type of extinguisher is finally selected, conformation with the appropriate British Standard specification (e.g. BS 5423) is a further requirement.

Fires are classified according to the type of fuel involved and appropriate extinguishing agents recommended for each fire type. Thus the European Standard BS-EN 2: 1972 classifications for fires are as given in Table 1, along with the recommended extinguishing agents. Fires involving gaseous fuels (Class C) can be overcome successfully only by turning off the supply of fuel at the valve or stopcock and then tackling any secondary fires using an appropriate extinguisher.

In museum laboratories and workshops the fuels are most likely to be ordinary combustible materials (paper, wood, etc.) and highly flammable liquids, so that protection is required for general and special risks. For general fire protection water is by far the most effective, since it has excellent cooling properties and can penetrate to

Table 1. Fire Classifications under European Standard BS-EN 2:1972

Type	Fuel	Extinguishing agent
Class A	Fires involving ordinary combustible materials (wood, paper, fabrics)	Water
Class B	Fires involving liquids	Foam, Halon, Carbon dioxide, Dry powder
Class C	Fires involving gases	–
Class D	Fires involving combustible metals	Special dry powder

deep-seated fires. Multipurpose dry powders based on ammonium phosphate are also effective on a range of fires. The special fire-risk activities in workrooms require extinguishing agents that are effective against both flammable liquid fires and those involving electrical or electronic equipment. Consideration should also be given to the damage that the extinguishing agent may cause to valuable artifacts and expensive equipment. Burning liquid fuels are sometimes contained or sometimes free-flowing over both horizontal and vertical surfaces. Dry powder is the best all-round agent for dealing with such fires, as it can deal with both free-flowing and contained liquids, and is more effective in comparative tests than other types. The dust deposits left after discharging a powder extinguisher are preferable to the damage caused by a small fire which gets out of control. Although the greatest priority is to extinguish a fire as quickly as possible, there may be occasions when it is necessary to avoid the damage and contamination caused by water, foam or powder, and in such instances a carbon dioxide extinguisher is recommended.

Fires originating in or involving live electrical equipment need special consideration. Isolating the electrical supply is the most effective course of action. This often extinguishes the fire so that a general-purpose agent can then be used. If, however, the electrical supply cannot be switched off, a non-conducting extinguishing agent must be used, preferably one which can penetrate to the interior of the equipment. Carbon dioxide and Halon agents are most effective in this respect, but it should be borne in mind that the Halon agents bromochlorodifluoromethane (BCF or Halon 1211) and bromotrifluoromethane (BTM or Halon 1301), form pyrolysis products that are not only toxic but also corrosive when used in unventilated or confined spaces.

As a general guide, most workrooms will be adequately protected if they are provided with three types of extinguisher: *water* for general-purpose (Class A) fires; *dry powder* for general-purpose and liquid (Classes A and B) fires; and *carbon dioxide* for flammable liquid (Class B) and electrical fires. Too many types will confuse, and some agents must not be used on certain types of fire. Thus, *do not use water or foam* on live electrical equipment; *do not use water* on flammable liquids; and *do not use carbon dioxide* on combustible metal fires. The old-fashioned sand-bucket still has its uses, although it is difficult for an untrained fire-fighter to extinguish anything but the smallest of fires with sand.

After selection of the type of extinguisher needed, the numbers required and their siting must then be considered. According to rules published by the Fire Offices' Committee (FOC), the fire rating of each extinguisher (assigned according to BS 5423:1980, and based on the type and weight of agent) is used so that for Class A fires the aggregate rating of all the Class A extinguishers should not be less than 0.065 times the floor area (m^2) for each floor of the building. For uncontained liquid fires, the aggregate Class B rating must be such that each area or workroom is provided with two extinguishers, each of which has a B rating of 10 times the volume, measured in litres, of the largest spillable liquid container. Further details may be found in the *Rules for the Provision of Fire Extinguisher Appliances* (FOC).

Extinguishers for general fire protection should be sited near the room exit, or on adjacent stairway landings, or on corridors—in conspicuous positions and accessible at all times. There should be a general-purpose extinguisher, or hose-reel, within 30 metres of any point within the workplace. In the case of special fire-risk activities the appropriate extinguishers should be positioned close to the point of risk.

Fire Drills and Training

Fire safety can be improved by providing fire protection systems, safe means of escape, and fire-resisting compartments and structures, but many of these measures will be wasted or ineffective if the staff are not instructed and trained in fire prevention techniques both in the use of fire extinguishers and in the actions expected of them in an emergency. Staff must be informed, and reminded at regular intervals, of the action to be taken if they discover a fire or if they hear the fire alarm. Training in the use of fire extinguishers involves instruction in the types of fire, the appropriate extinguishing agents, and methods of operation of the different extinguisher types.

Staff must be instructed in the means of escape from their place of work, including the normal and emergency exits. Evacuation drills should be carried out at least annually and under various conditions chosen to represent real fire situations. Special consideration must be given to disabled persons and to visitors who will be unfamiliar with the layout of the building. In large establishments a number of fire wardens may be appointed from among the staff to assist in the evacuation and the checking of rooms.

Sufficient escape routes and exits should be provided to enable the building to be cleared in 2½ minutes. This should be the target aimed at in practice drills because smoke can spread extremely quickly throughout a building once the fire has spread beyond the room of origin. About 40 per cent of fire casualties arise directly from the inhalation of smoke-borne carbon monoxide or other highly toxic combustion products, and concentrations of 1 per cent of carbon monoxide are likely to result in loss of consciousness in under 5 minutes.

Smoke rises over Hampton Court Palace in March, 1986, signalling the disastrous fire that caused damage running into millions of pounds, and the loss of one life. (Photo: Press Association)

Management Action

Museums as places of work are covered by the Health and Safety at Work Act, and employers and management carry onerous responsibility for protecting their staff from the hazard of fire. Accordingly, as part of the written Safety Policy, there should be a statement, backed up by appropriate provisions, outlining the arrangements for fire prevention and protection. Responsibility for enforcing the Safety Policy must be allocated to a manager with sufficient authority to act, and to activate others. Some of the immediate causes of laboratory and workshop fires have been mentioned above, but virtually all such fires are caused accidentally, and arson is rare. Control of people in the workplace is an important management function, and a museum with effective safety management will be more fire-safety conscious.

The following six-point action plan summarizes the steps which management ought to take in formulating and maintaining an effective fire-safety policy:

1. Identify the areas of high fire risk and the areas of high-value property.
2. Determine the precautions necessary to prevent fire and the loss-control systems to protect property.
3. Install and maintain the necessary fire-protection equipment.
4. Plan the action to be taken in the event of fire.
5. Instruct and train staff.
6. Compile a fire-safety checklist and set up an inspection programme to regularly monitor observance and remedy defects.

Bibliography

Information sources cited in this chapter can be located in the cumulative list on pp. 163–170. A full list of fire-related standards is available from the British Standards Institution at Linford Wood, Milton Keynes, Bucks 14 6LE, UK. Some of the most pertinent Standards are listed here:

BS 476 Fire Tests on Building Materials and Structures
Part 3: 1975 External fire exposure roof test
Part 4: 1970 Non-combustibility test for materials
Part 5: 1968 Ignitability test for materials
Part 6: 1968 Fire propagation tests for materials
Part 7: 1971 Surface spread of flame
Part 8: 1972 Test methods and criteria for the fire resistance of elements of building construction
BS 3116 Automatic Fire Alarms in Buildings
Part 1: 1970 Heat sensitive (point) detectors
Part 4: 1974 Control and indicating equipment
BS 4422 Glossary of Terms Associated with Fire
Part 1: 1969 The phenomenon of fire
Part 2: 1971 Building materials and structures
Part 3: 1972 Means of escape
Part 4: 1975 Fire protection equipment
Part 5: 1976 Miscellaneous terms
BS 4547 1972 Classification of Fires
BS 5266 Emergency Lighting of Premises
BS 5274 Fire Hose-reels for Portable Extinguishers
BS 5306 Code of Practice for Fire Extinguishing Installations and Equipment on Premises
Part 1: 1976 Hydrants systems, hose reels and foam inlets
Part 2: 1979 Sprinkler systems
Part 3: 1980 Portable fire extinguishers

Part 4: 1979 Carbon dioxide systems
Part 5: Section 5.1: 1982 Halon 1301 total flooding systems
BS 5345 Code of Practice for the Selection, Installation and Maintenance of Electrical Apparatus for Use in Potentially Explosive Atmospheres
Part 1: 1976 Basic requirements for all parts of the code
BS 5423 1981 Specification for Portable Fire Extinguishers
BS 5499 Fire Safety Signs, Notices and Graphic Symbols
Part 1: 1978 Specification for fire safety signs
BS 5588 Fire Precautions in the Design of Buildings
Part 4: Smoke control in protected escape routes
BS 5839 Fire Detection and Alarm Systems in Buildings
Part 1: 1980 Code of Practice for installation and servicing
BS 5908 1980 Code of Practice for Fire Precautions in Chemical Plant
BS 6165 Specification for Small Disposable Aerosol Fire Extinguishers
BS 6266 1982 Code of Practice for Fire Protection for Electronic Data Processing Installations (formerly CP 95)

CP 3 Chapter IV: 1948 Precautions against Fire
CP 402 Fire Fighting Installations and Equipment
CP 402: 201: 1952 Sprinkler Systems
CP 402: Part 3: 1964 Portable Fire Extinguishers for Buildings and Plant

3.5 Infection and Allergy in Museums

M. R. Bailey

Biological materials may introduce three distinct health hazards to museum workers. Live micro-organisms and viruses may cause infection. Organic material, either whole micro-organisms (live or dead), or the constituent parts of biological systems (e.g. proteins), may cause allergic reactions. Finally, the products of biological systems may be toxic. This chapter is concerned with where these hazards may arise and with how they should be controlled.

The sources of biological material which may give rise to health hazards in museum work can be conveniently divided into two groups: those associated with the work (exhibits, collections or specimens); and those associated with the museum buildings and their services. Control of work-associated health hazards depends upon both appropriate working practices and the individual workers. Hazards arising from the museum building and its services will be controlled only by correct management of the building.

Museum Work

Infection Hazards

Hazards of infection arising from museum work will normally be associated with preparatory work on biological specimens and some ethnographic material. Less frequently there will be exposure to human pathogens while human material is being handled. Animal, bird, fish and even invertebrate carcasses and skins may be contaminated with micro-organisms capable of producing human infection. Of particular concern are anthrax and leptospira bacteria associated with mammals, psitticosis and ornithosis associated with birds, and salmonella associated particularly with reptiles and amphibians. Such material may be encountered by archaeologists, anthropologists, ethnographers and natural historians, as well as staff working with medical collections.

The possibility of latent contamination with viable human pathogens may never be discounted, particularly when human material is handled. Recently a great deal of concern followed the excavation of human remains from a burial ground recorded to have been used for victims of smallpox. The time-limit for the survival of viruses like smallpox is unknown. It is thought possible that such viruses may remain viable for tens or hundreds of years, given the ideal conditions (cool, damp and undisturbed). Indeed, it is known that bacterial spores of anthrax do remain viable in the soil for many tens of years. The Ministry of Defence is currently disinfecting the anthrax-contaminated soil of Gruinard Island to make it habitable for the first time since it was used for biological weapons tests during World War II.

Whilst it is true that serious infection hazards will be encountered in museum work only infrequently, the potential for infection will often arise. The varied nature of museum work makes the specification of detailed safety rules impossible here, but the same general guidelines will be applicable to all situations. For human pathogens, guidance is published by the Advisory Committee on Dangerous Pathogens (*Categorisation of Pathogens According to Hazards and Categories of Containment*). This document is recognized by the Health and Safety Executive as representing good practice, and should be followed when appropriate.

1. Control of Infection. The proper control of occupational infection hazard requires an understanding of the routes of infection so that appropriate safe working practices may be devised. Infectious agents will not cause infection unless they enter the body in some way. These routes may be described as:

(a) contamination leading to ingestion (typical of gastro-intestinal infections such as those caused by salmonella bacteria);
(b) innoculation through intact skin or contamination of breaks in the skin (typical of staphylococcal infections, tetanus and leptospirosis);
(c) inhalation of infectious particles (typical of anthrax, psitticosis and ornithosis).

The principal object of all control arrangements is to avoid the worker becoming exposed to any of these routes of infection. The simplest way to achieve this is to kill the infectious agent before the worker has any contact with it. This is possible where the specimen or artifact is treated immediately on receipt with a preservative which also acts as a disinfectant, such as formalin or alcohol (the attendant toxic hazards of such materials should not be overlooked), or in some cases a fumigant such as ethylene oxide. Where such disinfectant treatment is not possible before the potentially infectious material is handled, the infection hazard must be assessed, and appropriate precautions taken. These will normally consist of the use of protective clothing (gloves and a laboratory coat or gown, supplemented with goggles if there is a hazard of eye contamination), together with arrangements for disinfecting working surfaces, equipment and waste at the end of the working session. As with all safe working arrangements, there must be a clear procedure to be followed in the event of accident or injury. The disinfectant to be used must be known to be effective for the infectious agent concerned, it should be freshly made up, and diluted according to the manufacturer's specification. It should go without saying that there must be no eating, smoking or drinking anywhere where potentially infectious materials are handled at any time. Personal hygiene is important, and hand-washing at the end of working sessions and particularly before eating, drinking or smoking is vital. The advice of the occupational health practitioner should be sought on infection control and vaccination.

If human pathogens are known to exist (or are strongly suspected), and the material cannot be disinfected before being handled, the Health and Safety Executive should be contacted for advice before the work commences. Specialized handling facilities, including microbiological safety cabinets, are required for work with serious infection hazards. However, the need for such arrangements will not normally arise in museum work. Human serotyping has been carried out in some museums.

Basic safety arrangements (good microbiological practice) may be summarized as follows:

(a) Disinfect material before handling whenever possible.
(b) Use laboratory coat, gloves and, when necessary, eye protection.

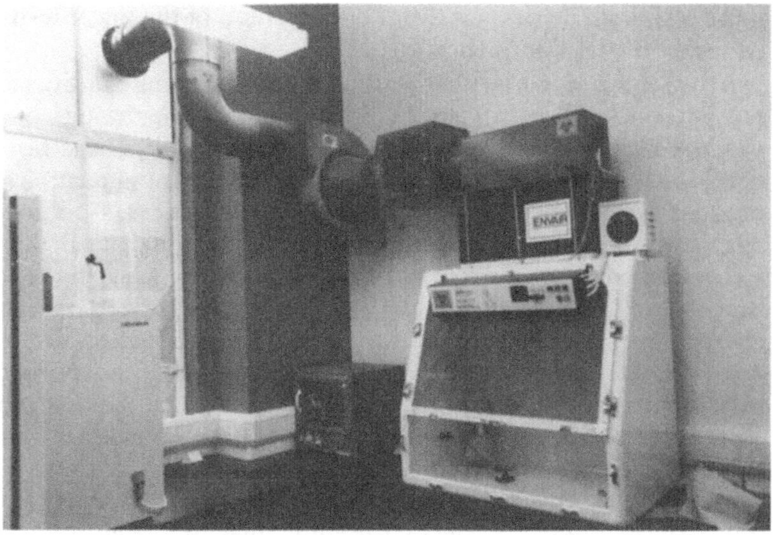

1. Microbiological safety cabinets should be used wherever there is a risk of airborne human pathogens.

(c) Have appropriate disinfectant at working dilution ready before starting work.
(d) Clean and disinfect surfaces and equipment at the end of each working session.
(e) Disinfect waste before disposal.
(f) No eating, drinking or smoking in the working area is to be permitted at any time.
(g) Wash hands at the end of each working session, or in the event of any contamination, and always before eating, drinking or smoking.
(h) Have a clear procedure for dealing with accidents and injuries, and ensure that it is known and understood by all staff working in the area.
(i) If in doubt, ask for advice from museum safety advisers, or from the Health and Safety Executive, before commencing work.
(j) Follow the advice of the occupational health practitioner on vaccination (e.g. tetanus).

2. *Biological Fieldwork.* Museum work sometimes takes place in the field, some of it overseas. The possibility of infection arising from local conditions should not be forgotten, and health advice should be sought before travelling, particularly when tropical regions are to be visited. If the work will involve the excavation of recent (within, say, 100 years) human remains, the advice of the Health and Safety Executive should be sought before commencing (see chapter references).

Allergy and Sensitization in Museum Work

The body's defence mechanism against invasion by foreign material is called its immune system. This system recognizes the foreign material (micro-organisms, biological molecules or inert material) and regulates the body's defensive responses. Allergy may be described as an unwanted immunological reaction. In some allergies the body's defences have been provoked by a harmless substance such as grass pollen or house-dust mites, in others the reaction to a mild irritant, such as bee venom, is excessive. Some allergies are a mild inconvenience whilst the most severe may be life-threatening. The most significant route of exposure is normally via inhalation, although exposure of the skin and eyes may provoke response. Allergic reactions may take the form of irritation of the nasal and upper respiratory passages (rhinitis), irritation of the lower respiratory tract (asthma), or irritation of the skin (urticaria).

All allergies begin with the individual becoming sensitized (the body learning to recognize the allergen), and then the allergy may progress so that the reaction is produced by smaller and smaller challenges. The degree of response and the sensitivity developed will depend to a large extent on the individual. Any foreign material may provoke an allergic reaction, although some materials do so particularly readily and frequently. In terms of exposure, materials of a size that can be inhaled (respirable) or of a chemical composition that will pass through the protective layer of the skin, are most hazardous. Once an individual has become sensitized the allergy may be properly controlled only by preventing further exposure. Short-term relief may be gained by the use of drugs such as sodium cromoglycate, but this approach is not a satisfactory solution to occupational allergy. It is vital that anyone showing signs of initial sensitization be referred to an occupational health physician so that further development of the allergy can be prevented.

The identity of the allergen may be determined by provocation testing, whereby the physician exposes the skin of the individual to a selection of common allergens and materials encountered in the workplace. This is done either as a patch test, by which the test materials are applied to the skin of the back, or by skin-prick testing, where the potential allergens are introduced under the outside layers of the skin of the arm. (It must be stressed that these tests are medical procedures and that they carry the hazard of inducing a sensitization which had not previously occurred.) In many situations the allergen is never properly identified. If control measures introduced to reduce exposure to materials in the workplace are effective, such an identification may not be necessary and may not justify the discomfort and risk of the provocation testing.

1. Control of Occupational Allergy. Ideally, occupational exposure to potential allergens should be controlled to such a degree that initial sensitization does not occur. This will never be possible for all cases, since some individuals react to minimal challenges from materials not normally recognized as allergens. However, work practices and conditions should be designed so that exposure to recognized allergens is minimized, and there is no excessive exposure to potentially allergenic material. Occupational allergens may be encountered in almost all museum disciplines. Regular exposure (e.g. taxidermy) or long-term exposure during a specific conservation project (e.g. fabric conservation) are most likely to give rise to problems. For all working situations the following guidelines should be applied:

(a) Exposure to respirable particles (dusts, vapours or aerosols) should always be minimized. This should be done by controlling the source of the particles rather than by providing workers with respiratory protective equipment.
(b) Whenever possible, potentially dusty operations should be carried out wet.
(c) Where respirable particles are produced, local extraction ventilation should be provided to remove the airborne material.
(d) If respiratory protective equipment is used, it must be of the correct type for the material in question, and it must be worn and maintained in accordance with the manufacturer's recommendations.
(e) Protective clothing for skin and eyes should be used whenever there is prolonged or excessive contamination. Particular care should be taken of eyes and broken skin and where the skin may be wetted or abraded.

(f) The potential for exposure from cleaning operations and from contaminated clothing should not be overlooked.
(g) Personal hygiene is important. Hands should be washed at the end of each working period and in the event of contamination.
(h) Occupational health advice should be sought if known allergens are handled and at the first sign of any sensitization.

2. *Toxic Biological Materials.* Some biological materials, notably reptile and insect venoms and plant and fungal toxins, will produce toxic effects. Many of these are hazardous in minute quantities, and most are well known as such. When work may involve contact with these substances, a safe working practice, together with appropriate protective clothing and a procedure for accidents and emergencies, must be prepared before the work commences. Advice should be sought from occupational health physicians and safety experts.

Museum Buildings

Infection Hazards

Recently there has been considerable public concern about 'Legionnaires' disease'. The causative organism, *Legionella pneumophila*, is widespread in the natural environment. It is also present in many buildings' water systems. It is the only cause of infection associated with buildings in the United Kingdom. Outbreaks of the disease are often associated with large public buildings (particularly hospitals), but museum managers should be aware of the aspects of building management which are important for the control of *Legionella* bacteria. It must be stressed that the problem of 'Legionnaires' disease' has not been specifically associated with museums, though in view of museums' extensive involvement with the general public, a cautious approach is recommended.

Infection by *Legionella pneumophila* can occur only as a result of exposure to an aerosol containing live bacteria, and such an aerosol may be produced only from a contaminated water system. It should also be remembered that old people, and those who are already ill, are most likely to develop an infection (which is why hospitals are so often involved). The process leading from a contaminated water system to a human infection may be broken into a number of steps. At each stage there are a number of control options available.

1. *Contamination of the Water System. Legionella* bacteria are ubiquitous, and as such must be expected to contaminate any water system at some time. Complete sterilization of a complex water system is often impossible and, since the contamination may be reintroduced from the environment, would be of little long-term value. The use of elevated temperatures (above 60° centigrade) to reduce the overall numbers of micro-organisms is widely practised in British hospitals following Department of Health advice. Bacterial numbers may also be controlled by maintaining a high turnover of the water in the system.

Chemical biocides can be effective only when applied to systems which are already clear of excessive amounts of organic material. Inert organic material, such as bacterial slime and wooden surfaces, will compete for the reactive chemical biocides and seriously reduce the chance of the target organisms being affected at all. The use of chemical

2. Cooling-towers come in all shapes and sizes. They should be kept clean and free of rust and limescale.

biocides should be carefully monitored by regular microbiological monitoring of the water quality. This must be carried out by a qualified biologist.

The specific examination of water samples for *Legionella* bacteria is not recommended unless the source of an infection is being sought. The laboratory procedure is both time-consuming and costly, and the results are difficult to interpret in terms of exposure and infection risk. A positive result will be unsurprising given the ubiquitous nature of the organism, while a negative result may indicate only the absence of the organism at the time of the sample or a failure of either the sampling techniques or the laboratory procedures to isolate the organism.

2. Growth of the Bacteria Within the Water System. The numbers of *Legionella* bacteria in the environment are generally low. For infection to occur, a relatively high density of the bacteria must be present in the source of the aerosol. This will be produced by growth of the bacteria within the water system, but such growth will occur only if suitable conditions are present. *Legionella* bacteria require a temperature between 20° and 50° centigrade, a source of organic nutrient, a source of iron salts, and time in which to grow. A carefully managed system will deprive the bacteria of many if not all of these requirements and thus prevent significant growth. Thus cold water should be stored and supplied below 20° centigrade, and hot water above 60° centigrade. Materials for the construction of a water system should be selected so as to avoid any which may support microbiological growth. The Water Authorities publish a directory of materials approved for use in water systems, and these have been tested and shown not to support microbiological growth.[1] They are specified by manufacturer and part number. Rust and limescale should be avoided, and removed periodically (at, say, six-monthly intervals) if they do occur. Care should be taken to prevent the system becoming contaminated with organic material, by covering water tanks and by maintaining filters where they are fitted.

3. Creation of Aerosols. Infection cannot arise, even from the most seriously contaminated systems, unless there is a means of disseminating the *Legionella* bacteria in an aerosol. Aerosols are produced by pressurizing liquid against a surface or through a small hole (as happens when tap-water hits the basin or bath and when a shower is used), or by blowing air through the liquid (which is what happens in wet cooling-towers). The aerosols produced by using taps and showers should not carry an infectious hazard if the water systems have been maintained in accordance with the advice given above. Aerosols from wet (evaporative) cooling-towers will be of more concern because it is very difficult to ensure that the cooling-towers remain free of contamination. Where museum buildings incorporate wet cooling-towers in their design, building managers should ensure that the spray (drift) from the cooling-towers is reduced as much as possible (by drift eliminators), and that it cannot be drawn into any ventilation system. It is also important that workers and the general public are prevented from having close access to any cooling-tower drift. When building engineers are working on, or close to, any cooling-tower, that tower should be shut down. All wet cooling-towers should be shut down and their internal surfaces cleaned of organic matter, limescale and rust at least twice per year.

4. Summary. The approach required of the building manager may be summarized as:

(a) Maintain a clean water system.
(b) Apply temperature controls.
(c) Use only materials specified in the Water Authorities' directory.
(d) Use chemical biocides if the system cannot otherwise be maintained sufficiently uncontaminated—it is stressed that this is in addition to maintaining a clean system. The addition of chemical biocides to dirty systems is a waste of time and money, and cannot be effective.
(e) Control drift from cooling-towers.

3. The drift from cooling-towers must be kept away from ventilation intakes. Here simple external ductwork has provided the solution.

(f) Ensure a rapid turnover of stored water; and pay particular attention to water outlets which are used infrequently or are at the ends of long runs of pipework.
(g) Regularly inspect all water systems, storage tanks and cooling-towers; clean as necessary.
(h) If in doubt seek advice from experts.

Allergy Hazards

Ventilation and humidification systems in buildings (particularly large and modern buildings) have been implicated in the exposure of their occupants to allergens. These allergens are usually of microbiological or fungal origin, although they do not need to be live at the time of exposure to promote allergic responses. Building managers should be

4. Water storage tanks should be as small as possible to ensure a rapid turnover of water to prevent stagnation. They should not be exposed to heat sources and sunlight, as illustrated here.

aware of the possibility of these health hazards, and should maintain their systems so as to avoid them. Distinct allergies associated with buildings are often termed 'humidifier fever' or 'Monday morning sickness'. Less specific health effects are covered by the description of 'sick building syndrome'. The exact allergen is rarely identified in outbreaks of these problems, but it is normally possible to remedy the situation by cleaning humidifiers and ventilation systems.

Humidification is necessary in air-conditioned buildings in the United Kingdom because the outside air which is drawn into the system normally has to be heated before being delivered. Cold air has a much lower capacity for holding moisture than warm air, so the warmed air will have a lower relative moisture content (relative humidity) than the cold air had. This low relative humidity would be uncomfortable to people in an unconditioned building and rehumidification will usually be required. The rehumidification may be an integral part of the air-conditioning system or it may be achieved by

5. All interior and exterior water storage tanks must be kept securely covered and free from such organic contamination as is shown here.

6. Drain points from ventilation systems and driptrays must be of adequate size. They should be regularly inspected for signs of microbiological growth.

7. Chemical water treatments will be effective only when used on well-maintained and cleaned systems. They must be regularly monitored to ensure their continued efficiency.

8. Steam humidification is the ideal method for many ventilation systems.

supplementary plant. In either case a system for introducing water to the warm air is required. This may take the form of a reservoir which is heated to evaporate the water, a spray of water directed into the airstream, or the introduction of steam. If steam is used there will be little danger of microbiological growth to give rise to problems of allergy (unless there is excessive condensation due to the amount of steam not being properly controlled). However, with humidification relying on reservoirs or sprays there will be warm wet conditions, which will inevitably encourage the growth of micro-organisms provided there are sufficient food sources available. These food sources may be unsuitable building materials, organic contamination from the environment or previous microbiological growth. It can be seen that once colonization of a system has begun it will be self-supporting until the conditions are changed or the system is cleaned. Since the object of humidification systems is to introduce the water into the building air, the addition of biocidal chemicals to that water is not recommended. These chemicals may produce their own problems of toxicity and sensitization of exposed people. Conversely, when building air is too warm, a chilling system may be incorporated into the ventilation arrangements. Cooling the air will reduce its moisture-holding capacity, and may result in water condensing onto the chiller elements. This condensate will be collected in drip-trays, which may also act as reservoirs of bacterial contamination if they are not adequately drained. The ideal approach for building managers may be summarized as:

9. The initial bag filters in the ventilation system should be well maintained. The filter room should be regularly inspected to ensure that it is clean.

10. Spray ponds have enormous potential for promoting microbiological growth. In a ventilation system, all surfaces which are in contact with water must be kept clean, and chemical treatments must not be added to spray ponds.

(a) Use steam humidification whenever possible.
(b) Where water reservoirs are used they should be kept clean and regularly flushed.
(c) All surfaces in contact with water in spray ponds should be kept clean, with particular attention paid to porous surfaces.
(d) Filters in the ventilation system should be maintained in good order to prevent organic contamination from the environment.
(e) Ventilation systems, humidifiers and chiller units should be regularly inspected and cleaned as necessary.

Notes

1. Guidance Notes on Monitoring and Controlling Microbial Growth in Recirculating Water Systems. Guidance Notes on Maintenance of Plumbing Systems, Microbiological Quality (TWA 2015). Thames Water Services, Water Quality Services, New River Head Laboratories, 177 Rosebery Avenue, London EC1R 4TP, UK.

Further Readings

Categorisation of Pathogens According to Hazard and Categories of Containment. London: HMSO Advisory Committee on Dangerous Pathogens.
Specification for Microbiological Safety Cabinets. British Standards Institution, BS5726:1979.

3.6 Physical Hazards in Workshops

Hani Raafat

Workshop Machinery Hazards[1]

A large proportion of accidents connected with workshop machinery can be prevented by the use of reasonably practicable precautions. Broadly, such preventable accidents are caused by a failure to identify potential hazards, inadequate physical or procedural safeguards, or the removal or misuse of the safety devices provided or the systems of work approved.

Legislation has accepted the premise that the design of totally hazard-free machinery is not practicable, and that rules should apply to the safeguarding of machines so as to minimize the risk of injury to machine users. In this way, the legal obligations have traditionally rested on employers—that is, the *users* of machinery—rather than the designers, producers and suppliers of machines and tools. The Factories Act, 1961 placed an absolute duty on employers to 'securely fence' all dangerous parts of machinery. The apparent stringency of this law has been whittled away by custom and practice, and by special regulations which exempt certain equipment, such as woodworking and milling machines and abrasive wheels, from the absolute duty to fence. To this extent the Health and Safety at Work Etc. Act 1974 is a significant departure from this tradition, as Section (6) requires 'any person who designs . . . any article for use at work to ensure, so far as is *reasonably practicable*, that the article is so designed as to be safe . . . when properly used'. The phrase 'reasonably practicable' is intended to ensure safety by balancing the risk of injury against the cost of removing potential hazards, thereby reducing that risk to an acceptable level.

Rational judgements about the acceptability of safety provisions for particular machines and processes can only be made when all the potential hazards have been identified, the likelihood of personnel exposure to these hazards has been assessed, and the extent of possible injuries estimated. Thus the long-term effectiveness of any safeguard depends intimately upon its detail design, and its compatibility with the operating procedures and function of the machine.

Identification of Machinery Hazards

The first point is to establish whether or not a machine is capable of causing injury. The best means of deciding which machinery parts are hazardous is to visualize the ways in which a person can be injured as a result of a sequence of events, and then to estimate the likely location and potential severity of the injury. This is helpful in the correct choice of safeguard. For example, it is essential to know the ways in which an abrasive wheel can cause harm in order to select relevant safety devices. The principal hazards involved in the operation of machinery can be divided into six categories:

1. *Impact.* This is the danger of a person being struck by a moving part of the machine or by its tools.
2. *Traps.* The limbs may be trapped between closing motions of machines, or between moving parts of the machine and fixed objects. In other cases, the trap occurs when the limbs are drawn between rotating components of a machine, e.g. gears, belt drives and chains.
3. *Contact.* Direct-contact injury can be caused by sharp or abrasive surfaces, or by energies (electrically live components can cause shock and hot surfaces can burn). This category includes contact with fast-moving saws and abrasive wheels.
4. *Entanglement.* These injuries involve the entanglement of loose clothes, hair, etc., in the rotary components of machinery, e.g. drills, lathes, milling machines.
5. *Ejection.* The previous categories are associated with hazards resulting from people reaching into danger areas of machines. In contrast, ejection involves hazards outside the machine components: a disintegrating abrasive wheel, or materials such as particles, swarf, chips, sparks or molten metal splash.
6. *Environmental hazards.* According to process applications, environmental conditions may present hazards including: dust; vapours and fumes; X-ray, laser, ultraviolet, ionizing and non-ionizing radiation; and flammable and explosive atmospheres.

Figure 1 illustrates some of the above hazards.

It is important to distinguish between hazards associated with normal operating conditions, where injury might result from human errors and the abuse of safe systems of work, and contingent hazards which follow directly from the failures of machine controls, components or safety devices. Safeguards must be selected to cope with both hazardous conditions.

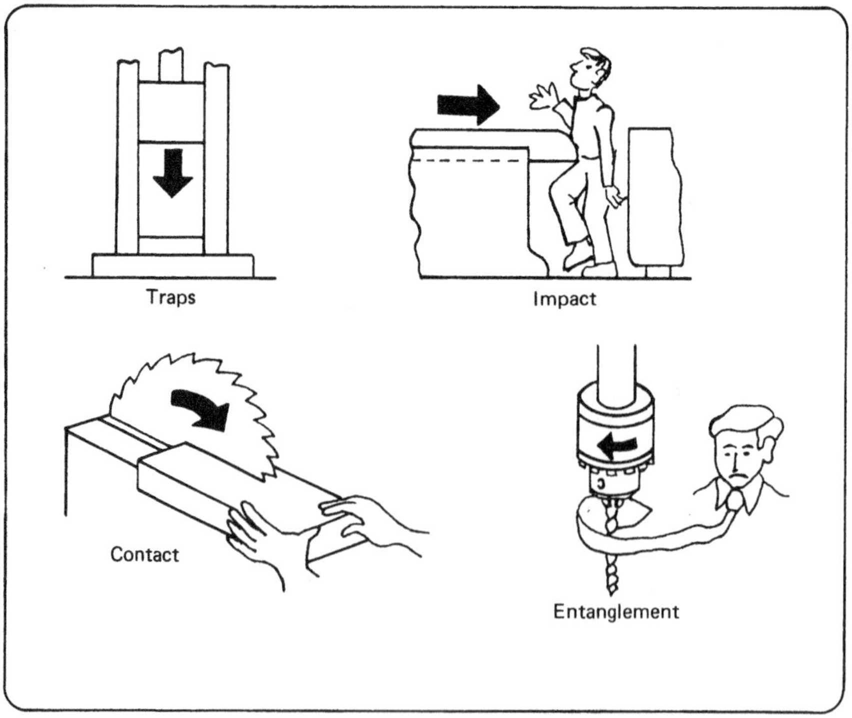

1. Machinery hazard identification.

Risk Assessment

Having identified all the steps involved in operating a particular piece of machinery, if its power, size and use suggest that risk of injury might result, then safeguards should be provided. Selection of the method of guarding and the need for safety devices and interlocking is then based on a risk assessment. The machine is considered in each of the different ways it can be operated—commissioning, normal operation, maintenance/repair, adjusting—and each mode is examined for normal and contingent hazards. Once the likelihood and consequences of these hazards have been assessed, appropriate safeguards can be applied. The factors in determining the risk include:

1. The frequency with which access to the danger area is required.
2. The likelihood and severity of injury should a safety device fail, taking into account: (a) the method of working; (b) the likely need for access; (c) the action of the parts safeguarded by an interlock that is used; and (d) the characteristics of the machine.

As an example of risk assessment, consider an unguarded grinding machine. Obviously such a machine must conform to The Abrasive Wheels Regulations 1970, which outline the legal requirements for protective measures against relevant hazards. The first step is to identify and examine all significant hazards at different stages of machine use, e.g. normal operation, inspection, turning and dressing, wheel balance and repair. Hazards associated with abrasive wheels are classified according to use as follows:

1. *Normal hazards,* associated with normal operating conditions, include:
   (a) entanglement in projected rotating parts of the machine;
   (b) direct contact with the abrasive surface of the wheel;
   (c) ejection of particles as a result of the grinding process;
   (d) trapping between the wheel and the work rest.
2. *Contingency hazards,* associated with process failures, include:
   (a) impact as a result of wheel breakages;
   (b) impact as a result of work breakages, or loss of grippage.

Some of the above hazards are illustrated in Figure 2, and having identified them, a full risk assessment is then conducted for each hazard, in order to rank them on a quantitative

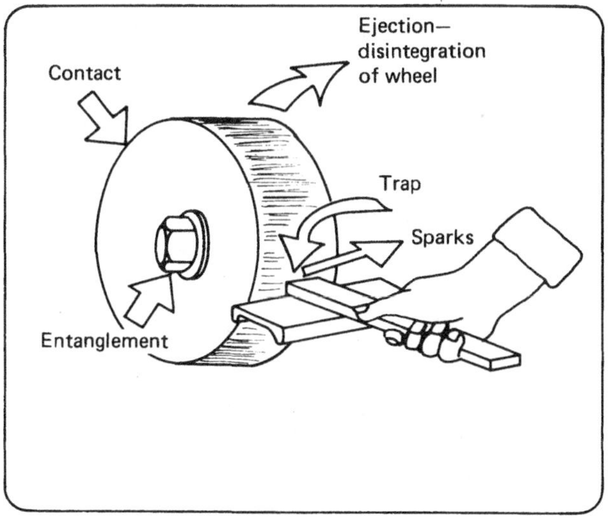

2. Hazards presented by abrasive wheels.

scale. This will provide a basis for priority in preventive measures, and a criterion for the acceptability of risk.

If, for example, as a result of hazard analysis, impact injury resulting from the wheel breaking during the calibration of speed were selected as a particularly serious hazard, risk assessment would be carried out as follows:

1. The likelihood or probability of the wheel breakage is calculated or estimated.
2. The frequency and duration of exposure to the impact hazard are estimated, e.g. how often is the wheel calibrated and how long does it take for each wheel?
3. The degree of resulting injury, e.g. fatal, loss of limb, hand, or finger, etc., is established.
4. The risk level is then calculated according to the equation:

$$\text{Risk} = \text{Probability of injury (per unit time)} \times \text{Degree of injury}$$

Risk is the expected injury loss per unit time, which is normally taken as one year.

In order to calculate the probability of injury as a result of the wheel breaking during calibration, it is necessary to calculate the probability of the wheel breaking (this may be obtained from historical data on similar wheels breaking), and the total man-hour exposure to this hazard during the wheel calibration. For example, if it were calculated that the probability of the wheel breaking was 0.001 per year, and the man-hours exposure during calibration was estimated to be 250 hours per year, then if the total operating time for the machine is 4000 hours per year:

$$\begin{aligned}\text{Probability of injury} &= \text{Probability of wheel breaking} \\ &\quad \times \text{Probability of operator exposed to hazard} \\ &= 0.001 \times 250/4000 \\ \text{Probability of injury} &= 0.001 \times 0.0625 \\ &= 0.004 \text{ per year}\end{aligned}$$

If the size of the wheel and its speed should suggest that the operator would be fatally injured as a result of the impact hazard, then;

$$\text{Risk} = 0.004 \times \text{fatal injury (per year)}$$

or it is expected that the operator would have a chance of a 4×10^{-3} per year of being killed as a result of the wheel breaking during calibration of the grinding machine. The risk function has to be minimized, whenever practicable, either by reducing the probability of a hazard occurring by providing safeguards, or by reducing personnel exposure to hazards.

The above criteria for risk assessment are proposed in the current review for the revision of the British Standard BS 5304:1975, for Safeguarding of Machinery.

Types of Safeguards

There are of course various safety features that can be built into the design of machines and equipment. However, it should be remembered that guards and safety devices are required only where the designer has failed to achieve 'intrinsic safety', that is, eliminating hazards at the design stage. The application of hazard analysis will identify those parts of the machine which will present an injury risk. As indicated earlier, when determining the type of safeguards to be adopted, consideration should be given to the need for access into hazardous areas, the frequency and duration of access, and the foreseeable risk and severity of injury. Methods of safeguarding may include fixed guards, interlocked guards, or trip devices.

Fixed Guards. A fixed guard should, when fitted to the machine, prevent all access to the hazard. However, the machine can still be operated when the guard is removed. Therefore, attention must be given to the method of fastening a fixed guard to the machine. Ideally a special tool should be required to remove the guard under supervision or a permit-to-work procedure. Furthermore, careful design of fixed guards is required to prevent traps being created between the guard and moving parts of the machine.

Interlocked Guards. Guards can be interlocked with the machine controls so that: (a) until the guard is closed, the machine cannot operate (except when access is required for maintenance and setting), and (b) either the guard remains locked closed, until dangerous movement of the machine has ceased, or, where overrun does not create hazard, opening the guard causes all movements to stop.

Interlocked guards can be hinged, sliding or removable. The crucial feature of the guard is the detail design of the interlocking mechanisms. The mechanism must be reliable, failure-to-danger modes must be identified and minimized in the events of all foreseeable machine failures, and the interlocking mechanism should be difficult to defeat or misuse.

The following example demonstrates the above considerations. Following a risk assessment, it was decided that the hypothetical machine shown in Figure 3 should have an interlocked guard to prevent the risk of injury as a result of access into the machine while in operation, as access is frequently required. The proposed design was to include a normally open electrical limit switch, as an interlocking element, connected in series with the machine power supply. By closing the guard, the limit switch is depressed, and the machine is ready to start operating. The proposed design for the interlocking arrangement is particularly unsatisfactory, for the following reasons:

1. The interlocking element (limit switch) can fail-to-danger as a result of spring failure or stem-bearing seizure.
2. The switch is easily defeated by simply depressing the stem by hand or using adhesive tape.

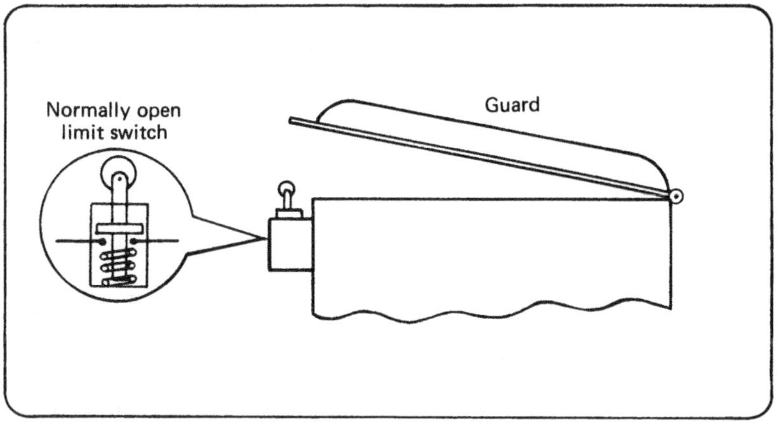

3. Normally open switch interlock.

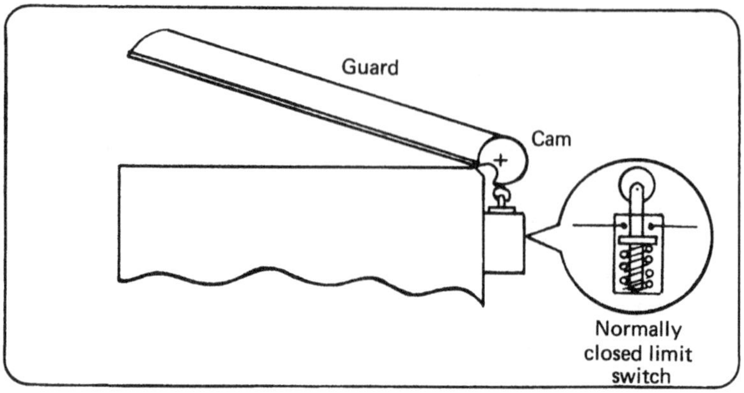

4. Normally closed switch interlock.

The normally closed limit switch is a more satisfactory arrangement as the switch cannot be readily defeated, as shown in Figure 4. The normally closed switch, however, can fail-to-danger as a result of wear on the cam or roller follower, overtravel, and lateral misalignment. Hence a system combining both types of limit switches is preferred.

Trip Devices. A trip device ensures that an approach beyond a safe limit (or, in some cases, the initiation of an entanglement) stops or reverses the machine movement, within a maximum prescribed time, usually 0.2 seconds. Trip devices include mechanical screens or barriers, which activate a switch upon trip, photo-electric (p–e) curtains, or pressure-sensitive mats. Trip devices differ from emergency stops in that they are activated by the involuntary action of the person at risk. The main problems associated with the use of trip devices are maladjustment of the device, or the machine's brake, or failure of these elements. The unproven reliability of some types of trip devices limit their use as secondary forms of guarding, or where limited access is required, e.g. for loading and unloading.

Machinery Safety Checklist

The following checklist may assist in deciding the appropriate form of guarding to prevent machinery accidents:

1. Can intrinsic safety be achieved? Mechanical hazards should be eliminated as far as possible at the design stage.
2. Reduce the need for approach. Review all causes for approach to dangerous parts of machines, and reduce them as far as possible.
3. Selection of guards and safety devices that:
   (a) should prevent all access to the hazard when fitted;
   (b) are difficult to defeat;
   (c) incorporate reliable components;
   (d) identify fail-to-danger modes of failures and minimize their effects;
   (e) can be easy to inspect;
   (f) are convenient for machine users.

The operating instructions for the machine should include details of maintenance requirements for all safety devices.

Bibliography (Machinery Safety)

Booth, R. T. (1975). Machinery Safeguarding, *Engineering*, December, 1979.
British Standards Institution, *Safeguarding of Machinery*, Code of Practice BS 5304: 1975.
Hale, A. R. and Hale, M. (1972). *Review of the Industrial Accident Research Literature*. HMSO, London, 1972.
Raafat, H. M. (1979). Basic Concepts of Hazards. *Occupational Health*, September.
Raafat, H. M. (1981). Fault-tree Accident Analysis. *Occupational Health*, August.
Safety and Health at Work (1972). Report of the Committee 1970–72, Chairman Lord Robens. HMSO, Cmnd. 5034, London.

Electrical Hazards

One of the greatest potential sources of accidents lies in electricity, by virtue of the fact that it cannot be seen, and its presence is not obvious. Although the output of electricity has been doubling every 10 years, the fatal accident rate as a result of shocks and burns remains remarkably steady, and has not risen with increased and widespread use. The types of hazard associated with electricity can be broadly classified into two categories:

1. health hazards, e.g. electric shock and burns;
2. secondary hazards, e.g. fires caused by electrical faults, and gas explosions due to sparking or, again, faulty equipment.

The primary legal requirements for electrical safety are governed, in the United Kingdom, by The Electricity Regulations (Factories Act), Special Regulations 1944. Other useful guides are produced by the Institution of Electrical Engineers, and relevant British Standards.

Causes of Electrical Hazards

Every electrical apparatus is designed to operate at a rated current, and if the current rises above this rated value, the apparatus and its supplying cables become overheated. The severity of that overheating depends on the amount and duration of the excess current. Even small excess currents for long or repeated periods will cause degradation of the installation of machines and cables, until a minor excess current could cause a major insulation breakdown or, indeed, fire. Excess current is mainly caused by:

1. mechanical overloading of machines;
2. electrical fault of line to earth, or line to line;
3. too low a rating of machine current and/or its cables.

Most British museum workshop machinery and tools are connected to 240 volt single-phase or 415 volt three-phase power supply systems, for which the following principles of protection apply.

Electrical Protective Devices

Electrical protective devices are used to protect machines and equipment from damage due to values of voltage or current exceeding design levels. They are also used to protect individuals from the risk of injury, by isolating electrical faults in part of the system. Electrical hazards associated with workshop machinery and tools may be caused by overload current, short-circuit current, or electric shocks to individuals arising from direct or indirect contact with live conductors. Overload current is an excessive current

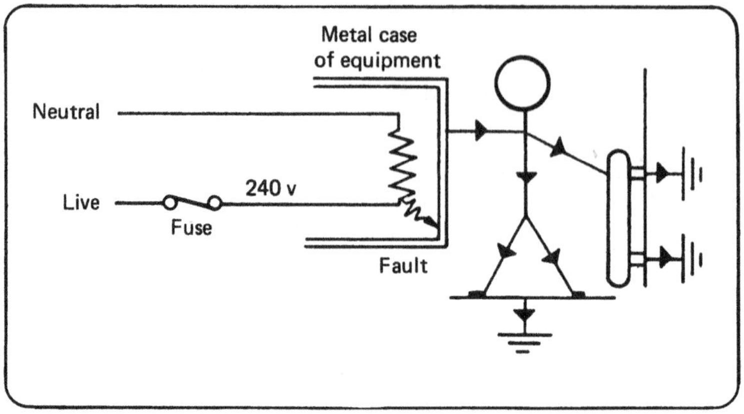

5. Electric shock sustained from direct contact.

flow in a circuit which exceeds maximum rated current. This occurs usually because too many pieces of equipment are connected to the circuit, or because a fault has developed in an individual piece of equipment. An overload condition can cause permanent damage to equipment and cables which could result in a fire. Short-circuit current is an excessive current flow in a circuit due to a direct contact made between any live conductor and a neutral conductor, or between conductors of different phases. Short-circuit currents can be very large, reaching several thousands of amperes. Electric shock as a result of indirect contact with live conductors is caused by equipment or circuit faults which result in parts of the electrical equipment becoming conductive, e.g. the metal casing of machines or portable tools. A voltage above earth potential is attained, and upon contact a person would receive an electric shock. An electric shock can also result from contact with live metalwork while a person is standing on concrete flooring, or by making simultaneous contact with two conductive parts, e.g. an unearthed radiator or faulty kettle, as illustrated in Figure 5.

Protection Against Overload Current. In order to protect against overload or excess current, the overloaded circuit, or part of the circuit, must be disconnected quickly. The most simple and common form of overload protection is the fuse. The fuse will offer close protection as it should melt within 4 hours if current of 1:5 times its rating flows (e.g. fuses to BS 88). The fuse should be located in the live side of the circuit only, and not in the earthed neutral side, because if the neutral fuse melts first, the apparatus will cease to operate and will appear 'dead', while in fact still being dangerously live. Circuit-breakers are also used for overload protection as an alternative to fuses. A circuit-breaker is an automatic switching device, which operates instantaneously when a significant overload current (typically 1.5 times rated current) is detected. Circuit-breakers are easily reset after a trip, but are more expensive than fuses.

Protection Against Short-circuit Current. A short circuit is a special case of excess current. However, a short-circuit failure differs from overload in that damage to the circuit and cables occurs very rapidly. Protective devices must therefore be able to respond quickly to these failures. As far as any type of fuse is concerned a short-circuit failure will cause it to operate more rapidly because of the increased thermal effect. Circuit-breakers, on the other hand, usually have a separate part of their operating characteristic which is specifically designed for short-circuit failures. A miniature circuit-breaker, incorporating a magnetic trip which responds directly to currents above a certain level, typically set at six times the rated current of the circuit-breaker, is integrated within the main circuit-breaker. The advantage of this arrangement is that trip occurs without delay once a certain current level is reached.

Protection Against Electric Shock. Fuses and circuit-breakers are overcurrent devices which offer protection to the circuit from the effects of overload current and short-circuit failures. They do not respond to earth fault currents below the rated current for which the device should trip. However, they play a secondary role in the protection against electric shock. The most effective method of protection against electric shock, as a result of indirect contact, is by earthing. This is achieved by connecting a protective conductor from the machine to the earthing point of an installation. In the case of machine faults that cause a live conductor to make contact with its earthed metallic parts, a very large current flows through the protective conductor. This results in the fuse or circuit-breaker rapidly disconnecting the circuit and isolating the faulty equipment. Earth fault currents arise as a result of:

(a) breakdown of isolation because of deterioration, physical damage, ingress of moisture or conductive deposits; or
(b) incorrect wiring of appliances or accessories.

The best form of protection against excess current due to earth fault is the earth-leakage circuit-breaker. This is a protective device designed to isolate the electrical supply when a fault on the circuit causes a current exceeding a preset level to leak to earth. A voltage-operated, earth-leakage circuit-breaker measures the voltage of the main earth terminal, i.e. apparatus casing, under earth fault conditions. When this reaches a maximum of 45 volts, the device trips and the circuit is made 'dead'. Earthing and earth-leakage circuit breakers will protect only against electric shock due to the indirect contact with faulty equipment.

Elecric shock as a result of direct contact, means that a person makes contact with part of the circuit which is intended to be live. The only form of protection against direct contact is to prevent such contact in the first place. This can be achieved by following the same principles of risk assessment and machinery safeguarding discussed earlier, namely to provide fixed guards, enclosures or insulation. However, if access is foreseeable, then permit-to-work systems should be operated. It should be remembered that intrinsic safety is an absolute priority in removing the risk of shock injury. This can be achieved by reducing the system voltage in areas of likely contact to such an extent that it cannot result in an electric shock.

In general terms, electrical protective devices in the United Kingdom must operate within a maximum prescribed time set by the Institution of Electrical Engineers Regulations. This is 5 seconds in the case of fixed equipment, and 0.4 seconds for portable tools when used inside a building.

Bibliography (Electrical Safety)

Electricity (Factories Act) Special Regulations, 1908 and 1944.
The Health and Safety at Work Etc Act, 1974.
Memorandum on The Electricity Regulations, SHW 928, HMSO, London.
Regulations for Electrical Equipment in Buildings, 14th ed., The Institution of Electrical Engineers, London.

Safety in Electrical Testing, SHW No. 31, HMSO, London.
Electrical Engineers' Reference Book, Newnes, London.

Notes

1. Hazard is defined as a physical situation with a potential for harm to life and limb; and is expressed as potential injury or fatality.

3.7 Use of Personal Safety Devices

IAN BARTLETT AND SHANE ROWLES

Personal protection[1] is required when a person cannot avoid the risk of being exposed to a contaminant which has the potential to cause harm. Since contaminants encompass physical hazards such as noise and radiation, and biological hazards such as micro-organisms, as well as the more familiar chemical hazards which include dust, solvent vapours and gases, the range of protective clothing and equipment available is extremely wide. Making the workplace safe has for long been considered preferable to relying upon personal protection, and indeed personal protection is often referred to as the 'last line of defence'. Thus, whenever possible, the preferred option is to engineer control of contaminants at source. Nevertheless, for a variety of reasons, personal protective clothing and equipment is widely used, and therefore it is essential to allocate both competent people and adequate resources to ensure that they are being used effectively.

Attention should be paid to both the quality of the personal protection available and any systems designed to underpin its use, i.e. personal protection schemes. All too often, unfortunately, personal protection is seen to be the low-cost option. Simply issuing a pair of gloves or a respirator, rather than installing air-handling equipment or ventilation, to protect staff may, in certain circumstances, be irresponsible. Besides any regulatory control of the process, this approach generally ignores the cost of cleaning, maintaining and repairing protective equipment and of training in its use. Wherever personal protective clothing or equipment is used, a comprehensive personal protection programme should be in force. In this chapter the elements vital to the success of personal protection programmes or schemes are discussed, as well as the use of particular types of protective equipment and clothing.

How is Protective Clothing and Equipment Chosen?

Personal protection is selected to provide a barrier between the user and a specific agent in the workplace that may cause harm. To assess its adequacy and to ensure that, in theory at least, it is capable of providing sufficient protection, it is necessary to obtain information about the nature and extent of the hazards likely to be present.

What Hazardous Agents Are Present?

Ideally, qualitative and quantitative information is required for each hazard present. For example, the sound level and frequency response of a source of noise needs to be assessed before the correct earmuffs or earplugs can be selected, whilst suitable gloves to protect against the degreasing action of a solvent cannot be chosen unless the chemical composition of the solvent is known. The chemical composition and concentration of airborne contaminants needs to be known before suitable respiratory protection can be selected. In addition, the work practices associated with the use of the agent need to be defined, so that the circumstances when personal protection is needed are clearly identified.

Information is required about the particular type of personal protective equipment or clothing to help in deciding whether it will reduce the hazardous agent to an acceptable level or eliminate it altogether. Such data are usually available from manufacturers or suppliers, and the information supplied will usually detail the results of tests performed under ideal, standardized conditions, such as those conforming to the relevant British or international standard for the particular type of protection required.

Is There an Acceptable Level for Exposure to a Harmful Agent?

For many agents there is no acceptable, safe level of exposure. For example, only *complete* protection of the eyes against acid splashes, or the skin from contact with caustic liquids, is tolerable. However, for many airborne contaminants, the occupational exposure limit (OEL) or some fraction of it is usually specified as the acceptable level.

Achieving the Necessary Degree of Protection

Once the required degree of protection is determined, it will not be achieved in practice unless:

1. the fit of the personal protection on the user is as good as the fit achieved during the original performance tests (it should be borne in mind, however, that British or international standard tests tend to be laboratory exercises, rather than field usage tests);
2. the equipment is adequately cleaned and maintained, and suitable facilities are available for storage, replacement and disposal;
3. those using the protective equipment or supervising its use receive adequate training;
4. the protection scheme is monitored; and
5. the effect on job performance is assessed.

The Fit of Protective Clothing and Equipment

Manufacturers' performance data are usually based upon the results of tests with relatively small samples of people, usually males, often of only one ethnic group, and invariably under laboratory conditions. It is therefore vital to check the fit of the protection when it is first issued to the user. Manufacturers usually do not produce the item required in a wide range of sizes, so it may be necessary to obtain a range of similar items from different suppliers, from which the best fit for the individual user can be selected. The user should then be trained to wear and operate the personal protection.

The calculated degree of protection will not be achieved in practice unless the protection is worn constantly during exposure to the hazard. It is important, therefore, that the equipment is compatible with the work in hand and with any other personal protection which has to be used concurrently. This requirement highlights the importance of comfort factors. Personal protection which affords a high degree of protection but which is uncomfortable to wear, and therefore removed frequently or dispensed with, provides less protection in practice than items which in theory are slightly less effective but which are more comfortable and therefore worn for a higher proportion of the time. If the user is involved in choosing the protection, he or she is far more likely to find wearing it acceptable.

Maintenance

Cleaning and maintenance are very important if a high degree of protection is to be maintained. Cleaning equipment should be the responsibility of the user; however, maintenance and inspection of equipment (apart from the user's own checks every time he or she wears it) is better left to the appointed, responsible person, as a lessening of the degree of protection can easily go unnoticed by the user.

Training

Users, supervisors and those responsible for maintenance have to be trained if the protection scheme is going to work. In developing a training programme, consideration should be given to the following:

(a) the nature of the hazardous agent and why protection is required, i.e. what happens if the person is directly exposed to it;
(b) the reasons why personal protection is the chosen option for contamination control, whether it is a stop-gap or the chosen long-term option;
(c) why the particular equipment was chosen;
(d) the equipment's capabilities, e.g. nominal protection factors for respirators (see later), and its limitations, e.g. so-called 'general-purpose' gloves which should be used only for dry materials;
(e) instruction and training in the use of the equipment, including 'classroom' and field training, which should encompass recognition of emergencies and how to cope with them;
(f) how to fit the equipment and how to clean it; when to have it replaced; where to store the equipment when it is not in use; and how to dispose of the equipment.

Inspection

As well as routine maintenance and checks, protective equipment should be monitored through spot checks, and procedures should be established for investigating the reasons why some people do not use the protection. Areas where personal protection is required should be identified with prominent signs in order to remind people entering that they must obtain the appropriate protective equipment; but care should also be taken in setting the limits of each area. Subjective impressions of where the risk lies in a certain area, and then creating a boundary to reflect that risk (bearing in mind the actual risk area), are often far more effective than making complete workshops into personal protection areas.

The Effect of Personal Protection on Work Performance

In many cases the use of personal protection makes a job more difficult to perform. Vision may be reduced by visors, the olfactory senses will be impaired by the use of respirators, and wearing gloves will reduce the sense of touch, but, as far as possible, equipment should be chosen to be compatible with the job. People soon become accustomed to wearing personal protection, and learn to make use of sensory information which is slightly modified by that equipment. Safety considerations stemming from the use of particular equipment should be considered during the initial selection.

Ongoing Personal Protection Schemes

Once a scheme is set up and operational, whoever manages the job for which personal protection is required should have established procedures for updating that protection to cope with changes to the process itself or to the materials used in it, reductions in the occupational exposure limit, any change of personnel, the availability of new systems of protection or the lack of availability of current types of protection. Written procedures concerning the scheme should be made available.

Respiratory Protective Equipment

Respiratory protective equipment (RPE) should be worn where there is an unavoidable risk of exposure to harmful airborne contamination, or a shortage of oxygen is likely to be encountered. Breathing apparatus fed with compressed air, or self-contained breathing apparatus (open and closed circuit) to BS 4667, must be used in oxygen-deficient atmospheres, though special training is required for their use. In certain circumstances RPE may be the preferred method of protection and it is commonly used:

(a) for infrequent work;
(b) for intermittent work of short duration with low-toxicity materials;
(c) for work with nuisance (non-toxic) materials;
(d) as an intermediate method of controlling exposure;
(e) where no other method of controlling the hazard is practicable, e.g. chemical vessel cleaning, asbestos removal.

In circumstances where respiratory protective equipment is used it is essential that appropriate equipment is selected, and a wide range is currently available in the United Kingdom. Selection of the most appropriate type of equipment for a given situation will require knowledge of:

(a) the contaminant;
(b) the concentration of the contaminant in the working atmosphere;
(c) the occupational exposure limit (OEL) for the contaminant;
(d) the work practices of the wearer.

The degree of protection required will be the factor by which it is necessary to reduce the airborne concentration of the contaminant in order to limit the exposure to below the occupational exposure limit. A fraction of the OEL, i.e. one-tenth, is usually chosen as a suitable level of protection. The degree of protection provided by a specified piece of RPE is given by a designated nominal protection factor (NPF), which is defined as the ratio of the concentration of contaminant present in the ambient atmosphere to the calculated concentration in the breathing zone when the RPE is being worn.

$$\text{NPF} = \frac{\text{ambient air concentration}}{\text{concentration in breathing zone}}$$

An NPF of 100 means that one-hundredth of the airborne concentration outside the RPE will be present in the breathing zone. The NPF is a measure of the 'total inward leakage' occurring through the filter, air-exchange valves and around the edges of the equipment. The most suitable type of RPE with a sufficient NPF should be selected to provide the required degree of protection for a given circumstance. The approximate NPF for a range of different RPE is given in Table 1.

Table 1. Approximate Nominal Protection Factors (NPF) for Various Types of Respiratory Protective Equipment (RPE)

Type of RPE	Applicable BS	NPF
Disposable filtering face-piece	BS6016	5–10
Half-mask (orinasal) for dusts	BS2091	7–10
High-efficiency full-face respirators	BS4555	900–1000
Cartridge-type gas respirators	BS2091	20
Canister-type gas respirators	BS2091	400
Positive-pressure-powered respirator (std efficiency) including half-masks, full face-masks, blouses and suits	BS4558/BS4771	20
Positive-pressure respirator (high efficiency):		
(a) half-masks	BS4558	20
(b) full face-masks	BS4558	2500
(c) hoods, blouses and suits	BS4771	20–2500
Ventilated helmets or visor	No current BS	10–100
Air-fed ventilated helmet	No current BS	500
Fresh-air hose breathing apparatus (without or without blower)	BS4667	2000
Compressed airline breathing apparatus	BS4667	1000–2000
Self-contained breathing apparatus (open and closed circuit)	BS4667	2000

Manufacturers of RPE normally indicate the NPF for their equipment. In the United Kingdom, the NPF is determined on the basis of British Standard Institution recommended test procedures. Estimated NPFs for a range of different equipment are given in BS4275 (1974). The Health and Safety Executive produces certificates of approval for RPE, breathing apparatus and canister gas respirators. These documents are updated annually and provide information on the degree of protection provided by specific manufacturers' equipment.

RPE may be divided broadly into two categories:

1. *Respirators.* These purify the air by drawing the air through a medium that removes the contaminants. Respirators can be used to provide protection against dusts (including mists and fumes), gases and vapours. Respirators should not be used in atmospheres immediately dangerous to life.
2. *Breathing apparatus.* These provide air from an uncontaminated source and are commonly used to provide protection against oxygen-deficient atmospheres, when high levels of very toxic materials are present in the atmosphere, or for escape purposes.

Respirators

A number of different types of respirator are currently available:

(a) The disposable filtering face-mask is designed to cover the nose and mouth and is made wholly from the filtering material. The masks should be worn only once, by a single person and for not longer than a single shift, prior to disposal. These masks are used normally for protection against low levels of contaminants of low toxicity. Nuisance-dust masks are similar in appearance but should be used only for comfort purposes to exclude large particles of non-toxic materials.

(b) Half-mask or orinasal respirators consist of a plastic or rubber mask designed to cover the nose and mouth. This type of mask may be used for protection against dusts, gases and vapours, depending upon the type of filter cartridge fitted. Pre-filters, capable of removing large dust particles, are commonly available for use with most models.

(c) High-efficiency dust respirators consist of a rubber or plastic full face-piece which covers the eyes, nose and mouth. This type of mask is suitable for dusts, gases and

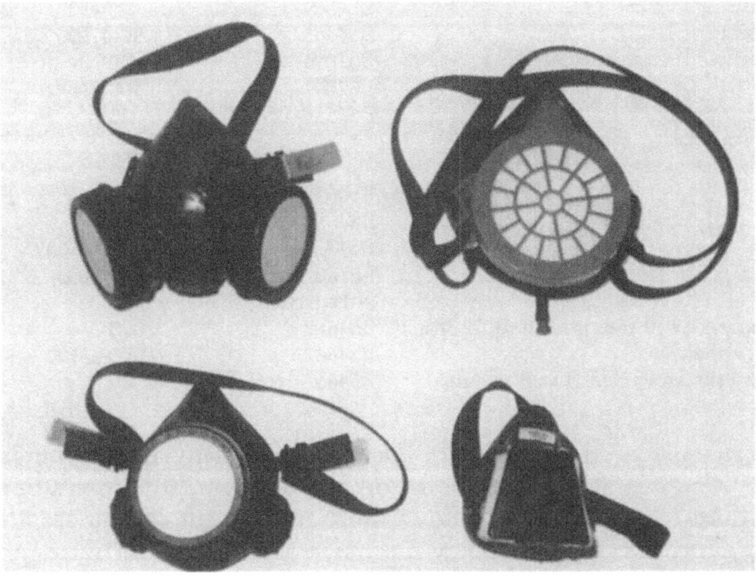

1. A selection of half-mask (orinasal) dust respirators (NPF = 10).

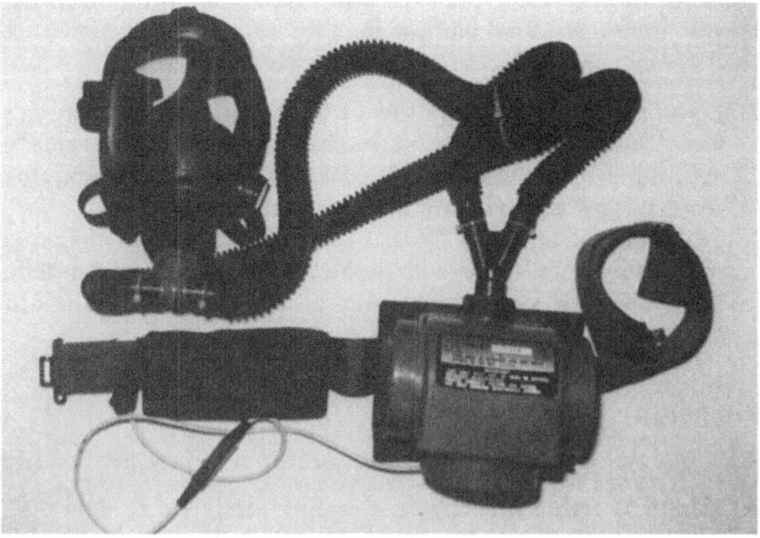

2. An example of a high-efficiency, positive-pressure, powered respirator.

vapours depending upon the type of replaceable cartridge or canister used. A list of cartridge and canister types for various gases (including duration times) is given in BS2091 and in the HSE certificate of approval for 'canister gas respirators'.

(d) Positive-pressure powered respirators are those in which air is drawn through a filtration medium by a battery-powered fan and supplied to the breathing zone. The powered filtration unit can be used to supply air into a half dust-mask, full face-piece, hood, blouse, half suit or full suit. The breathing zone is predominantly under 'positive pressure' and consequently any leakage of air is normally outward.

(e) Ventilated helmets and visors pass filtered air between the face and a visor. The fan and filters may be housed in a helmet or worn on a harness. Air-fed ventilated helmets are also available.

Breathing Apparatus

A few situations in museums require breathing apparatus, and there are basically three types of breathing apparatus in use:

(a) Fresh-air hose apparatus, in which air is drawn along a hose by the breathing action of the wearer.

(b) Compressed airline apparatus, where air is supplied to the breathing zone by a compressed-air line (filtered).

(c) Self-contained apparatus provides air from pressurized gas cylinders, normally carried on a harness.

RPE will provide full protection only if it fits the wearer snugly. At least three different manufacturers' products, in a range of sizes, should be made available to the workforce in order to accommodate most individuals. A simple test can be performed when a person is fitted with certain types of RPE incorporating face-pieces, which involves closing the inlet with a wet hand, inhaling gently so that the face-piece collapses, and then holding the breath for 10 seconds. The face-piece should remain in its slightly collapsed position. If not, it or the head-straps may need to be adjusted, but not to the

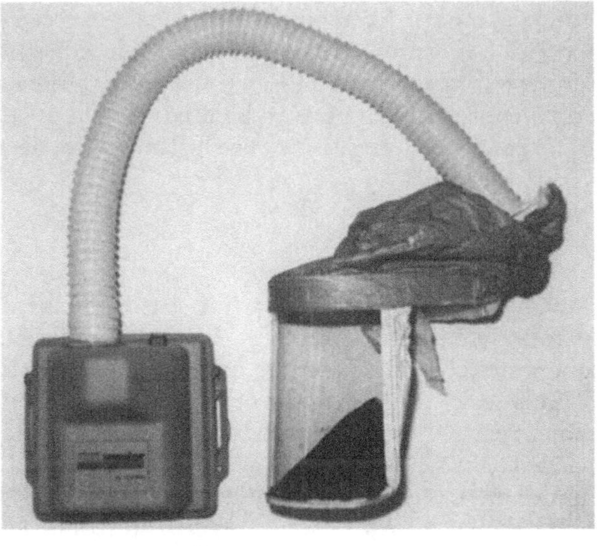

3. Ventilated visor (NPF = 20).

point of making the respirator uncomfortable to wear. This method also serves as a test for leaks caused by poor sealing of the exhalation valve or a badly fitting filter cartridge. This technique is not appropriate for ventilated visors, hoods, blouses or suits.

The required degree of protection will not be achieved unless the RPE is worn during the whole of the period of exposure. The wearer should be informed about the nature of the hazard and the reasons for using the RPE in order to encourage correct use of the equipment. If the RPE is uncomfortable, does not fit properly or greatly affects the work of the wearer, it is unlikely to be used correctly, and incorrect use will pose safety problems. The higher the NPF of the RPE, the more marked will be the reduction in the degree of protection provided by the RPE if it is not used effectively over the total exposure period. As stressed earlier, a comprehensive personal protection programme should be established for the use of all protective equipment to encompass:

(a) cleaning of the RPE;
(b) maintenance of the RPE;
(c) storage of the RPE when not in use;
(d) replacement of the RPE or disposable parts, i.e. the regular replacement of filter cartridges;
(e) decontamination of the RPE, where highly toxic materials have been used;
(f) supervision of personnel.

All users and supervisors must be given adequate training in the use of the equipment, including fitting the RPE, and instructed clearly as to the procedures specified in the protection programme. It is essential that all users and supervisors are aware when RPE is required, what type of RPE and filter system are suitable and the duration of exposure permissible for the work. Adequate facilities will be required to implement effectively every part of the programme, i.e. suitable cleaning materials, storage areas and so forth. If several persons need to wear RPE then a central system of cleaning, maintenance and storage may be advisable. In these circumstances one or two competent and trained persons should be given the responsibility for ensuring the integrity of the RPE.

Spectacles and beards reduce the effectiveness of certain types of RPE. Full face-pieces and half masks should not be used by persons with beards, and spectacles cause leakage around the sides of full face-pieces. Even one or two days' growth of stubble may lower substantially the degree of protection provided by face-piece respirators. Extremes of temperature may alter the effectiveness of RPE, e.g. freezing of the exhalation valve, and manufacturers should be consulted if RPE is to be used in such conditions. Intrinsically safe RPE must be used where explosive or inflammable atmospheres may be encountered.

Eye Protection

Eye protection is usually selected purely on the basis of the type of hazard or combination of hazards present in the workplace. A complete survey of the workplace is advisable in order to identify all work practices where there is a risk of eye injury. The Protection of Eyes Regulations, 1974 specify work practices for which eye protection is mandatory or recommended, and many conservation processes fall into this category. The HSE have produced certificates of approval (Parts One and Two) for the eye protectors required under these regulations. The certificates of approval are based on the current British Standards for various types of eye protectors. The British Standard BS2092 defines recommended tests to evaluate the effectiveness of eye protectors against

4. A protective visor, goggles and spectacles.

various hazards, namely: impact, flying particles (including molten metal), gases, dusts (including chemical dusts), and chemical splashes or droplets. It is advisable when selecting eye protection to refer to the manufacturers' data to ensure that the eye protectors provide adequate protection against the hazard and conform to the British Standard. Other British Standards specify the requirement for eye protection used for welding (BS1542), radiation (BS679) or for sunglare (BS2724).

There are three basic types of eye protection:

(a) Spectacles. These usually have side-shields and are commonly used for general-purpose protection against impact or low-velocity projectiles. Prescription lenses of hardened glass conforming to BS2092 may be used, and tinted protection lenses for specific ultraviolet or infrared hazards are available. Safety spectacles do not give adequate protection from chemical splashes or dust.
(b) Goggles. A wide range of cup- and box-type (wide vision) goggles are available. These are normally held in place by a head-strap and are obtainable with protected ventilation ports. Goggles may be used to provide protection against a wide variety of mechanical, chemical and radiation hazards.
(c) Face shields. These may be hand-held or attached to helmets, but more often they are fixed independently to a rigid headpiece. Face shields provide eye protection against most hazards except irritant dust, gases and vapours.

To be effective, eye protectors, like all protective equipment and clothing, must fit the wearer. Badly fitting eye protectors may result in discomfort, pressure sores, malalignment of the lenses, or a greatly reduced field of vision. As with other equipment, a range of different sizes should be available to the wearer, with a combination of different sizes of frames, side-arms and bridge fittings. Eye protectors should be included in the personal protection programme for the workplace. Facilities should be available for cleaning and storing the eye protectors, and procedures defined for maintenance and replacements. Supervision and training is an essential part of a protection programme. It should be remembered that eye protectors may interact with other forms of protective equipment, e.g. spectacle side-arms may reduce the effectiveness of hearing or respiratory protection. The major problems with eye protection are a reduction in the visual field, and misting of the lenses or face shield. These factors need to be considered in the initial selection of eye protectors.

Hearing Protection

Noise-induced hearing loss can result from exposure to elevated noise levels. The Code of Practice for Reducing the Exposure of Employed Persons to Noise, 1972 (Department of Employment) recommends that hearing protection should be worn when persons are unavoidably exposed to a sound level of 90dB(A) or more for 8 hours (Leq). This standard is likely to be reduced to 85dB(A) in the near future. The attenuation provided by hearing protection is dependent upon the frequencies of the noise conditions in which it is worn, and most hearing protection will reduce high-frequency noise to a greater extent than low-frequency noise. In order to select the most appropriate hearing protection, the noise levels need to be measured at specified octave band-centre frequencies and matched to the degree of attenuation provided by the hearing protectors at those frequencies.

In the United Kingdom, the attenuation provided by hearing protection is determined on the basis of British Standard BS5108 recommended tests, where the threshold of hearing is measured on subjects with and without hearing protectors being worn. If the hearing protectors are a poor fit or removed for even a short time, the degree of attenuation provided by the protectors will be markedly reduced. It is essential that the ear defenders fit the wearer to avoid discomfort or a reduction in effective attenuation. The specifications for the manufacture of hearing protection are given in BS6344.

A range of hearing protectors should be made available to the user, who should be trained in fitting the hearing protector and informed of the risks of noise-induced hearing loss. Supervision of the wearer is vital in ensuring that the hearing protector is worn for the whole duration of exposure. A comprehensive hearing-protection programme should include facilities for cleaning and storage of the hearing protectors and procedures for their maintenance and replacement. There are three types of hearing protectors:

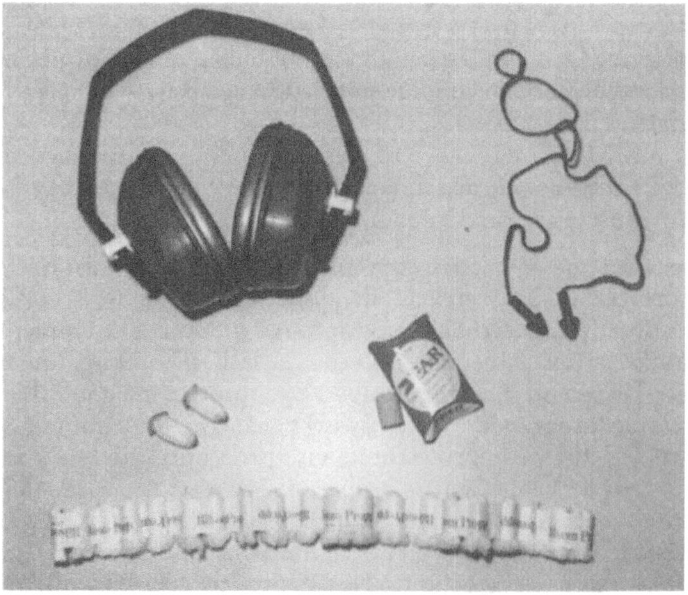

5. Earmuffs and earplugs.

(a) Earplugs are inserted into the ear canal, and may consist of waxed cotton or glass down, compressible foamed plastic, or premoulded plastic. Earplugs are usually disposable and dispensed from machines adjacent to the working area. Unhygienic use of earplugs by reuse or sharing can give rise to infection.
(b) Earmuffs fit over and enclose the ear, sealing against the side of the head. Some types seal against the ear itself. The ear cups are usually lined with absorbent material and fitted with soft sealing cushions or air seals. The earmuffs are normally held in place by an adjustable rigid headband designed to press the seals firmly against the head. In warm environments the seals may cause some discomfort, resulting in the earmuff being frequently removed.
(c) Helmets are made from specially shaped acoustic insulation material and are normally used in areas where very high noise levels exist.

Earmuffs require regular inspection and maintenance, and particular attention should be paid to the cushion or air seals, adjustable headband and internal lining of the cups. Exposure to excessive heat may distort the shape of the cups. Protective helmets or spectacles may alter the attenuation provided by the hearing protectors, and these factors should be considered in the initial selection of the hearing protectors. Speech understanding will usually be affected by the use of hearing protectors, although alternative modes of communication are often evolved by the wearers. Safety implications arising from the use of hearing protection will also need to be examined when developing a hearing protection programme.

Clothing

Body Protection

Various types of clothing may be required for protection against extremes of temperature, corrosive or dangerous chemicals, oils, molten metal splash or water penetration. Protective clothing is commonly made from PVC-coated fabrics, rubber,

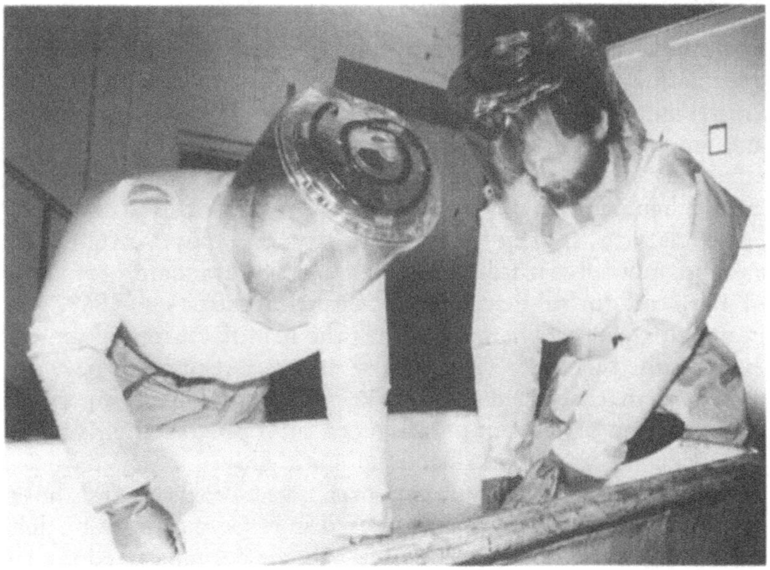

6. Fresh-air fed RPE comprising chemical-resistant blouse with integral hood for work with specimens in formalin.

synthetic materials such as nylon or terylene, cotton, wool or leather. Various garments are available, including coats, overalls, smocks, aprons, boilersuits, bib-and-brace overalls, leggings and full suits. The selection of the most appropriate material and garment design will depend upon the nature of the hazards and the work practice of the user (ideally, work practices should be designed to minimize reliance on protective clothing).

In varying circumstances consideration may need to be given to:

(a) the permeability of the material to specific chemicals or oils;
(b) requirements for welded seams;
(c) flame-proofing;
(d) air and water vapour permeability;
(e) anti-static materials;
(f) the visibility of the garment;
(g) wind and water penetration;
(h) the possible reduction in mobility of the wearer;
(i) the flexibility and robustness of the garment with regard to its crack, tear and abrasion resistance;
(j) the comfort of the clothing, particularly in regard to thermal comfort (air vents or loose-fitting garments facilitate heat loss from the body).

The different elements of the garment assembly may need to overlap each other, particularly if toxic chemical or dust hazards are present. Complete assemblies of the same manufacturer's clothing are normally preferable to purchasing individual items, which may be incompatible, from different suppliers.

Facilities for changing and washing the protective clothing should be available, bearing in mind that it may need to be washed prior to undressing if it has been contaminated with toxic materials. A wide range of British Standards (about 350) exist for textile and clothing manufacturers, and the British Standards Institution produces a list (SL33) stating the relevant standards for textiles and clothing.

Hand Protection

Hand protection may be required to prevent physical injury to the hands, skin diseases (dermatitis) or skin absorption of certain chemicals. The hazards may be a combination of irritant or corrosive chemicals, oils, abrasions, cuts, impact, heat or cold, radiation, molten metal splash or high-voltage electricity. Various materials are used in glove manufacture, including PVC, rubber, leather, chrome leather, cotton, felt, molecloth, or metal chainmail. A wide choice of gloves is normally available to provide protection from most hazards, but it is possible to have gloves tailored for a specific hazard or combination of hazards. There are British Standards for industrial glove maintenance (B1651) and for rubber gloves for electrical purposes (BS697). If gloves are to be used for protection against chemicals or oil the manufacturers' chemical resistance charts should be consulted in order to select the most appropriate type.

Gloves may be lined to improve comfort by absorbing sweat, whilst matt coatings to improve grip or prevent abrasion can be applied to their surfaces. Flame-proofed gloves are available, as are anti-bacterial static gloves which reduce the risk of dermatitis to sensitive skins. Gloves will, however, affect dexterity and the tactile senses of the hands, and these factors must be considered in respect of light or delicate work. All too often gloves are taken off, misplaced, or become contaminated internally and are then reused.

Instructions and training should be given to the wearer to prevent unhygienic use of the gloves, and as mentioned earlier in this chapter, gloves should be included in the personal protection programme.

Other Protective Equipment

Head Protection

In selecting head protection, the hazard(s) must be correctly identified. Head protection may be required against falling objects, impact, sideways crush, chemical splash, excessive heat or contact with hot surfaces. There may be a requirement also to protect the face and neck, as well as attachments for other forms of equipment, e.g. face shields. The compatibility of the head protector with other protective equipment, e.g. face mask, must be considered in the initial selection. There are basically two types of head protector:

(a) Helmets may have a peak at the front or a brim all the way around. The performance of helmets is based on mandatory British Standard tests (BS5240), and further optional tests may also be requested. Helmets are commonly constructed of aluminium alloy, laminated material such as glass fibre, or plastics, and selection of the type of material will depend upon projected use, e.g. some plastics may deform if subjected to excessive heat.
(b) Caps, in the form of scalp protectors or bump caps, are commonly used as protection against minor injury, such as abrasion or bruising, and they are particularly useful for work in confined spaces. Specifications for the manufacture of industrial scalp protectors are given in BS4033.

Foot Protection

Risk of injury to the foot and lower leg may arise from falling objects, slipping, impact, contact with hot surfaces, chemicals or oil, molten metal and from penetration by various means through the sole. Foot protection may be in the form of shoes, boots, wellingtons or thigh boots, and is usually available with metal toe-caps and insoles. During the selection of appropriate footwear, consideration should be given to the materials and construction of both the uppers and the soles, and the methods used for sole attachment, to ensure the footwear will tolerate the working conditions and provide sound footing. British Standards BS1870, BS933 and BS953 provide general specifications for the construction and testing of foot protection and internal or external steel caps. In certain circumstances, anti-static, conductive or electrically resistant foot protection will be necessary, and reference should be made to the manufacturers' data and the relevant British Standard.

Notes

1. Personal protection (UK) is synonymous with personal protection (USA). Some standards for personal safety equipment used in the United States are included in the bibliographical listings at the end of this volume.

Bibliography

British Standards Institution

BS679	Filters (eyepiece) for use during welding and similar industrial processes.
BS697	Specification for rubber gloves for electrical purposes.
BS953	Methods of test for safety and protective footwear.
BS1542	Equipment for eye, face and neck protection against radiation arising during welding and similar operations.
BS1651	Industrial gloves.
BS1870	Safety footwear.
BS2091	Respirators for protection against harmful dusts, vapours and gases.
BS2092	Industrial eye-protectors.
BS2724	Filters (eyepiece) for protection against intense sunglare.
BS4275	Recommendations for the selection, use and maintenance of respiratory protective equipment.
BS4033	Specification for industrial scalp protectors (light duty).
BS4555	High efficiency dust respirators.
BS4558	Positive pressured powdered dust respirators.
BS4667	Breathing apparatus.
BS4771	Positive pressure, powered dust hoods and blouses.
BS5108	Method of measurement of attenuation of hearing protectors at threshold.
BS5240	General purpose industrial safety helmets.
BS6016	Specification for filtering facepiece dust respirators.
BS6344	Industrial hearing protectors.

BS list SL33 gives the British Standards for Textile and Clothing Manufacture.

Health and Safety Executive (available from HMSO)

Certificate of Approval, breathing apparatus (F2501).
Certificate of Approval, canister gas respirators (F2502).
Certificate of Approval, respiratory protective equipment (F2486).
Codes of practice for reducing the exposure of employed persons to noise.
Environmental Hygiene 27, Acrylonitrile: personal protective equipment.
Environmental Hygiene 41, Respiratory protective equipment for use with asbestos.
Health and Safety at Work Series 18, Industrial Dermatitis: precautionary measures.
The Protection of Eyes Regulations 1974: Certificates of Approval No. 1 (F2457) and No. 2 (2489).

Books

Industrial Safety (Protective Equipment) Manufacturers' Association (ISPEMA), *Reference Book of Protective Equipment*, 69 Cannon Street, London EC4, UK.

Occupational Hygiene (Chapter 13), Waldren and Harrington, Blackwell Scientific Publications, Oxford, UK.

Section 4. Information Sources and Training in Safety

The provision of information on hazards, especially of the environmental type, has perhaps never been so topical a concern as it is today. Over the past decade, Flixborough, Seveso, Bhopal and Chernobyl have helped to polarize public opinion in questioning the quality of both official propaganda and the 'expert' advisory committees set up as public watchdogs. On a smaller scale, the provision of information on all types of occupational safety matters is no less fraught with problems. The sheer volume of the available literature, which includes legislation, guidance, codes of practice, standards and an ever-increasing number of computer databases, is daunting in the extreme. It has been suggested that in the United Kingdom alone more than 10 000 pages of health and safety legislation and guidance are published every year. In addition, manufacturers and suppliers produce hazard data sheets of varying quality. This information explosion in safety legislation and guidance during the past decade has resulted in the demise of the all-round safety adviser.

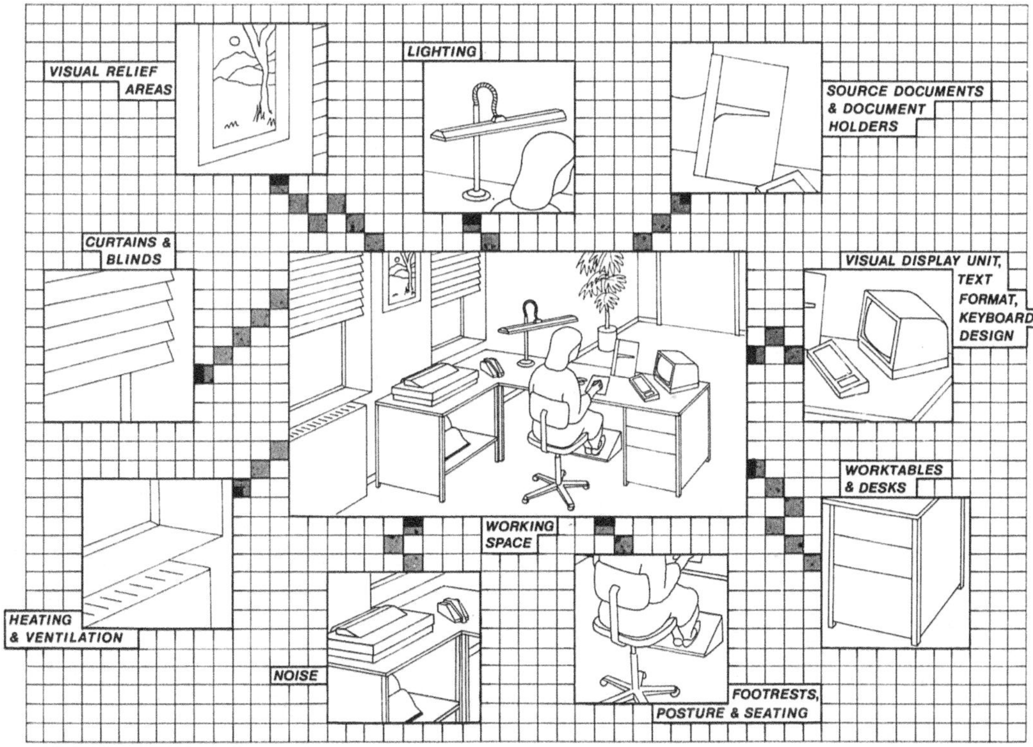

Workplace ergonomics applied to the office to reduce some of the hazards arising from the use of information technology equipment. (Copyright the Trustees of the British Museum, Natural History)

This section covers the following topics:

- Primary safety literature sources
- Safety journals
- Secondary sources of safety information
- Computerized safety information—HSELINE and PRESTEL
- Microfiche information

4.1 Access to Health and Safety Information for Museum Workers

Sheila Pantry

So much information is available today that the imperative becomes how to get the right information to the right person at the right time. What follows is a breakdown of printed and database information sources that should help users identify and select what they need from the plethora of mandatory and advisory material available.

Legislation

Obviously, one of the most important parts of occupational health, safety and hygiene information is the Health and Safety at Work Etc. Act 1974 and the 500 or so pieces of safety legislation. The HSE Library and Information Service (HSE/LIS) will supply copies, free of charge, of lists of all the Statutory Instruments both pre and post the Health and Safety at Work Act[1] (for HSE addresses). Butterworths have recently published a cumulative supplement to update *Redgrave's Health and Safety in Factories* by Ian Ffyfe and E. Anthony Machin. Codes of Practice are issued by the Health and Safety Commission, and the Codes of Practice of other organizations are also very important. The HSC Codes are mandatory and must be complied with, unless an equally safe procedure can be proved. A number of publications which will assist in understanding the implications of the law on health and safety at work are described in *Health and Safety: A Guide to Sources of Information.*[2]

Basic Literature

Any attempt to highlight basic texts in occupational health and hygiene is fraught with difficulties, but the following are known to be of use:

L. Bretherick, *Handbook of Reactive Chemical Hazards*, Butterworths, 1986.

N. I. Sax et al., *Dangerous Properties of Industrial Materials*, 6th ed., Van Nostrand Reinhold, 1984.

G. D. Clayton and F. E. Patty, *Industrial Hygiene and Toxicology*, Wiley. (Volumes 2a, 2b and 2c are especially useful on toxicology data.)

J. Doull et al., *Casarett and Doull's Toxicology: The Basic Sciences of Poison*, Macmillan, 1986.

Health and Safety Executive, *Occupational Exposure Limits EH40.* (Produced on an annual basis and updated by the Toxic Substances Bulletin twice per annum.)

There are many others listed in Pantry (1985).[2]

Journals

Many journals are published on health and safety at work. HSE/LIS maintains a list of journals which are scanned on a regular basis for items to be added to HSELINE. This list is available from HSE in the HSELINE users' guide.[3] Many new journals are being produced. These are indexed in HSELINE as and when they appear (details below). Other journals are listed in Pantry (1985).[2]

Standard Specifications

Standard specifications are absolutely vital to the work of the Health and Safety Executive. The British Standards Institution has produced a database which is available on Pergamon Infoline.[4] All British standard specifications are listed within BSI Standardline, and a list of published British Standards is available from the BSI.

Secondary Sources

Abstracting services and bulletins are a very good way of keeping up to date with information if subscribing to a host of journals is not practical.

Safety and Health Bulletin: ILO/CIS Bulletin. Issued by the International Labour Office, Geneva, 7 or 8 times per year, each issue contains an abstract and a full reference for each document covered, and a detailed subject index. This journal is available on subscription, and as a database, CISDOC.[5] The Health and Safety Executive Library and Information Service at Sheffield is the UK National Centre for the ILO/CIS.

Chemical Hazards in Industry. Published monthly by the Royal Society of Chemistry,[6] the bulletin gives information on the hazards caused by chemicals likely to be encountered in the chemical and allied industries, and how they might adversely affect health and safety.

Excerpta Medica (Occupational Health and Industrial Medicine Section 35).[7] Published by Elsevier, this has worldwide coverage of all aspects of occupational health and industrial medicine, and is available online as EMBASE.

Laboratory Hazards Bulletin. Another Royal Society of Chemistry publication, this bulletin gives information from the literature on hazards likely to be encountered by chemical and biochemical laboratory research workers which might adversely affect the health and safety of such personnel.

Ergonomics Abstracts. Produced by the Ergonomic Information Centre Department of Engineering Production, University of Birmingham, this has very informative abstracts on all aspects of work and working conditions.

Computerized Information

There are over 3000 readily available databases in the world today, all of which can be accessed very quickly. Some large museum libraries, university libraries and local government information units, or even the local public library, will have access to all these databases, some of which are listed here:

BIOSIS, which covers all aspects of biological sciences, includes chemistry and medicine
CANCERLIT, CANCERPROJ and CANCERPROT are databases giving information on cancer and related topics
CHEMICAL ABSTRACTS has an extremely wide subject area, covering all aspects of biochemistry, chemistry, chemical engineering and toxicology
CISDOC covers occupational hygiene, medicine, physiology, industrial toxicology and accident prevention
EMBASE (*Excerpta Medica*) gives worldwide coverage of medical and pharmacological areas, including drugs and chemical compounds; useful for searching for specific toxic effects
HSELINE deals with all aspects of occupational health, hygiene and medicine
MEDICAL RESEARCH DIRECTORY records all current and recent medical and nursing research being conducted in the UK
MEDLINE/MEDLARS offers biomedical information, including public health
OCCUPATIONAL SAFETY AND HEALTH (NIOSH) deals with all aspects of occupational health
RTECS covers the toxic effects of chemical substances
TOXLINE deals with toxicology, chemical analysis of toxic substances, chemical hazards, mutagenicity and teratology

For further information see Pantry (1985).[2]

Links with Other Organizations

The Health and Safety Executive Library and Information Service links up in the United Kingdom and internationally with organizations who are concerned with health and safety information. Amongst those contacted on a regular basis are the Royal Society for the Prevention of Accidents, the National Radiological Protection Board, various unions and the Royal College of Nursing in the UK; and the National Institute of Occupational Safety and Health, the Environmental Protection Agency and the Occupational Safety and Health Administration in the USA. Links are also maintained with other occupational health and safety institutions and governmental organizations in the following countries: Sweden, Finland, Denmark, the Netherlands, France, Germany, Switzerland, Australia, Canada, New Zealand, etc. HSE/LIS maintains a list of organizations concerned with occupational health and safety.

Microfiche Information

The Barbour Health and Safety Library[8] provides vital reference information for occupational health and safety information-seekers. The library is reproduced on microfiche and contains the full text of publications ranging from legislation to standards and codes, advisory leaflets and data sheets. Another useful service is the catalogue of British Official Publications not published by HMSO, produced by Chadwyck Healey.[9] This catalogue covers the publications of over 400 organizations financed or controlled, completely or partially, by the British government.

Keeping Up to Date

Many individuals and organizations experience difficulty in keeping up to date with the publications of the Health and Safety Commission and the Executive. The *Health and Safety Commission Newsletter* is produced 6 times a year and contains information on legislation, publications, films and other new initiatives. The Health and Safety Commission and Executive Press Releases are available as a 'news bulletin service'[10] and this is dispatched on a weekly basis. All information coming through from the Executive and Commission is usually picked up by the trade and technical press. Documents which are published through HMSO are listed in the HMSO Daily List and on HMSO Prestel. All HSC/HSE publications are listed in *Publications in Series,* published twice per annum, free of charge, from HSE/LIS. Additionally, there are a number of catalogues—agriculture, asbestos, chemicals, construction, medical and hygiene—all available from the Public Enquiry Points.

Prestel

HSE Library and Information Service has an extensive programme on Prestel. Currently it has 1200 frames of information which are changed daily, giving new publications, initiatives, new legislation, hazards information and news releases, as well as keeping hard facts, such as names, addresses and telephone numbers of area offices. The HSE/LIS is rapidly developing this service. There is a Diary of Events giving courses, UK national conferences, overseas conferences and exhibitions. Also there is full text of some of the most frequently requested free leaflets. In addition, there is a facility to order free leaflets and press releases. HSE's Prestel service links into the HMSO Prestel service, enabling the user to order direct—a very useful, quick way of receiving information from HMSO. There is also a 'Talkback' facility where the Prestel user can send messages to HSE/LIS. A brochure describing Prestel is available from HSE/LIS's Public Enquiry Points.[1]

HSELINE

HSELINE is HSE's publicly available database which was started in 1977. The information is gathered within HSE for the use of inspectors, doctors, scientists and engineers, with the objective of making it publicly available. This was achieved in 1981. It is now available on three host services, the European Space Agency Information Retrieval Service operating through the Department of Trade and Industry,[11] and also on Pergamon Infoline,[4] and Datastat.[12] Anyone looking for medical or chemical information would find HSELINE extremely useful. Items from over 250 journals are regularly scanned. In addition, references to books, reports, legislation, codes of practice and standard specifications are inputted, with 12 500 references added per year and a monthly update on HSELINE. Two examples of references are given below:

> 4179 714
> MUSEUMS : OCCUPATIONAL HAZARDS.
> Hatton, A.
> Safety Practitioner. Apr.1986, vol.4, no.4,
> 5-9.
> Examines: health and safety in museums as a management function; health and safety risks in the natural sciences; chemicals used in conservation; obtaining, cleaning and repairing specimens; security; design of buildings and exhibitions.

A180 754
MOULD EXPOSURE IN MUSEUM PERSONNEL.
Kolmodin-Hedman, B. Blomquist, G. and others.
International Archives of Occupational and Environmental Health. 1986, vol.57, no.4,
321-323.
In the basement archives of a local arts and crafts museum where the books and bookkeeping registers were handled, a woman on the museum staff had had ten attacks of fever, chill, nausea and cough during one year. The symptoms appeared at the end of the working day and disappeared after one to three days at home. No symptoms could be detected during the summer holidays. The books stored in the basement archives had earlier been stored in a small house with a leaky roof, which had led to the growth of mould on the books. When the books were handled at the museum, they were still covered with mould.

Each reference is indexed so that retrieval can be by title of the article or publication; by authors, both personal and corporate; and by journal title. Publisher, data publication and pagination are also given. Where the title is inadequate, extra keywords are added to describe the document more fully. All journal articles have an abstract of up to 100 words. One of the advantages of using computerized information services is that, for an individual with a particular subject interest, a 'profile' or key words can be logged into the computer, and regular access to the relevant database, using these keywords or profile, will produce a printout of any new items on that particular subject. This saves much research time and effort.[13]

International Labour Office—Occupational Safety and Health Information Centres (ILO/CIS)

The headquarters of the HSE Library and Information Service in Sheffield acts as the UK national centre for the ILO Health and Safety Service. Through the CIS, HSE enjoys links with 50 national centres in other countries. The ILO/CIS publishes their *Safety and Health Bulletin* and also various bibliographies which are available to subscribers. CIS also has a database CISDOC which is available on the European Space Agency Information Retrieval service in Italy (and available in the UK via the Department of Trade and Industry)[11] and also Telesysteme Questel in France. Anyone accessing ESA/IRS will be able to move quickly from one database, such as HSELINE, to another, such as CISDOC. The latter is a very good source for standards and legislation produced by other countries. There is a descriptive brochure, a sample of CIS abstracts and a list of publications on occupational health and safety produced by ILO available from any of the Enquiry Points above.

Notes

1. Health and Safety Executive Library and Information Services (HSE/LIS), UK Public Enquiry Points:
   Broad Lane, Sheffield S3 7HQ. Tel: (0742) 752539.
   Baynards House, 1 Chepstow Place, London W2 4TF. Tel: (01) 221 0870.
   St Hugh's House, Stanley Precinct, Bootle, Merseyside L20 3QY. Tel: (051) 951 4381.

2. S. Pantry, *Health and Safety: A Guide to Sources of Information,* CPI Information Review no. 6, 2nd fully revised and updated edition, 1985, £10.00, ISBN 0 906011 29 9. Capital Planning Information, The Grey House, Broad Street, Stamford, Lincs PE9 1PR, UK.
3. *HSELINE User Guide,* Health and Safety Executive Library and Information Services (free).
4. Pergamon Infoline, 12 Vandy Street, London EC2A 2DE, UK. Tel: (01) 377 4650.
5. CISDOC; Further information from HSE/LIS.
6. The Royal Society of Chemistry, The University, Nottingham NG7 2RD, UK.
7. *Excerpta Medica,* PO Box 1211, 1000 AE Amsterdam, The Netherlands.
8. Barbour Index Limited, New Lodge, Drift Road, Windsor, Berks SL4 4RQ, UK.
9. Chadwyck Healey Limited, 20 Newmarket Road, Cambridge CB5 8DT, UK.
10. HSE News Bulletin Service (£50 per annum subscription, cash with order). Order from: Health and Safety Executive, Sales Point, St Hugh's House, Stanley Precinct, Trinity Road, Bootle, Merseyside, UK.
11. IRS DIALTECH, Department of Trade and Industry, Room 392, Ashdown House, 123 Victoria Street, London SW1E 6RB, UK. Tel: (01) 212 5638.
12. Datastar, D-S Marketing Ltd, Plaza Suite, 114 Jermyn Street, London SW1Y 6HJ, UK. Tel: (01) 930 5503.
13. Since this paper was presented, HSELINE and CISDOC are now available on compact disc read only memory (CDROM). For information about this exciting new and easy way of accessing data from an IBM personal computer with a CD scanner, contact the HSE Enquiry Point at Sheffield.

4.2 Most Safe Places

G. F. Chapman

Since the Health and Safety at Work Etc. Act 1974 we have been subjected to an information explosion on all aspects of health, safety and welfare. Statutory requirements, new codes of practice and advisory notes seem to be a daily occurrence. Under the same Act we are also required to keep abreast of current developments and not be too slow in applying them. The result is that we are in danger of being overwhelmed by the information. From time to time it is perhaps prudent to stand back and assess the situation; to ask the question 'Is the work that we are doing actually reducing accidents and ill health at work?'

The information explosion does not appear to have made the impact on the accident statistics that one would have expected, perhaps because much of this information and legislation has been directed at areas where there is a high potential for danger but little accident experience, or where the media have raised issues they claim to be 'of public concern'. However, there has been a reduction in fatal and serious injury accidents during the past 10 years, but this reduction has been in the 'ordinary' industrial-type accidents and not the 'high tech' high-profile industries which have featured so prominently in the information explosion. There are many accidents which can be prevented if we look again at where accidents are occurring. The majority of fatal and injury accidents stem from the same causative factors that prevailed in our fathers' day, and probably in their fathers' day. Use of the mnemonic 'MOST SAFE PLACES' can assist in highlighting those areas of potential hazard by identifying the unsafe place or unsafe act.

Machinery	Structure	Pressure Vessels
Openings	Attire	Ladders
Stacks	Fire	Atmosphere
Tools	Electricity	Cranes
		Explosives
		Signs

M: *Machinery.* 15 per cent of industrial injuries involve machinery. Some hazards like gears, rotating shafts and spindles with projecting keys, intakes between vee-belts and pulleys, or chains over sprockets, are easy to recognize. Others are not so obvious, such as parts which are dangerous only during maintenance, cleaning, repairing and testing.

O: *Openings.* In many industries people may have to enter tanks, vessels or other confined spaces where there may be dangerous fumes or lack of oxygen. Others may be working in excavations, tunnels or coffer dams, each with a high risk potential. The other major hazard, more relevant to museums, is falling through unguarded openings in floors.

S: *Stacks.* Improved materials handling techniques and the rising cost of space means that more things are being stacked on top of each other than ever before. Falls of material account for a high proportion of severe industrial accidents and an increasing number of injury and damage accidents at all places of work.

T: *Tools.* Hand tools are widely used and account for about 7 per cent of notifiable accidents. Very few are fatal, but in many cases the accidents are disabling and may result in permanent damage to the person involved. Hammers, chisels, knives, screwdrivers, scalpels, etc., are common causes of injury. Inspection of toolkits should be high on the list of priorities when visiting workplaces.

S: *Structures.* The working environment is covered in this section, which spans painting and repainting, washing down of walls and windows, good housekeeping, and cleaning of toilet and cloakroom facilities.

A: *Attire* (or protective clothing or equipment). Many organizations adopt the 'Safe Person Strategy', believing it to be less costly than the 'Safe Place Strategy'. They fail to appreciate that protective clothing does not prevent accidents. At best it can reduce the amount of damage or injury sustained, and then only if it was being worn at the time. Consequently this is often one of management's biggest problems—ensuring equipment provided is being worn.

F: *Fire.* Fire is the greatest single cause of loss in industry. It can kill, maim and, in the case of small organizations, put them out of business. Alarms, drills, extinguishers and good housekeeping can reduce the number of incidents and the magnitude of the fire. However, management and employees all too often fail to appreciate the speed at which a spark can become a conflagration.

E: *Electricity.* Few businesses could survive without electricity. It supplies heating, lighting and ventilation, and it provides power for machinery. It is an essential element in the communications network, but it kills. One in three electrical injuries results in death, but trained and competent personnel, and proper maintenance plus the correct selection and use of equipment, can tame the deadly potential to within acceptable limits.

P: *Pressure Vessels.* Boilers, steam receivers, air receivers, compressors, compressed gas cylinders and bottles are all bombs waiting to explode. Selection, use, maintenance, storage, training, competent persons and adequate supervision are all essential to maintaining a safe place of work.

L: *Ladders.* Ladders, steps, scaffolding and other means of access are widely used in industry and commerce. Working from ladders and temporary scaffolding accounts for some 10 per cent of industrial and construction accidents, many of them fatal. Poor equipment, badly maintained, erected and used by untrained personnel, with insufficient supervision, are the main causes of falls.

A: *Atmosphere.* Health is becoming a major issue today. Substances which a few years ago were considered safe are now banned in the United Kingdom because of their potential to cause death and ill-health. Many of these substances are still with us, including asbestos, for example. An awareness of the potential is required if the harm from these substances is to be contained. Training, competent persons, supervision, safe practices in the use and disposal of waste are all essential items in setting up a safe place and safe systems strategy.

C: *Cranes.* Cranes, ropes, slings, chains and all types of lifting tackle are used by museums as well as industry and commerce. There are legal requirements for having identification marks, safe working load, etc., marked on equipment. Equipment has to be examined by competent persons at the intervals of time fixed by statute. In spite of this, overturned cranes and failures of equipment when in use continue to make headlines in the press.

E: *Explosives.* Many of the substances used in museums and in industry have the potential to explode when meeting a source of ignition. Most dusts will explode if finely divided. Liquid propane gas containers, 'empty' drums, and tanks which once contained flammable substances, may detonate during maintenance or repair. We need to examine safe procedures.

S: *Signs.* In the cosmopolitan business world, we use articles and substances from many countries, and the information and instructions may be in many languages. To overcome the interpretation problem, much wider use is being made of pictograms to convey to the user the way in which the product should be used or stored. The Hazchem code is widely used by the petrochemical industry and emergency services. There are indications, however, that the message is still not always understood by the user.

These categories can do no more than touch on the potential hazards that abound in museums, as well as in industry and commerce. They may, however, form the basis of a more sophisticated audit checklist.[1]

Note

1. A model safety checklist appears in the appendices to this volume.

Appendix 1. Safety Checklists for Use in Museums and Galleries

The following lists are intended as general guidelines only. They may not apply in their entirety to your establishment; on the other hand, additional items may be required.

Two checklists are given. The first comprises a safety policy checklist covering the policy statement, and the organization and arrangements for applying the policy in the museum situation. The second is a safety audit checklist. A safety audit is a sophisticated form of hazard spotting and may be found useful in formulating an approach to the regular safety 'self-inspection' procedures required under the HASAWA and OSHA regulations.

1. Safety Policy Checklist

Statement of Policy Intent

— Is a clear commitment to safety given?
— Is the level of signatory or authorization at the highest level?
— Does the policy identify *all* the persons to be protected (including public visitors to galleries, etc.)?
— How often and by whom is the policy reviewed (not just the written statement of policy)?
— Are staff/unions consulted on preparation and review of policy?

Organization for Safety

The policy should clearly identify the need for the following items:
(a) final responsibility in all safety matters to be at highest possible level of management;
(b) delegation of duties to be hierarchical; responsibilities to be clearly identified as line management duties;
(c) professional and specialist advisers to be identified;
(d) the role of specialists to be clearly identified;
(e) means of liaising with contractors, etc., to be effective;
(f) adequate arrangements for consultation with workforce through safety committees and safety representatives;
(g) adequate arrangements for the safety of visitors to galleries, etc.

Arrangements

Does the policy identify and refer to measures for the control of hazards in the following:
— layout, structure and use of storerooms, workshops, laboratories, offices, passages and galleries;
— operations carried out in the above areas;
— articles and substances used;
— environmental consideration for staff and visitors;
— systems of work;
— disposal of waste;
— production of exhibits;

— supply of sale items;
— services to outside organizations and individuals.

Does the policy identify the need for:
— regular workplace inspections;
— accident and incident investigation;
— occupational health cover including first aid arrangements for workforce;
— safety training at all levels;
— fire safety requirements;
— contingency arrangements (bomb, flood, etc.);
— monitoring known and suspected hazardous procedures;
— liaison with regulatory bodies (HSE, OSHA);
— safe systems of work;
— occupational hygiene monitoring;
— adequate communication;
— keeping statutory records;
— safety in fieldwork activities.

2. Safety Audit Checklist

General

— Is the safety policy appropriate and up to date?
— Are all staff and visitors, as necessary, aware of the policy contents?
— Are safety officers, advisers and representatives, first-aiders, medical staff, etc., named?
— Is there a central noticeboard for safety information?
— Are up-to-date evacuation notices displayed adequately?

Fire Safety

— Has a fire certificate been issued for the museum or gallery?
— Are the means of escape adequate, clearly signed and free of obstruction?
— Are all flammable materials correctly stored?
— Is an adequate fire-alarm system installed (i.e. can it be heard in workshops, etc.)?
— Are fire evacuation drills held regularly?
— Are all fire-extinguishers of the correct type and located where needed?

First Aid

— Are up-to-date first aid stocks available?
— Are first aid arrangements adequate (i.e. a trained first-aider is required when 150 or more work on one museum site)?
— Is an accessible accident book provided?
— Is an accident and near-miss recording system in operation?
— Are special first aid facilities provided in areas where acids, etc., are used (e.g. eye-wash, poison antidotes and instructions)?

Welfare and Working Conditions

— Are facilities for eating and drinking provided away from areas where hazardous substances are used?
— Are washing and sanitary facilities adequate?
— Are floors, stairs, passageways and doorways clear of obstruction and properly maintained?

— Is ventilation (window or mechanical) sufficient to keep the air odour-free?
— Are the air-change rates adequate for the purpose of the room (e.g. laboratories 6–12 air changes per hour, darkrooms 8–12, etc.)
— Is the working temperature at or above 16°C within an hour of starting work?
— Is lighting adequate for the type of work carried out (e.g. studio or lab work 750–1000 Lux, general work 500 Lux, storerooms 100–250 Lux, passageways min. 50 Lux)?
— Is emergency lighting (where provided) adequate?
— Are properly designed seats and tables provided for work in hand (e.g. adjustable workstations for VDU operation)?

Laboratory, Studio and Workshop Areas

— Are benches of correct height, width and spaced adequately?
— Are services (gas, electricity, compressed air, etc.) adequate and safe in use?
— Are solid toxic chemicals stored adequately and securely?
— Are corrosives and inflammable solvents stored in permissible quantities, in adequate containers at low level (i.e. not at or above chest level)?
— Are fumecupboards and ventilation systems suitable for work in hand?
— Are machines guarded where necessary (e.g. bench grinding wheels, bench drills, etc.)?
— Is equipment checked regularly for hazards (e.g. electrical safety checks, gas cylinder fittings and pressure/vacuum vessels for leakage or fault, tools for defects, etc.)?
— Is X-ray equipment properly interlocked, and are staff monitored where necessary?
— Is personal safety equipment properly stored and maintained?

Storage Areas

— Are cupboards properly constructed for intended use?
— Are correct floor-loading levels adhered to?
— Are passage-ways kept clear?
— Are heavy objects stored at or below chest level?
— Is lifting equipment (where provided) adequately maintained, inspected and marked with safe working load?

This audit checklist should be considered as guidance only for the preparation of suitable checklists for application in your museum or gallery. Safety audits are usually evaluated by using a system of 'points scoring'. Answers to questions are assessed by the person making the report and compared to a known or reasonable standard. For example, responses to the first question, 'Is the safety policy appropriate and up to date?', could be:

No policy exists	Poor response	Score 0
No written policy	Fair response	Score 5
Policy written, but not up to date	Good response	Score 15
Up-to-date policy Known to all staff	Excellent response	Score 20

For a full description of the use and applications of safety audits, see: H. W. Heinrich, D. Peterson and N. Roos, *Industrial Accident Prevention* (New York, McGraw Hill, 1980), pp. 208–219

Appendix 2. Bibliography

Law Relating to Safety and Health in Museums and Galleries

Major United Kingdom Acts of Parliament

Building Act 1984
Consumer Protection Act 1987
Control of Pollution Act 1974
Employers' Liability (Compulsory Insurance) Act 1969
Factories Act 1961
Fire Precaution Act 1971
Health and Safety at Work Etc. Act 1974
Occupier's Liability Act 1957
Occupier's Liability Act 1984
Offices, Shops and Railway Premises Act 1963
Public Health Act 1936
Radioactive Substances Act 1960
Sale of Goods Act 1979
Social Security Act 1975
Unfair Contract Terms Act 1977
Workman's Compensation Act 1925

Major United States Laws

Clean Air Act 1983
Consumer Product Safety Act 1972
Federal Employees Compensation Act
Federal Environmental Pesticide Control Act 1972
Federal Hazardous Substances Act 1981
Federal Insecticide, Fungicide and Rodenticide Act 1947
Federal Pesticide Act 1978
Flammable Fabrics Act 1954
Hazardous Materials Transportation Act 1979
Occupational Safety and Health Act 1970
Toxic Substances Control Act 1976
Noise Control Act 1972

Regulations Applicable to Working in Museums

United Kingdom Regulations

These are some of the principal regulations currently applicable to working in museums in the United Kingdom. Guidance notes (see p. 164) explaining most of these regulations are available through HMSO or from BSI (see p. 172 for address).

Abrasive Wheels Regulations 1970 (SI No. 535)
Asbestos Regulations 1969 (SI No. 690)

Building Regulations 1985
Classification Packaging and Labelling of Dangerous Substances Regulations 1984 (SI No. 1244)
Construction (General Provision) Regulations 1961 (SI No. 1580)
Construction (Lifting Operation) Regulations 1961 (SI No. 1581)
Control of Lead at Work Regulation 1980 (SI No. 1581)
Control of Pesticides Regulations 1986 (SI No. 1510)
Control of Pollution (Special Waste) Regulations 1980 (SI No. 1709)
Electrically Operated Lifts (EEC Requirements) Regulations 1986 (SI No. 1500)
Electricity (Factories Act) Special Regulations 1908–1944 (SI No. 739)
Fire Precautions (Applicable for Certificate) Regulations 1976 (SI No. 2008)
Fire Precautions (Factories, Offices, Shops and Railway Premises) Regulations 1976 (SI No. 2009)
Food Hygiene (General) Regulations 1970 (SI No. 1172)
Health and Safety (Emissions into the Atmosphere Regulation) 1983 (SI No. 2023)
Health and Safety (Enforcing) Regulations 1977 (SI No. 746)
Health and Safety (First-Aid) Regulation 1981 (SI No. 917)
Highly Flammable Liquids and Liquified Petroleum Gases Regulation 1972 (SI No. 917)
Ionizing Radiations Regulations 1985 (SI No. 1333)
Protection of Eyes Regulations 1974 (SI No. 168) 1975 Amendment (SI No. 303)
Reporting of Injuries, Diseases and Dangerous Occurrences Regulations 1985 (SI No. 1333)
Safety Representatives and Safety Committees Regulations 1977 (SI No. 500)
Safety Signs Regulation 1980 (SI No. 1471)
Woodworking Machines Regulations 1974 (SI No. 903)

Some United States Regulations and Orders

The two principal codes of federal regulations generated by the OSH Act are 29 CFR 1910 and 29 CFR 1926. Some examples of these and other regulations and orders are listed below.

29 CFR 1910, General Industry Standards
29 CFR 1910:1200, Hazard Communication Standard
29 CFR 1910:1000, Permissible Exposure Limits
29 CFR 1910:134, Standard for Respirator Programs
29 CFR 1926, Health and Safety Regulations for Construction, 1971
EO 12088, Federal Compliance with Pollution Control Standards, 1978
EO 12316, Responses to Environmental Damage, 1981
52 FR 2882, Radiation Protection Guidance to Federal Agencies for Occupational Exposure
29 CFR 1990, Identification, Classification and Regulation of Potential Occupational Carcinogens, 1980
49 CFR 397, Transportation of Hazardous Materials, 1971
16 CFR 1500, Hazardous Substances and Articles; Administration and Enforcement Regulations, 1973
21 CFR 1230, Regulations under the Federal Caustic Poisons Act, 1973
46 CFR 34, Fire-fighting Equipment, 1965
46 CFR 95, Fire Protection Equipment, 1965

In many parts of the US, safety rules and regulations are based on the appropriate American National Standard. These are some examples of standards relevant to Museums and Galleries.

ANSI/UL 900: 1982, Air Filter Units, Safety Standard
ANSI A58.1: 1982, Design Loads for Buildings and other Strcutures
ANSI A117.1: 1986, Buildings and Facilities- Providing Accessibility and Usability for Physically Handicapped People

ANSI/NFDA 491M: 1985, Manual of Hazardous Chemical Reactions
ANSI 2129.1: 1982, Precautionary Labelling of Hazardous Industrial Chemicals
ANSI/UL/NFPA 4913: 1979, Hazardous Locations, Intrinsically Safe Apparatus and Associated Apparatus for use in Class 1, II and III, Division I
ANSI C2: 1987, National Electrical Safety Code
ANSI 29.2: 1979, Design and Operation of Local Exhaust Systems, Fundamentals Governing the
ANSI/NFPA 30: 1984, Flammable and Combustible Liquids Code
ANSI/NFPA 911: 1985 Museums and Museum Collections, Protection of
ANSI/NFPA 45: 1986 Fire Protection for Laboratories using Chemicals
ANSI/A14. 1-A14.4, Safety Requirements for ladders
ANSI 787.1: 1979, Practice for Occupational and Educational Eye and Face Protection
ANSI/NFPA 43D: 1986, Storage of Pesticides in Portable Containers
ANSI N13.2: 1969, Administrative Practices in Radiation Monitoring
ANSI 288.2: 1980, Practices for Respiratory Protection
ANSI K13.1: 1973, Identification of Air-Purifying Respirator Canisters and Cartridges
ANSI/UL 1322: 1984, Fabricated Scaffold Planks and Stages
ANSI A92.1: 1977, Mobile Ladder Stands and Scaffolds (Towers) Manually Propelled
ANSI 01.1a: 1979, Woodworking Machinery, Safety Requirements for

HSE Guidance Notes published by HMSO

Chemical Safety

CS 1 Industrial use of flammable gas detectors (1979)
CS 2 Storage of highly flammable liquids (1977)
CS 3 Storage and use of sodium chlorate and other similar strong oxidants (1985)
CS 4 Keeping of LPG in cylinders and similar containers (1986)
CS 5 Storage of LPG at fixed installations (1981)
CS 6 Storage and use of LPG on construction sites (1981)
CS 7 Odorisation of bulk oxygen supplies in shipyards (1983)
CS 8 Small scale storage and display of LPG at retail premises (1985)
CS 9 Bulk storage and use of liquid carbon dioxide: hazards and procedures (1985)
CS 10 Fumigation using phosphine (1986)
CS 12 Fumigation using methyl bromide (bromomethane) (1986)
CS 15 Cleaning and gas freeing of tanks containing flammable residues (1985)
CS 16 Chlorine vaporisers (1985)
CS 17 Storage of packaged dangerous substances (1986)
CS 18 Storage and handling of ammonium nitrate (1986)

Environmental Hygiene

EH 1 Cadmium – health and safety precautions (1986)
EH 2 Chromium – health and safety precautions (1977)
EH 4 Aniline – health and safety precautions (1979)
EH 5 Trichloroethylene: health and safety precautions (1985)
EH 6 Chromic acid concentrations in air (1977)
EH 7 Petroleum based adhesives in building operations (1977)
EH 8 Arsenic – health and safety precautions (1987)
EH 9 Spraying of highly flammable liquids (1977)
EH 10 Asbestos – control limits and measurement of airborne dust concentrations (1984)
EH 11 Arsine – health and safety precautions (1977)
EH 12 Stibnine – health and safety precautions (1977)

EH 13 Beryllium – health and safety precautions (1977)
EH 14 Level of training for technicians making noise surveys (1977)
EH 16 Isocyanates: toxic hazards and precautions (1984)
EH 17 Mercury – health and safety precautions (1977)
EH 18 Toxic substances: a precautionary policy (1977)
EH 19 Antimony – health and safety precautions (1978)
EH 20 Phosphine – health and safety precautions (1979)
EH 21 Carbon dust – health and safety precautions (1979)
EH 22 Ventilation of buildings: fresh air requirements (1979)
EH 23 Anthrax: health hazards (1979)
EH 24 Dust and accidents in malthouses (1979)
EH 25 Cotton dust sampling (1980)
EH 26 Occupational skin diseases: health and safety precautions (1981)
EH 27 Acrylonitrile: personal protective equipment (1981)
EH 28 Control of lead: air sampling techniques and strategies (1986)
EH 29 Control of lead: outside workers (1981)
EH 30 Control of lead: pottery and related industries (1981)
EH 31 Control of exposure to polyvinyl chloride dust (1982)
EH 32 Control of exposure to talc dust (1982)
EH 33 Atmospheric pollution in car parks (1982)
EH 34 Benzidine based dyes: health and safety precautions (1982)
EH 35 Probable asbestos dust concentrations at construction processes (1984)
EH 36 Work with asbestos cement (1984)
EH 37 Work with asbestos insulating board (1984)
EH 38 Ozone: health hazards and precautionary measures (1983)
EH 40 Occupational exposure limits 1987 (1987)
EH 41 Respiratory protective equipment for use against asbestos (1985)
EH 42 Monitoring strategies for toxic substances 1984 (1984)
EH 43 Carbon monoxide (1984)
EH 44 Dust in the workplace: general principles of protection (1984)
EH 45 Carbon disulphide: control of exposure in the viscose industry (1984)
EH 46 Exposure to mineral wools (1986)
EH 47 Provision, use and maintenance of hygiene facilities for work with asbestos insulation and coatings (1986)
EH 48 Legionnaires' diseases (1987)

General Series

GS 2 Metrication of construction safety regulations (1976)
GS 3 Fire risk in the storage and industrial use of cellular plastics (1976)
GS 4 Safety in pressure testing (1976)
GS 5 Entry into confined spaces (1977)
GS 6 Avoidance of danger from overhead electrical lines (1980)
GS 7 Accidents to children on construction sites (1977)
GS 8 Articles and substances for use at work – guidance for designers, manufacturers, importers, suppliers, erectors and installers (1977)
GS 9 Road transport in factories (1978)
GS 10 Roofwork: prevention of falls (1979)
GS 11 Whisky cask racking (1980)
GS 12 Effluent storage on farms (1981)
GS 15 General access scaffolds (1982)
GS 16 Gaseous fire extinguishing systems: precautions for toxic and asphyxiating hazards (1984)

GS 17 Safe custody and handling of stock bulls on farms and at artificial insemination centres (1982; O/P see GS 35)
GS 18 Commercial ultraviolet tanning equipment (1982)
GS 19 General fire precautions aboard ships being fitted out or under repair (1983)
GS 20 Fire precautions in pressurised workings (1983)
GS 21 Assessment of the radio frequency ignition hazard to process plants where flammable atmospheres may occur (1983; O/P replaced by BS 6656:1986)
GS 23 Electrical safety in schools (1983)
GS 24 Electricity on construction sites (1983)
GS 25 Prevention of falls to window cleaners (1983)
GS 26 Access to road tankers (1983)
GS 27 Protection against electric shock (1984)
GS 28/1 Safe erection of structures. Part 1: initial planning and design (1984)
GS 28/2 Safe erection of structures. Part 2: Site management and procedures (1985)
GS 28/3 Safe erection of structures. Part 3: working places and access (1986)
GS 28/4 Safe erection of structures. Part 4: Legislation and training (1986)
GS 29/1 Health and safety in demolition work. Part 1: preparation and planning (1984)
GS 29/2 Health and safety in demolition work. Part 2: Legislation (1984)
GS 29/3 Health and safety in demolition work. Part 3: techniques (1984)
GS 29/4 Health and safety in demolition work. Part 4: health hazards (1985)
GS 30 Health and safety hazards associated with pig husbandry (1984)
GS 31 Safe use of ladders, step ladders and trestles (1984)
GS 32 Health and safety in shoe repair premises (1984)
GS 33 Avoiding danger from buried electricity cables (1985)
GS 34 Electrical safety in departments of electrical engineering (1986)
GS 35 Safe custody and handling of bulls on farms and similar premises (1985)
GS 36 Safe custody and handling of bulls at agricultural shows, markets and similar premises off the farm (1985)
GS 37 Flexible leads, plugs, sockets, etc. (1985)
GS 38 Electrical test equipment for use by electricians (1986)
GS 39 Training of crane drivers and slingers (1986)
GS 40 Loading and unloading of bulk flammable liquids and gases at harbours and inland waterways (1986)
GS 41 Radiation safety in underwater radiography (1986)

Medical Series

MS 4 Organic dust surveys (1977)
MS 5 Lung function (1977)
MS 6 Chest X-rays in dust diseases (1977)
MS 7 Colour vision (1977)
MS 8 Isocyanates: medical surveillance (1983)
MS 9 Byssinosis (1977)
MS 10 Beat conditions, tenosynovitis (1977)
MS 12 Mercury – medical surveillance (1978)
MS 13 Asbestos (1977)
MS 15 Welding (1978)
MS 16 Training of offshore sick-bay attendants (1978)
MS 17 Health surveillance of workers exposed to organo-phosphorus and carbamate pesticides (1986)
MS 18 Health surveillance by routine procedures
MS 20 Pre-employment health screening (1982)
MS 21 Precautions for the safe handling of cytotoxic drugs (1983)
MS 22 Medical monitoring of workers exposed to platinum salts (1983)

Plant and Machinery

PM 1 Guarding of portable pipe-threading machines (1984)
PM 2 Guards for planing machines (1976)
PM 3 Erection and dismantling of tower cranes (1976)
PM 4 High temperature dyeing machines (1980)
PM 5 Automatically controlled steam and hot water boilers (1977)
PM 6 Dough dividers (1976)
PM 7 Lifts: thorough examination and testing (1982)
PM 8 Passenger-carrying paternosters (1977)
PM 9 Access to tower cranes (1979)
PM 10 Tripping devices for radial and heavy vertical drilling machines (1977)
PM 13 Zinc embrittlement of austenitic stainless steel (1977)
PM 14 Safety in the use of cartridge operated tools (1978)
PM 15 Safety in the use of timber pallets
PM 16 Eyebolts (1978)
PM 17 Pneumatic nailing and stapling tools (1979)
PM 18 Locomotive boilers (1980)
PM 19 Use of lasers for display purposes (1980)
PM 20 Cable-laid slings and grommets (1981)
PM 21 Safety in the use of woodworking machines (1981)
PM 22 Training advice on the mounting of abrasive wheels (1983)
PM 23 Photo-electric safety systems (1981)
PM 24 Safety at rack and pinion hoists (1981)
PM 25 Vehicle finishing units: fire and explosion hazards (1981)
PM 26 Safety at lift landings (1981)
PM 27 Construction hoists (1981)
PM 28 Working platforms on forklift trucks (1981)
PM 29 Electrical hazards from steam/water pressure cleaners etc. (1981)
PM 30 Suspended access equipment (1983)
PM 31 Chain saws (1982)
PM 32 Safe use of portable electrical apparatus (electrical safety) (1983)
PM 33 Safety of bandsaws in the food industry (1983)
PM 34 Safety in the use of escalators (1983)
PM 35 Safety in the use of reversing dough brakes (1983)
PM 36 Weld defect acceptance levels for in service non destructive examination of set-in endplate to furnace and shell connections of shell boilers (1984)
PM 37 Electrical installations in motor vehicle repair premises and amendment sheet (1984)
PM 38 Selection and use of electric handlamps (1984)
PM 39 Hydrogen embrittlement of grade T chain (1984)
PM 40 Protection of workers at welded steel tube mills (1984)
PM 41 Application of photo-electric safety systems to machinery (1984)
PM 42 Excavators used as cranes (1984)
PM 43 Scotch derrick cranes (1984)
PM 45 Escalators: periodic thorough examination (1984)
PM 46 Wedge and socket anchorages for wire ropes (1985)
PM 47 Safe operation of passenger-carrying amusement devices – the waltzer (1985)
PM 48 Safe operation of passenger-carrying amusement devices – the octopus (1985)
PM 49 Safe operation of passenger-carrying amusement devices – the cyclone twist (1985)
PM 51 Safety in the use of radio-frequency dielectric heating equipment (1986)
PM 52 Safety in the use of refuse compaction vehicles (1985)
PM 53 Emergency private generation: electrical safety (1985)
PM 54 Lifting gear standards (1985)
PM 55 Safe working with overhead travelling cranes (1985)

PM 56 Noise from pneumatic systems (1985)
PM 57 Safe operation of passenger-carrying amusement devices – the big wheel (1986)
PM 58 Diesel engined lift trucks in hazardous areas (1986)
PM 59 Safe operation of passenger-carrying amusement devices – the paratrooper (1986)
PM 61 Safe operation of passenger-carrying amusement devices – the chair-o-plane (1986)
PM 62 Expanded polystyrene moulding machines (1986)
PM 64 Electrical safety in arc welding (1986)
PM 66 Scrap baling machines (1986)
PM 69 Safety in the use of freight containers (1987)

Further Readings

General Subjects

American Conference of Governmental Industrial Hygienists (1984). *Industrial Ventilation.* Cincinnati: ACGIH.
Bretherick, L. (1984). *Hazards in the Chemical Laboratory.* Nottingham: Royal Chemical Society.
Challis, T. and Roberts, G. (eds) (1984). *Caution: A Guide to Safe Practice in the Arts and Crafts.* Sunderland, UK: Sunderland Polytechnic Faculty of Art and Design.
Chemical Industries Association and Chemical Industry Safety and Health Council (1977). *A Guide to Hazard and Operability Studies.* London: CIA.
Egan, B. (1979). *Safety Policies,* New Commercial Publishing Company, New Law Guidances Series Number 11. London: Brehan Press.
Fife, I. and Machin, E. (1980). *Health and Safety at Work.* London: Butterworths.
Fife, I. and Machin, E. (1985). *Redgrave's Health and Safety in Factories.* London: Butterworths.
Fordham-Cooper, W. (1986). *Electrical Safety Engineering.* London: Butterworths.
Health and Safety Commission (1987). *Draft Regulations: Control of Substances Hazardous to Health.* London: HMSO.
Heinrich, H. W., Petersen, D. and Roos, N. (1980). *Industrial Accident Prevention – A Safety Management Approach.* New York: McGraw-Hill.
Hunter, D. (1976). *The Diseases of Occupations.* London: Hodder and Stoughton.
International Labour Office (1983). *Encyclopaedia of Occupational Health and Safety.* Geneva: ILO.
James, D. (1986). *Fire Prevention Handbook.* London: Butterworths.
King, R. W. and Hudson, R. (1985). *Construction Hazard and Safety Handbook.* London: Butterworths.
McCann, M. (1979). *Artist Beware.* New York: Watson Gupthill Publications.
Powell-Smith, V. and Billington, M. J. (1986). *The Building Regulations: Explained and Illustrated.* London: Collins.
Ridley, J. (1986). *Safety at Work.* London: Butterworths.
Schilling, R. S. F. (ed.) (1981). *Occupational Health Practice.* London: Butterworths.
Waring, A. E. (ed.) (1982). *Micro Computers for Safety Practitioners.* Institution of Occupational Safety and Health, Primer Series Booklet No. 1. Leicester: IOSH.

Museum Sources

Abrams, D. S., Reist, P. C. and Dement, J. (1986). An evaluation of the effectiveness of a recirculating laboratory hood. *American Industrial Hygiene Association, 47*(1), 22–26.
Anderson, S. (1982). Freeze-drying: a new hazard. *Museums Bulletin, 21*(11), 224–225.
Anonymous (1983). DDT exposures in a natural history museum in Colorado. *Morbidity and Mortality Weekly Report, 32*(34), 443–444.

Anonymous (1983). Glossary of health and safety terms. *The Paper Conservator, 7*, 73–82.
Baer, N. S. (1984). Risk assessment as applied to the setting of solvent toxicity limits. *Adhesives and Consolidants*, Preprints of the Contribution to the Paris Congress 1984, pp. 26–31.
Barton, D. N. (1985). *An Ounce of Prevention: A Handbook on Disaster Contingency Planning for Archives, Libraries and Record Centres.* Toronto: Area Archivists' Group Education Foundation.
Briggs, D., Sell, P. D., et al. (1983). Mercury vapour: a health hazard in herbaria. *New Phytologist, 94*, 453–457.
Center for Occupational Hazards (1984). Arsenic in taxidermy specimens. *Arts Hazards News, 7*(5), 4.
Clark, N., Cutter, T. and McGrane, J. (1984). *Ventilation: A Practical Guide.* New York: Center for Occupational Hazards.
Commoner, L. (1984). Personal protective equipment for conservators: gloves and hand protection. *Journal of the American Institute for Conservation, 23*(2), 153–158.
Clydesdale, A. (1982). *Chemicals in Conservation: A Guide to Possible Hazards and Safe Use.* Edinburgh: Conservation Bureau of the Scottish Development Agency and the Scottish Society for Conservation and Restoration.
Davies, T. D., Ramer, B., et al. (1984). Indoor/outdoor ozone concentrations at a contemporary art gallery. *Journal of the Air Pollution Control Association, 34*(2), 135–137.
Diamond, P. and Petheridge, G. (1981). Storage and disposal of toxic and flammable material. *The Paper Conservator, 5/6*, 38–50.
Dixon, D. W. (1983). *Radiation Hazards to Collectors of Geological Specimens Containing Natural Radioactivity NRPB-R131.* Didcot, UK: National Radiological Protection Board.
Edwards, S. R., Bell, B. M. and King, M. E. (1981). *Pest Control in Museums: A Status Report.* Kansas: The Association of Systematics Collections.
Fischbein, A., Wallace, J., et al. (1982). Lead poisoning in an art conservator. *Journal of the American Medical Association, 247*(14), 2007–2009.
Frølich, K. W., Andersen, L. M., et al. (1984). Phenoxyethanol as a nontoxic substitute for formaldehyde in long-term preservation of human anatomical specimens for dissection and demonstration purposes. *The Anatomical Record, 208*, 271–278.
Gallo, F. P. (1978). Methyl bromide, ethylene oxide and formaldehyde: biological and toxicological problems related to treatment of library materials. *Nuovi Annali Igiene e Microbiologia, 29*(1), 51–82.
Gombos, B., Murinova, O., et al. (1982). Severe accidental poisoning by arsenic (in Czech). *Pracovni Lekarstvi, 34*, 28–31.
Hawks, C. A. and Williams, S. L. (1986). Arsenic in natural history collections. *Leather Conservation News, 2*(2), 1–4.
Hatton, A. (1986). Museums: occupational hazards. *The Safety Practitioner, 4*(4), 5–9.
Health and Safety Executive (1982). *General Access Scaffolds*, Guidance Note GS 15. London: HMSO.
Health and Safety Executive (1987). *Tower Scaffolds*, Guidance Note GS42. London: HMSO.
Hey, M. (1981). Paper conservation processes hazardous to health. *The Paper Conservator, 5/6*, 5–13.
Hillman, D. (1983). Health and safety: fumigation in the BC provincial museum. *IIC-CC Newsletter, 9*(2), 6–9.
Howie, F. (1985). New occupational exposure limit for formaldehyde: significance for museums. *Newsletter, Biological Curators' Group, 4*(2), 21.
Howie, F. M. P. (1986). Exhaust ventilation systems for museums: some basic principles. *UKIC – Conservation News, 29*, 17–19.

Howie, F. M. P. (1987). Safety considerations for the geological conservator. *The Geological Conservator, 4*(7), 379–401.

Irvin, A. D., Cooper, J. E. and Hedges, S. R. (1972). Possible health hazards associated with the collection and handling of post-mortem zoological material. *Mammal Review, 2*(2), 43–54.

Johnson, W. M., Sheppard, L. E. and Barton, D. N. (1977). A downdraft fume hood for the control of toxic vapours of heavy liquids used for mineral separation. *Canadian Journal of Earth Sciences, 14*, 2422–2424.

Kannemeyer, S. K. and Schaefer, N. (1986). Safety in the museum laboratory and workshop. *SAMAB, 17*(2), 41–92.

McCann, M. (1979). The impact of hazards in art on female workers. *Preventative Medicine, 7*, 338–348.

McDermot, H. J. (1985). *Handbook of Ventilation for Contaminant Control.* Ann Arbor: Science Press.

McGiffin, R. F. (1985). Health and safety in the museum workplace. *Museum News, 64*(2), 36–43.

Muir, D., Lovell, M., et al. (1981). Health hazards in natural history museum work. *Museums Journal, 80*(4), 205–206.

Oil and Chemical Plant Constructors Association (1986). *Radiation Safety for Site Radiography*. Amsterdam: Kluwer Verlag.

Pascoe, M. (1980). Toxic hazards from solvents in conservation. *The Conservator, 4*, 25–28.

Petheridge, G. (1981). Physical hazards in the paper conservation workshop. *The Paper Conservator, 5/6*, 15–20.

Petheridge, G. (1981). Protective clothing and equipment. *The Paper Conservator, 5/6*, 51–64.

Petheridge, G. and Harrington, M. J. (ed.) (1981). *Safety and health in the paper conservation laboratory. The Paper Conservator* (London), special issue, 184 pp.

Pryor, P. (1983). *NTIS Health Hazard Evaluation Report, no. HETA 82-027-1281.* Denver, Colorado: Denver Museum of National History (PB84-210392).

Puffer, J. H. D. (1980). Toxic minerals. *The Mineralogical Record*, 5–11.

Ruhe, R. L. (1977). *Hazard Evaluation and Technical Assistance Report no. TA 76-92*, Harpurs Ferry Center Museum Laboratory, West Virginia. NTIS (PB-278842).

Rycroft, R. (1981). Skin problems at work. *The Paper Conservator, 5/6*, 83–84.

Scott, I. C. (1986). Hazardous raw materials used in the paint and ink industries. *Oil and Colour Chemists Association Journal, 69*(11), 310–313.

Scottish Society for Conservation and Restoration (1986). *Health and Safety*, Bulletin no. 6.

Smithsonian Institution (1980). *Safety Handbook*, SSH 620. Washington, DC: Smithsonian Institution.

Walsh, T. and Keane, D. (1980). Technical note: the dangers of fumigation of archives with ethylene oxide. *Archives and Manuscripts, 8*(1), 62–63.

Watkinson, D. E. and Leigh, D. (1978). Polyurethane foam: a health hazard. *IIC-CG Newsletter, 4*(1); 5–6.

Wheeler, G. (1980). Chemical hazards in the arts. *Journal of Chemical Education, 57*(4), 281–282.

Williams, T. (1984). Exposure of embalmers to formaldehyde and other chemicals. *American Industrial Hygiene Association Journal, 45*(3), 172–176.

Appendix 3. Sources of Information, Training and Legal Advice

Handbooks and Guides

Barbour Microfile: Health and Safety (1987). Microfiche Library, Barbour Index, Windsor, UK.

Best's Safety Directory (1982). A. M. Best and Co, Oldwick, New Jersey.

Handbook of the Co-ordinating Committee for the Professional Occupational Health and Safety Organization.

Publications in Series: List Jan. 1987. Library and Information Services, Health and Safety Executive, Sheffield, UK.

The Safety Practitioners' Year Book (2nd ed. 1987). The Institution of Occupational Safety and Health (IOSH), Paramount Publishing, Boreham Wood, UK.

Sax, N. I. (1984). *Dangerous Properties of Industrial Materials.* London/New York: Van Nostrand-Reinhold.

Sources of Information

United Kingdom

The British Occupational Hygiene Society: Secretariat (BOHS), London School of Hygiene and Tropical Medicine, Keppel Street, London WC1E 7HT. (Resources include: specialist members' meetings, technology guides, education and training booklets, and BOHS Journal – *The Annals of Occupational Hygiene.)*

Fire Protection Association (FPA): 140 Aldersgate Street, London EC1A 4HX. (Produces videos and films on fire safety, publishes guides and booklets, and organizes training for work people.)

Institute of Occupational Hygienists: Secretary to Council, Institute of Occupational Hygienists, Pixie Close, Noke, Oxford OX3 9TT. (Professional institute for qualified occupational hygienists.)

Institute of University Safety Officers: Hon. Secretary, IUSO, c/o Safety Office, University of Southampton, Southampton SO9 5NH.

Institution of Chemical Engineers (ICE): Geo E. Davis Building, 105–171 Railway Terrace, Rugby CV21 3HQ. (Guides and books on ventilation and safety engineering.)

Institution of Occupational Safety and Health (IOSH): 222 Uppingham Road, Leicester LE5 0QG. (Professional association for safety officers; runs conferences, and publishes a journal – *The Safety Practitioner* – and booklets on safety.)

Royal Society for the Prevention of Accidents (RoSPA): Cannon House, The Priory, Queensway, Birmingham B4 6BS. (Membership services, training centre, and publishes a journal – *Occupational Safety and Health.)*

United States

American Conference of Governmental Industrial Hygienists (ACGIH): 500 Glenway Avenue, Building D5, Cincinnati OH 45211. (Publishes guides on Ventilation and Threshold Limit Values Documentation.)

American Industrial Hygiene Association (AIHE): 66 South Miller Road, Akron OH 44313. (Publishes guides on chemical use and a journal.)
American Society of Safety Engineers (ASSE): 850 Busse Highway, Park Ridge IL 60068. (Sets standards for professional competence.)
National Fire Protection Association (NFPA): Battery March Park, Quincy MA 02269. (Publishes guides and codes on fire protection for libraries and museums.)
National Safety Council (NSC): 444 North Michigan Avenue, Chicago IL 60611.

Governmental Sources (UK)

British Standards Institution (BSI): 2 Park Street, London W1A 2BS; and Linford Wood, Milton Keynes, Bucks 14 6LE.
Health and Safety Agency for Northern Ireland: Canada House, 22 North Street, Belfast BT1 1NW.
Health and Safety Commission (HSC): Regina House, 259 Old Marylebone Road, London NW1 5RR.
Health and Safety Executive (HSE): Baynards House, 1 Chepstow Place, London W2 4TF.
Health and Safety Executive Accident Prevention Advisory Unit: 1st Floor, St Hugh's House, Stanley Precinct, Bootle, Merseyside L20 3QY.
National Radiological Protection Board (NRPB): Chilton, Didcot, Oxon.

Governmental sources (US)

American National Standards Institute (ANSI): 1430 Broadway, New York NY 10018.
Consumer Product Safety Commission (CPSC): Washington DC 20207.
Environmental Protection Agency: 401 Main Street SW, Washington DC 20460.
National Institute for Occupational Safety and Health (NIOSH): 4676 Columbia Parkway, Cincinnati, OH 45226.
Occupational Safety and Health Agency (OSHA): US Department of Labor, Washington DC 20210.

Training

United Kingdom

Institutions offering basic level and professional qualifying courses (non-graduate) on safety:

British Safety Council: National Safety Centre, 62 Chancellor's Road, London W6 9RS.
Coventry Management Training Centre: Woodland Grange, Leamington Spa, Warwickshire CV32 6RN.
HASTAM Ltd: Aston Science Park, Love Lane, Aston Triangle, Birmingham B7 4BJ.
Loughborough University of Technology: Centre for Extension Studies, Loughborough, Leicester LE11 3TU.
Occupational Health and Safety Service: London School of Hygiene and Tropical Medicine, Keppel St, London WC1.
Portsmouth Polytechnic: Occupational Health and Safety Open Learning, Buckingham Building, Lion Terrace, Portsmouth PO1 3HE.
Royal Society for the Prevention of Accidents: Training Centre, 22 Summer Road, Acocks Green, Birmingham B27 7UT.

University-level courses (graduate and postgraduate):

Heriot-Watt University: Riecarton, Edinburgh RH14 4AS.
London University: School of Hygiene and Tropical Medicine, Keppel Street, London WC1.
Polytechnic of the South Bank: Centre for Industrial Health and Hygiene, Borough Road, London SE1.

University of Aston: Health and Safety Unit, Dept of Chemical Engineering, Gosta Green, Birmingham B4 7ET.

United States of America

National Institute for Occupational Safety and Health: Robert A Taft Laboratories, 4676 Columbia Parkway, Cincinnati, Ohio 45226.
School of Hygiene and Public Health: The John Hopkins University, Baltimore, Maryland.
Institute of Safety and Systems Management: University of Southern California, Los Angeles, California.

Legal Advice

United Kingdom

Contact the following bodies for guidance:

Confederation of British Industry: Centre Point, New Oxford Street, London WC1.
Department of Employment (Enterprise and Deregulation Unit): Caxton House, Tothill Street, London W1.
Department of Trade (Small Businesses Development Unit): 1–19 Victoria Street, London SW1.
Health and Safety Executive Area Offices (about 21). Contact, in the first instance, the central enquiry point at: HSE, Baynards House, 1 Chepstow Place, London W2.
International Labour Office: 96 Marsham Street, London W1.
Trades Union Congress: Great Russell Street, London WC1.
Solicitors and Barristers specializing in health and safety matters can be contacted via The Law Society, 113 Chancery Lane, London WC2.

United States of America

Department of Labor, 200 Constitution Ave, Washington DC 20210.
National Safety Council, 444 North Michigan Ave, Chicago, Illinois 60611.
Occupational Safety and Health Administration, 200 Constitution Ave NW, Washington DC 20210.

International Journal of Museum Management and Curatorship

Safety in Museums and Galleries

Index

Note: Page numbers in italic type refer to illustrations.

Printed in France by Amazon
Brétigny-sur-Orge, FR

51786471R00112